An Economic History
of Europe Since 1700

VERA ZAMAGNI

agenda
publishing

English translation © Agenda Publishing Ltd 2017

Translated by N. Michael Brennen

First published as *Perché l'Europa ha cambiato il mondo. Una storia economica*

© Società editrice il Mulino, 2015

First English-language edition published in 2017 by Agenda Publishing

Agenda Publishing Limited
The Core
Science Central
Bath Lane
Newcastle upon Tyne
NE4 5TF

www.agendapub.com

ISBN 978-1-911116-38-7 (hardcover)
ISBN 978-1-911116-39-4 (paperback)

British Library Cataloguing-in-Publication Data
A catalogue record for this book is available from the British Library

Typeset by Patty Rennie in Adobe Garamond
Printed and bound in the UK by CPI Group (UK) Ltd, Croydon, CR0 4YY

Contents

Preface

Every person has a natural obligation to seek his own happiness and, being the political body made up of such persons, the political body too is obliged to do everything it can to contribute to the common prosperity, without breaching the rights of any civil body. This obligation with appropriate and divine bond reverberates from the civil body back to every family and every person through the common societal pacts ... We can add [to these two obligations, the natural and the societal] a third obligation, namely self-utility. It will eternally be true ... that the true utility is the daughter of virtue, because it is eternally true that at the heart of man, where his utmost value resides, there is the love of those with whom he lives, a love that is the son of virtue.

ANTONIO GENOVESI,
Lezioni di commercio o sia d'economia civile (1765)

This English edition of my book, originally published in Italian in 2015, stems from the consideration that a succinct and agile textbook of modern economic growth over the long run has been missing. Numerous textbooks exist of considerable size, as do more specialized treatments, but none try to summarize the basic factors contributing to economic progress over the centuries leading up to the present day in a manageable number of pages, that could be widely read.

The book concentrates on the implications of the three industrial revolutions. The first two chapters explore the prerequisites of the first industrial revolution, which took place in eighteenth-century Britain, namely the flourishing of the self-governed city-states in the Middle Ages and the impact of the geographical explorations of the sixteenth and seventeenth centuries. These two chapters are significant for understanding the meaning of "the great divergence" between Europe and the rest of the world, a topic that has recently commanded a growing literature. Chapter 3 explores the key features of the British experience, while Chapters 4–8 chart the spread of the first industrial revolution across the European continent and to Japan, the birth of the second industrial revolution in the United States, the emergence of an international economy in the nineteenth century, and a synthesis of the literature on British decline, which had already begun in the second half of the same century.

Economic progress has not avoided conflict or policy mistakes, so Chapters 9–12 discuss the impact on the world economy of the two world wars and the 1929 crisis, with a chapter dedicated to the birth of the Soviet Union and its alternative model of economic development. Chapters 13–17 concentrate on the major events unfolding between the mid-twentieth century and the beginning of the present day. These encompass the spread of the second industrial revolution beyond the United States, the reorganization of the European nations inside the framework of the European Union, the impact of the third industrial revolution and the processes of globalization, the failure of the Soviet model and the reawakening of Asia, and the insurgence of a second world crisis.

In order to maintain a concise and manageable overview in the face of such vast material I have had to point the reader to secondary sources to pursue the detail. I have given priority to conceptual and interpretative material, arranged thematically within a broad chronological framework in order to help students and readers form ideas on the way economic and social advancements were achieved, on why certain communities were more progressive than others in different times and contexts, on the part played by institutions, on the costs and benefits of certain solutions, and on the forces that run against progress.

There is a thesis underlying this book: that the industrial revolutions could only have been born inside a European culture that exalted human freedom while at the same time preaching justice and fraternity, and which placed checks on the abuse of power through equalitarian legislation, shared government and the support of those who could not help themselves. It is only in a context in which there is freedom, but at the same time empowerment of people, that *competition* can truly develop, defeating rent-seeking and monopolies. The innovations that brought about the three industrial revolutions charted in this book, born inside this type of culture, made a number of European states first, then the United States and Japan, the wealthiest countries in the world. Imitation was certainly possible in countries where a different culture prevailed, although to date some, like the Soviet Union, have failed and are now trying, with severe difficulties, to adopt a "European"-type culture, while others, such as China and India, have yet to complete their transition. However, as I will argue in the Epilogue, the future might well afford us some surprises.

The jealous defence of independence, self-determination and the acquisition of world power by means of conquest on the part of European nation states has cost Europe the loss of leadership to the United States. States in the USA were federated very early in the country's history and were able to avoid major military confrontations (the exception was the civil war), while at the same time the country was able to develop a rapidly enlarging domestic market, with a single currency and a single foreign policy. The process of European economic integration since the Second World War must be seen as a redemption for the mistakes done in Europe with excessive conflicts, but, although beneficial for Europe itself and for the world at large, it has not allowed Europe to overcome entirely its fragmentation even today, as the ailing common currency and the lack of a common foreign policy illustrate.

This book is the result of a long career of teaching economic history in various Italian universities, at SAIS Europe of the Johns Hopkins University (Bologna, Italy) and at Dickinson College (Bologna) to students from all parts of the world. As Newton once said, the important thing for a scholar is to learn and not to teach; therefore I thank all my students for much that I have learned from them. I also thank my economist husband, Stefano Zamagni, for all the heated intellectual discussions I have had with him over the years and for his excellent cooking abilities, two things that have made my everyday life very enjoyable. I dedicate this book to my grandchildren Alice, Matteo, Federico and Margherita, from whom I expect a contribution to make this world happier and more hospitable.

VERA ZAMAGNI

I

Advanced agricultural and mercantile civilizations before the modern era

1.1 *World economic development and the role of institutions over the long term*

To fully appreciate the profound discontinuity imprinted by the industrial revolution on human life, one must turn to long-term studies that trace the course of human civilizations from an economic perspective. Mankind lived for tens of thousands of years in an economic system based on hunting, fishing and gathering. It was a nomadic life in continuous movement that did not allow permanent settlements, because what nature spontaneously offered was quickly exhausted. Caves were the most common shelter, followed by rapidly constructed tents or huts. Life expectancy at birth was between 20 and 25 years, and the possibility of population growth was low due to the harsh living conditions (see Table 1.1). People lived in small scattered groups with a very simple social organization. In many areas this situation, which we can doubtlessly define as primitive, showed only faint signs of evolving. Some handicrafts, particularly textiles, developed here and there, but people frequently used skins to cover themselves when they could not remain naked because of the rigours of the climate. That is why warm places were the most suitable. It was therefore a wandering civilization that could neither accumulate nor put down roots, at most able to orally transmit its traditions.

In some areas, especially those in the more temperate climates of Asia, Europe, America and north Africa, about 9000 BCE an agro-pastoral civilization evolved in which people cultivated the land and raised animals, initially in transhumance and later in fixed locations. This permitted the earliest forms of permanent dwelling. The earliest remains of villages have been identified in Jericho, Palestine and the Middle East around 7000 BCE. In later times there

I

Table 1.1 Population (millions).

Region	1000	1500	1600	1700	1820	1870	1911	1952	2008	Index 2008 (1500 = 1)
Western Europe	26	57	74	81	169	233	335	399	520	9
United States	1	2	1.5	1	10	40	94	183	303	151
Japan	7.5	15.5	18.5	27	31	34	50	87	127	8
China	60	103	160	138	381	358	428	569	1,327	13
India	75	110	135	165	209	253	303	372	1,125	10
Latin America	–	–	–	–	22	40	78	175	575	–
Mexico	4.5	7.5	2.5	4	6.5	9	15	30	110	15
Brazil	1	1	1	1	4.5	10	22	55	192	192
Soviet Union (former)	7	17	21	27	55	89	156	186	287	17
Russian Federation									142	

Source: Angus Maddison's original database, made available by the University of Groningen, www.ggdc.net/maddison (hereafter cited as "Maddison database" in table sources).

are signs of settlements in Central America, South Asia and China. From these places, what Cipolla defined as the "agricultural revolution" spread into many parts of Europe and the East. The agro-pastoral civilization showed a remarkable capacity to accumulate; cities and empires blossomed, the population expanded and "culture" spread in both a material sense of methods of improved cultivation and in a spiritual sense. Writing developed – although not everywhere – as well as the love of knowledge, which could be more easily transmitted through writing; famous libraries emerged. The limited ability to control the environment (such as natural events or epidemics due to over-crowding in cities) and a heightened propensity towards conflict, generated by settlements able to sustain powerful armies for both defence and offence, held life expectancy at a level not substantially different than primitive societies; however, there was no comparison between the two societies either in terms of population expansion or in terms of evolutionary capabilities. Where primitive civilizations did not know if they would survive, agrico-pastoral civilizations quickly revealed a taste for the new, as Ulysses's adventure illustrates, even though the new was risky and always just out of reach ahead.

Between frightening setbacks and periods of stagnation, and through fasci-nating adventures such as those of the Greek, Roman, Arab, Indian, Chinese, Inca and Aztec civilizations, millennia passed before the progress inherent in accumulating knowledge came to transform the agro-pastoral civilization into an industrial civilization. This happened in Europe between the sixteenth and eighteenth centuries CE after about nine millennia of agro-pastoral civiliza-tion. In this new industrial civilization, which to date has existed for only the brief span of three centuries, life expectancy has tripled, the world's popula-tion has exceeded seven billion, and urbanization is aggressively expanding; however, the ways we work and live have changed most of all, as we will see in detail in this work. What we should immediately note here is that such a comparatively very young industrial civilization has been surprisingly capable of a radical transformation in an incomparably shorter time than preceding civilizations. It is precisely for this transformative capacity that it has been described as a "revolution". This was certainly not for the time span over which it happened, which was slower than political revolutions; in the latter the word "revolution" denotes not only a radical but also a rapid change of regime. In economics all "revolutionary" transformations play out over the long term, though in more recent times the pace has quickened.

It is with such a long-range approach, although more focused on geograph-ical and historical viewpoints, that we are able to explain why an event such as the industrial revolution happened in Europe and not in another of the world's many agrico-pastoral civilizations. To address that matter, it will be useful to precede it with a few considerations regarding the elements generally held to be foundational for economically and socially "progressive" civilizations. The following explanatory elements are those that scholars have held to be significant: climate, geographic location, natural resources, the philosophical and religious vision of the world, and the organization of society, with the creation of the appropriate institutions. Studies have now shown that the first three elements played a facilitating role within societies that were already dynamic due to other factors. Indeed, it has been noted that the most dynamic civilizations were located in areas with a mild climate and watercourses that facilitated transportation, irrigation and community life, but also that there were many such areas that did not develop until very recently. Scholars have ascertained that the world is full of areas rich in natural resources that did not develop until the arrival of immigrants, because the local peoples were not able to grasp the opportunities offered by available resources or to effectively take advantage of them. The most obvious example is North America, where until the sixteenth century a dispersed population lived that had reached a semi-nomadic level of civilization. The development of this enormous area happened only after European settlers arrived in the sixteenth century who, on the basis of the cultural milieu they brought with them, brought an unprecedented dynamism to bear on it.

The real strategic role in determining the degree of progress of the various societies was therefore played by philosophical and religious worldviews and by the social organization of the society that derived from them, along with the various political and economic institutions that followed. This institutional approach to various civilizations is now shared not only by historians, but also by scholars in different disciplines, such as anthropologists, sociologists, and economists. In the forefront of these we find Douglass North, an American economic historian who received the 1993 Nobel Prize in economics for his historical analysis of economic institutions. In his 2005 book he pointed out that:

> The central focus of this study, and the key to improving economic performance, is the deliberate effort of human beings to control their environment. Therefore, priority is given here to institutional change, with the consequent incentive implications for demographic and stock of knowledge changes.[1]

---

1. North, *Understanding the Process of Economic Change*, 1.

After having clarified that "the institutional structure ... is a combination of formal rules, informal constraints, and their enforcement characteristics",[2] North insisted on the fact that the culture from which institutions and their economic decisions derive goes well beyond the "instrumental rationality" – that is, a means–ends logic – used by so-called mainstream economists in their models. In North's words:

> Beliefs and the way they evolve are at the heart of the theoretical issues of this book. For the most part, economists, with a few important exceptions such as Friedrich Hayek, have ignored the role of ideas in making choice. The rationality assumption has served economists ... well for a limited range of issues in micro theory, but is a shortcoming in dealing with the issues central to this study. Indeed the uncritical acceptance of the rationality assumption is devastating for most of the major issues confronting social scientists and is a major stumbling block in the path of future progress.[3]

To understand how the discourse on institutions and the culture that determines them goes well beyond merely a basis of instrumental rationality, it is necessary to introduce the concept of path dependence. This concept was developed by Paul David, who argued that the explanation for many technological and institutional configurations originates over a particular historical course rather than in universally valid rational economic laws.[4] Chains of events, some of which are random, end up closing off alternatives that were initially possible and limiting the range of choices to a particular configuration that crystallizes. This is obviously true in all undeveloped countries; only historical inertia and remaining locked into their own traditional world explain why a country does not progress when others do. It is also true in

---

2. *Ibid.*, 6.

3. *Ibid.*, 5. For a more general discussion on the topic of institutions, see Furubotn & Richter, *Institutions and Economic Theory*.

4. David, "Clio and the Economics of QWERTY". QWERTY is David's well-known example; these are the first six letters initially of the typewriter, then of keyboards. The keys were placed in that order due to the typewriter's mechanical problem of the typebars striking on top of each other. When these problems disappeared with the advent of a new technology the order of the letters remained unchanged, even after it was shown to be inefficient, because by then everyone was accustomed to it. More recently David has offered a summary of his long work, recommending that economists take a greater interest in dynamic matters; these imply a "historical" time and not just a time reduced to space, which one can pursue in any direction; see David, "Path Dependence".

developing countries, which tend to remain bound to the particular form of their early development even when a particularly forceful institutional innovation emerges that commends itself for adoption, and so a process of decline sets in.

So with these interpretive tools we will attempt to compare the advanced stages of the principal agrarian civilizations to understand the culture, beliefs and institutions, that, between the sixteenth and eighteenth centuries, determined their different economic destiny.

1.2   *An institutional comparison of advanced agricultural economies*

Traditionally, and largely in North's work as well, institutional analysis has been applied only to the Western world of European origins to explain why Britain was the first to industrialize – a theme we will take up in Chapter 3 – and why the United States took over leadership from Britain – a theme we will extensively cover in various chapters. The recent economic ascent of China and India, however, has given rise to a highly interesting literature that sets itself a more global goal of explaining why Europe was the first to industrialize and not China, India, or the Islamic world, even speculating on the possibility that Western hegemony can be considered temporary because it does not emerge from a structural superiority.[5] This section will summarize this new literature, but before proceeding we must briefly dwell on the definition of Europe.

As is known, Europe has never existed as a unified state, even in the time of the Roman Empire, which extended to include north Africa and Asia Minor but had poor control over its areas to the north and east. Even its cultural matrix, which derived from Greece and Rome (with its various contributions that were not strictly Latin), did not come just from the areas recognized as Europe: Christianity, a decisive component, originated in Palestine. Nonetheless, for geographical (the western boundary with a protective but also limiting ocean), historical (the development of Islam to the southwest of the Mediterranean) and religious (the spread of Christianity to the Slavic peoples) reasons, Europe became a continent, one bounded on the west, south and north by seas; the eastern boundary was much less distinct, determined more by cultural factors (the spread of Christianity) than by geographic factors. The eastern boundary was the more porous, with

---

5. Goody, *The Eurasian Miracle*.

significant Islamic and even Asian settlements.[6] Within this continent an intense dynamic developed of cross-cultural influences, military clashes and economic exchanges among states that linked their destinies in many ways.[7] So it is correct to speak of "Europe", because all the states that historically composed it have had an interconnected political, economic and cultural life, even though the continent was never politically united – still today a topic of great importance. Naturally, in Europe as in all the other large areas of the world, there were significant internal differences, as we will see in later chapters.

The institutional comparison we propose is summarized in Table 1.2, in which only three areas appear: Europe, the Islamic world and China. The Central American agrarian civilizations (the Incas, Aztecs and Mayas) are not considered because they were isolated, largely illiterate and with little commerce. Furthermore, they were heavily dominated by Europeans in a not very advanced phase of their development, with no ability to resist; consequently they are not eligible for a possible comparison with European civilization on the prerequisites that led to industrialization. The exclusion of India is different and less clearly defensible. India had a complex agrarian civilization until the third millennium BCE that was linked in many ways to both China and Europe. Over the course of the centuries we are considering it also had some complex commercial activity that was fairly successful. As has been authoritatively clarified by Amartya Sen, its intellectual and religious life was original in many ways, as it had some elements of a secular state and a pluralism absent in other parts of Asia that were the basis of its democratic evolution in the twentieth century.[8] However, it was not able to defend its cultural traditions and economy either politically or militarily. First it was not able to resist the Muslim conquest, which established the Moghul empire that endured for over five hundred years until the seventeenth century. Later it was dominated by the British, which began with the incursion of the East

---

6. Although the southern boundary had Islamic settlements and major military conflicts and, despite always being in the eye of the storm, in the end it proved to be a defined border.

7. As previously cited, North wrote in this regard: "To treat the Netherlands and England as success stories in isolation from the stimulus received from the rest of Europe ... is to miss a vital part of the explanation. Italian city states, Portugal, and Germanic states all fell behind the Netherlands and England; but banking, artistic development, improvements in navigation and printing were just a few of the obvious contributions that the former states made to European advancement" (North, *Understanding*, 138).

8. Sen, *The Argumentative Indian*.

Table 1.2 Comparison between advanced agrarian civilizations with respect to several strategic factors for economic development.

	China, 6th–16th century	Islamic world, 8th–16th century	Europe, 11th–16th century
Liberty	Absolutist government; unified empire; upper class bureaucracy; lower class merchants; caste system	Theocratic government; political fragmentation prior to the Ottoman Empire; unstable boundaries; merchants had no political power; less functional business organization (clan based, with unlimited liability)	City-states self-governed by merchants; political fragmentation; western boundary protective but limiting, with a large inland sea; functional business organization (non-familial, with limited liability)
Order	Stable; army for defence only	Instability prior to the Ottoman Empire; wars of conquest	General state of war to defend autonomous entities, but also for conquest
Justice	Protected rights to cultivate land, but generally the emperor's arbitrariness	Will of the elite	Impersonal, based on codes and *habeas corpus*; protection of property rights
Taxation	Light, often unpredictable (confiscation)	Light	Always increasing, but *no taxation without representation*; development of public debt, large fiscal capacity
Public goods	Some (e.g. dams, the Great Wall)	Few	Increasing number: infrastructure, education, hospitals, commercial, economic institutions, and welfare (poor laws)

India Company (see Chapter 2) in the seventeenth century.[9] As a consequence India is ineligible for our comparison with other civilizations on the possibility of developing an industrial revolution because it lacked the institutional prerequisites, mainly political, that the other areas considered had.

So let us move on to a comment on Table 1.2. The three civilizations described here had long developed writing, manufacturing (in the original sense of the term as products made by hand, but with the aid of mechanical devices as well) and commerce, and thus a civil life, although agriculture was the most widespread activity. They were based on different religions and philosophies, but they shared a belief in human rationality, an ethic of virtues (although parsed in very different ways), and in the dissemination of culture and the arts. On the basis of these traits they were capable of producing important technological and scientific advancements and of conducting business. The different historical span taken into account in the tables testifies to the fact that the fall of the Roman Empire had created a delay in Europe that was bridged only with great effort. Indeed, recent literature clarifies that until the end of the eleventh century China and the Arab world were more advanced than Europe, as is also demonstrated by their ability to support a large population. They were the stagnant countries that much Eurocentric literature from Adam Smith and Marx down to Max Weber had maintained. They were equipped with complex military machines, flourishing commercial activities and skilled manufacturing in textiles and ceramics, but they demonstrated a different ability to sustain the pace of development over the centuries.

To understand the reasons for the "great divergence", a felicitous expression coined by Pomeranz, Table 1.2 compares several foundational dimensions of the three societies.[10] The first line details the form of government: liberal or absolutist. In China an absolutist government has always dominated, one that paternalistically protected its subjects, but it gave them no voice. In the case of the Islamic world the government was – and still is – subordinated to religious precepts, with laws that always descend from above. It is clear that not all absolutist governments are rapacious and opposed to economic

---

9. See Metcalf & Metcalf, *A Concise History of Modern India.* These authors highlight India's flourishing economy until the seventeenth century, which was not accompanied by a state organization capable of confronting emerging challenges. Paradoxically, it was precisely its flourishing commerce that prompted the Indians to come to terms with the British, who by then dominated international trade and ended up dominating the Indians through their powerful trading company.

10. Pomeranz, *The Great Divergence.*

development. Rather, many of them seek to promote development, primarily for the purpose of enriching the elite in power with their bureaucracies, arming the military and attaining an international power status. But laws emanating from above are never as favourable to individual economic activity as those designed by the economic actors themselves, which is what happened in the cities, and later in the states, that were self-governed by an economic elite or governed with the participation of an economic elite. Furthermore, the liberty enjoyed by individuals in societies with representative governments cannot be compared to that allowed in societies with absolutist governments. Chapters 2 and 3 will provide extensive documentation of these claims. As North (among many others) well wrote:

> The lack of large-scale political and economic order [in Europe] created the essential environment hospitable to economic growth and ultimately human freedom. In that competitive decentralized environment lots of alternatives were pursued …the key to the story is the variety of the options pursued and the increased likelihood (as compared to a single unified policy) that some would turn out to produce economic growth.[11]

Still, absolutist governments create "extractive" institutions, to the harm of "inclusive" ones, much more easily than in governments that are participatory or in some measure democratic. Comparing extractive and inclusive institutions is at the heart of Acemoglu and Robinson's work.[12] They define extractive institutions as those that place the economic surplus produced in the service of enriching the few through the extraction of rents, primarily by taxation and finance. Inclusive institutions are those that allow a great many people to participate with equal opportunity in economic activities. According to Acemoglu and Robinson, the development produced by extractive institutions is inevitably limited over time, while that of inclusive institutions is sustainable and cumulative. Ultimately the political fragmentation typical of Europe, by creating small states, provided an incentive for governments to seek the best way to increase wealth, whether from a technological or an organizational and military point of view.[13]

---

11. North, *Understanding*, 137–8.
12. Acemoglu & Robinson, *Why Nations Fail*.
13. This is the thesis of Rosenthal & Wong, *Before and Beyond Divergence*, who conclude that "European advantages were unintended consequences of political differences with China" (*ibid.*, 9).

Order, the second dimension, follows directly from the first. Large states such as China have many internal resources, and interest is concentrated on maintaining the status quo, which favours isolationist and defensive tendencies, while small states always seek to become larger and to field campaigns of conquest. From this angle, the perennial state of war in Europe between the Middle Ages and the twentieth century was a price to pay for the fragmentation that created far greater incentives for economic growth than those reported in China. Geographical explorations in the Age of Discovery, which will be discussed in Chapter 2, were also a result of political fragmentation and the competition to increase the wealth of small European states, which had very limited resources.[14]

The Islamic world was in wars of conquest much more similar to Europe than China because prior to the Ottoman Empire it was long fragmented internally. Its geographic location did not help. On one side it collided with the Europeans, who arrested it to the west and north; on the other it collided with India and the Asiatic peoples to the east. India was actually conquered by Islam (the Moghul Empire, mentioned above), but the Asiatic peoples (first Genghis Khan and then the Ottoman Turks) instead conquered and occasionally destroyed Islamic states, even though they converted to Islam. In the end, the Ottoman Turks built an Islamic empire in the sixteenth century on the ruins of the previous states. It quickly entered difficult times, however, primarily because its economic sources dried up (the Mediterranean and the Red Sea, were both largely replaced by the Atlantic routes and the emergence of the New World), but due also to its absolutist government. Furthermore, its geographic location discouraged the Islamic world from participating in geographic exploration, a fate which was also shared by the Italian cities.

The third dimension – justice in the legal sense – is highly significant when seen in conjunction with the system of government. If the latter is absolutist, justice will be arbitrary, while if it is representative, and then democratic, it will be "equal for all", at least in principle, and it will not give rise to privileges. The Roman Empire's legal tradition (*habeas corpus*, that is, no one may be prosecuted without evidence of guilt), which Europe inherited, was in this sense very positive.

With the last two dimensions we come to the role of the state, a theme

---

14. Parthasarathi (*Why Europe Grew Rich and Asia Did Not*) maintains that European development was an unintended consequence of economic pressures due to the scarcity of resources in the small states; here he is in agreement with Rosenthal and Bin, who however emphasize the political implications more than fragmentation.

which will be discussed in Chapter 4. Europe is noted for higher and more efficient taxation. This was initially necessary for military purposes, but it was also used to increase the production of goods and services that were not convenient to produce by private parties (the so-called "public goods"); eventually it came to be seen as strategic for development. This is a type of integrative public activity that does not replace private initiative. Even within Europe itself it was ascertained that the most representative states also taxed their citizens more in order to better defend them and to offer greater military support for carrying out their activities. Precisely due to the high level of taxes demanded by European states, the populations ended up imposing limits on their use, according to the famous phrase coined in the American colonies before the Revolutionary War: no taxation without representation.[15] This is also why increasingly widespread and extended forms of participation emerged in conducting the affairs of the state, which were no longer the exclusive domain of the "sovereign"; over time these participatory forms led to a true political democracy.

What emerges from the comparison between the three civilizations in Table 1.2 is that Europe clearly stands out as the area in which individual liberties were better safeguarded, primarily through the existence of political institutions that not only respected the individual but which were also ready to understand the significance of and to support individuals' economic initiatives. This was done through a plurality of cultural institutions in which intellectuals not only had a way to publicly state their different points of view, but also to teach them to new generations of students who could move from one university to another (the so-called *clerici vagantes*) to acquire a critical knowledge. It is precisely the liberty of thought and enterprise that underlies self-sustaining economic progress and the multiplicity of economic entities that create competition – the most powerful driver of continual improvement in the use of resources.

We can conclude that Europe knew how to develop an environment conducive to technological and institutional innovation because there was greater liberty and greater legal certainty, which gave a more solid foundation for investment related economic calculation.[16] Moreover, it provided greater subsidiary support for individual initiative by public authorities at both the military and political level and the economic level (public goods). The philosophical and religious foundations of Europe proved to be strategic

---

15. In this regard see Findlay & O'Rourke, *Power and Plenty*, 350.
16. See the exhaustive work by Mokyr, *The Lever of Riches* as well as Rosenberg & Birdzell, *How the West Grew Rich*.

in creating and sustaining this political, cultural and economic dynamic.[17] They can be summarized in four points.

The first foundation was the definition of the human person as having unique and absolute value, in that according to Christianity human beings were created in the image of God, and composed of a body and a soul, or material and spiritual aspects, that coexist. Liberty and justice derive from this centrality of the person. The more this principle was asserted, the more absolutism and slavery were abandoned and privileges and discrimination were eliminated. Ultimately the equality of all persons was declared – whether male or female, child or old person, rich or poor, sick or healthy, weak or strong – with fundamental implications for politics (representative government, then democracy) and economics (the liberty of individual initiative).[18] Beginning with St Benedict (*Ora et labora*), the concept of work itself was revisited as an activity not of slaves, but of free persons. The Benedictine and Cistercian monastic experiences were the first to put this new concept of work into practice, which, when done by free and thinking people, tends to improve productivity. All the early treatises on machines that could replace or complement human labour were written by monks.

The second foundation follows from the first. If each human person is in the image of God, then the basic relationship between persons is a horizontal relationship. Solidarity, trust, and business relationships are not limited to the clan, but rather they extend universally. This was the origin of institutions that are elective (i.e. not bound to the family and clan) and impersonal (in the sense that they extend to persons whom one does not know), which entailed implementing mechanisms for formal sanctions (i.e. specialized courts) and assurance of public trust (i.e. the notary system; see Chapter 2). Christianity was (and remains) a powerful and influential hub of this universal fraternity. The Franciscans elaborated the concept of the "common good", which ultimately saw the purpose of merchants' and manufacturers' activities as the prosperity of the local community, justifying individual enrichment only as a consequence.[19] The "expansive" mindset of European merchants originated from this foundation; it drove them to overcome limits by any means possible to expand their volume of business.[20] The "civil" economy was born, an

---

17. In the latest economic literature there is a growing appreciation of culture as a determining factor of economic success or failure. See the review in Lopez-Claros & Perotti, *Does Culture Matter for Growth?* and Mitterauer, *Why Europe?*.
18. On this theme see Bruni & Zamagni, *Civil Economy*.
19. See Todeschini, *Franciscan Wealth* and S. Zamagni, *Mercato*.
20. A summary source of all preceding works on the Franciscans' theoretical elaboration in Zamagni & Porta, *Economia*.

economy in service of the city, in which each one found her role through work done well, competent and fair transactions, the division of labour and common responsibility for the needs of the city.[21]

The third foundation is the exaltation of the spirit as having the capacity to reason, from which followed the birth of science (the scientific revolution), the spread of learning (universities, literacy schools and printing), and mankind's control over nature (*homo faber*, which led to technology). Humanists and the great scientists and artists of the Renaissance were the interpreters of this principle, initially in Italy and then in Europe.[22] The systematic ordering of knowledge, the experimental method of searching for proofs and the comparative critical analysis that were developed during that time led to an accumulation of scientific results that has not ceased since. As Newton said, "If I have seen further than others, it is by standing upon the shoulders of giants".[23]

Finally, the fourth element, the separation of powers, was crucial to avoid the concentration of too much power in too few hands and to allow space for a system of checks and balances. In its early phase the separation of powers meant a distinction between civil and religious power, which was not achieved in Europe without opposition and heavy conflict; this distinction was instead rejected by the Islamic world and irrelevant in China. In a second phase it meant the articulation of society into "corporations" or guilds – intermediate entities – that enjoyed broad autonomy. Later, it came to mean the separation of legislative, judicial and executive powers, an articulation that did not exist in absolutist states.[24]

These were the characteristics of European society that, amid opposition and setbacks, permitted the emergence of broadly inclusive economic practices that gave Europe an advantage even prior to the industrial revolution.[25] For example, a widely debated question in the recent literature is the impact of plague – the Black Death – in the fourteenth century; we can define that event as worldwide and it spread throughout the Eurasian continent. The death of tens of millions of people resulted in increased wages everywhere, but in later centuries that increase was sustained only in some European

---

21. Grief, "The Birth of Impersonal Exchange".
22. Garin, *L'uomo del Rinascimento*.
23. Newton was actually drawing from a tradition that goes back to the medieval theologians; see Casini, *Newton e la coscienza europea*.
24. John Locke (1632–1704) gave formal status to the separation of powers, and with Montesquieu (1689–1755) it became an actual theory; see Felice, *Oppressione e libertà: Filosofia e anatomia del dispotismo nel pensiero di Montesquieu*.
25. For additional details on the peculiarities of Europe, see Goldstone, *Why Europe?*

Table 1.3 Gross domestic product per capita (1990 US dollars).

Region	1000	1500	1600	1700	1820	1870	1911	1952	2003	Index (USA = 100)	2003 Index 1500 = 1
Western Europe	425	772	889	987	1,110	1,960	3,457	4,719	16,821	58	22
United States	400	400	400	527	1,257	2,445	5,301	10,316	29,037	100	73
Japan	425	500	520	570	669	737	1,387	2,336	21,218	73	42
China	466	600	600	600	600	530	562	538	4,803	17	8
India	450	550	550	550	533	533	673	629	2,160	7	4
Latin America	–	–	–	–	691	742	1,618	2,588	5,786	20	–
Mexico	400	425	454	568	759	674	1,732	2,504	7,137	25	17
Brazil	–	400	428	459	646	713	811	1,752	5,563	19	14
Former Soviet Union	400	499	552	610	688	943	1,488	2,937	5,397	19	11
Russian Federation									6,323	22	
Ottoman Empire and predecessors	600	660	–	770	740	825	1,213	–	–	–	–

Note: Maddison based his estimates on the value of the 1990 dollar as a benchmark. Other values expressed in different currencies are converted to dollars without using exchange rates, which, as is well-known, are volatile and may not accurately reflect relative price structures. For the purposes of international comparisons of the size of national accounts, a system of "purchasing power parity" exchange rates was developed calculated on a representative basket of goods and services valued at current prices in the countries included in the comparison. The UN was the first to develop this method, which was then applied by the European Union and now used by historians. Maddison's estimates are therefore in purchasing power parity.

Sources: Maddison database; for the Ottoman Empire, Bolt & Van Zanden, *The First Update to the Maddison Project.*

countries. In other areas, however, it was a relatively short-lived event that left no trace.[26] These primed economic processes that led to the industrial revolution; we will examine in Chapter 3. But before doing so we will focus in Chapter 2, on the institutions and economic practices that facilitated the creation of the European advantage, institutions and practices which took shape first in the Italian city-states prior to the international trade triggered by the Age of Discovery.

Table 1.3 shows Europe's backwardness relative to other countries around the year 1000 and its growing advantage prior to the industrial revolution. We should note a few observations about the table. Throughout this volume we will primarily use GDP, or gross domestic product, an indicator that is by now universally accepted, for the purpose of comparing economic development. It gives an account of the production of goods and services within a chosen geographical area (usually a nation, but also a region, as we will see) for a given year, standardized per capita for comparative purposes. Although as the basic indicator it has various defects, we do not yet have a better one for representing the degree of economic advancement; today it is often cited along with other indicators to offer a more penetrating analysis.[27] The use of GDP as an indicator spread primarily in the last century, but thanks to Angus Maddison, a great English scholar who worked for many years at Groningen in the Netherlands, today a homogeneous database exists that has brought together many historians' work regarding earlier centuries than the one just passed. For centuries before those in which we have actual data we only have estimates of GDP, but these have been constructed on a solid and consistent base. The quantitative basis of this work is drawn from that database.

---

26. Findlay & O'Rourke, *Power and Plenty.*
27. For a highly interesting presentation and discussion, see Lepenies, *The Power of a Single Number.*

2

From the Italian city-states
to the Age of Discovery

2.1 *The new system of European citizenship*

It is widely recognized that, beginning in the twelfth century, the cities that formed in Europe had different characteristics to Islamic, Indian and Chinese cities. Merchants played a dominant economic role in cities everywhere, which were a mélange of people dedicated for the most part to non-agricultural activities, such as manufacturing, services and bureaucracies. But there were also cities in Europe that enjoyed either total political independence (as in Italy, the Netherlands, Switzerland, or the Hansa) or extensive autonomy; this is why the banners of many European, and particularly Italian, cities carry the word *libertas*. Businessmen in these cities play a political role of self-government, which was unknown outside Europe.[1] We will examine in some detail how they operated and the institutional implications that made European cities, and Italian cities in particular, centres of innovation, with consequent wealth accumulation (as shown in Table 1.3) and technological and organizational changes.

The economic system of the city was based on two pillars: the craft guilds and the chambers of merchants. Craftsmen did not normally produce goods

---

1. Mielants, in *Origins of Capitalism*, insists on this point. European cities not only left their merchants free, they also actively supported their business activities both internally, through legislation and tending to let them govern the surrounding countryside as well, and externally, through diplomatic and military backing. "Independent urban institutions that favoured policies that would facilitate capital accumulation were not established [in Asia] ... and most cities did not envisage implementing a systematic colonization strategy similar to their Western European counterparts" (*ibid.*, 147).

for inventory, but rather to order from merchants, who sometimes provided the raw materials. A close relationship formed between the merchants who developed the business (and who frequently accumulated raw materials and finished goods in their *fondachi*, or warehouses) and the artisans who had the tools and the know-how to work with them. Manufacturing production quickly benefitted from important technological innovations. Beginning in the thirteenth century hydraulic power was used to operate mechanisms in various fields such as ironworking, timber sawing, paper processing and spinning. Sometimes these were innovations already known in the Islamic world or China, which Europeans introduced or reinvented. But the two most important areas in which medieval European technology made important developments were navigation and clockmaking.

In navigation, the widespread use of the magnetic compass, the creation of nautical charts and compiling trigonometric tables allowed navigation by instruments or mathematics that, in conjunction with the stern helm, made sea travel much more precise and feasible even in less favourable weather conditions. These innovations were already known in China. However, it was the revolution in mechanical clocks that had incalculable consequences. Time had been traditionally measured by the hourglass and the sundial, but beginning in the thirteenth century a mechanical solution was sought in Europe. There is not agreement on where the first clocks were built; the most probable area was in northern Italy, but Germany also claims to be the first. The fact remains that in the fourteenth century the mechanical clock spread rapidly throughout Europe, with mechanical masterpieces that not only automatically marked hours and minutes, but also days, months, years, and even the planetary orbits, frequently accompanied by sound and by pirouettes of angels, Madonnas and other characters who were revealed and concealed at pre-established times. The advent of the mechanical clock established the "mechanical" way of thinking in the West that was the basis of its fortunes. The mechanical clock was an original European invention that was unknown elsewhere.

The leading European areas in which cities developed manufacturing capabilities were north-central Italy and the southern Netherlands (Flanders and Brabant). Italy took advantage of its geographical location as a natural bridge between Europe, North Africa and the Near East. The Netherlands were at the centre of roads and routes between the North Sea and the Atlantic coast of France and Spain. Italian merchants were the ones who most developed these new commercial routes. A document from 1127 mentions the "Lombards" (the people of north-central Italy) as participants in fairs promoted by local lords. The first fairs took place in north Italy in the twelfth century and then spread to many other places in Europe, such as Champagne, Provence, Frankfurt, Scotland and Ireland.

The Flemish – the inhabitants of Flanders – pushed primarily into Germany, where native merchants very quickly became active, but they also arrived in Italy. The Gotthard Pass opened in the first half of the thirteenth century with the audacious construction of a bridge, called the "Devil's Bridge", built along a cliff face and over a deep gorge, became a crucial passage for goods; this brought Switzerland into commercial activity. Participation in European commerce is precisely what allowed the Swiss cantons to become politically autonomous. Other passes subsequently opened through the Alps. However, toward the end of the thirteenth century Italians were regularly transporting goods by sea between the Mediterranean and the North Sea by circumnavigating the Iberian Peninsula and France. Land and sea transport companies were created, as well as courier services to carry messages.

Trying to keep out the Flemish and hold other competitors at bay, the Italians – particularly from Venice, Pisa and Genoa – built impressive trade routes in the southern and eastern Mediterranean, in part following the Crusades. Venice became the "gateway to the East", not only because it colonized vast areas of the eastern Mediterranean, but because it sponsored expeditions to the Black Sea and Crimea, as well as Central Asia, India and China. Venetian trading communities settled in Egypt, Syria, Tunisia, Trabzon, Constantinople, Thessalonika, Bulgaria, Romania, Greece, Cyprus, Famagusta, Nicosia and Crimea, as well as Central Asia, India and China.[2] Multiple sea routes opened to India and China in addition to the traditional land routes, such as the Silk Road. They departed from Arabia and sailed through the Red Sea, entering the Indian Ocean at Aden; they stopped in south India or Sri Lanka and then sailing along the Indonesian islands they reached Guangzhou, or Canton, in south China. Europeans quickly specialized in foreign trade because their cities were too small to offer markets sufficiently large for the production and exchange abilities they were able to develop.

The great freedom these merchants enjoyed also brought about significant innovations in economic institutions, contracts and money management; some were adaptations of existing practices in the Islamic world, but with their spread and refinement in Europe they quickly became incomparable. The following are among the most important:

- The *commenda* (also known in Venice as *collegantia*). The twelfth century saw the development, primarily in the maritime cities, of a form of capital

---

2. For a general overview see Cardini & Montesano, *Storia Medioevale*.

association that permitted someone who did not want to work directly for a company to finance it, advancing part of the necessary capital and receiving an adequate compensation in return. This was the beginning of the practice of raising capital from people unrelated by family in order to employ it under the responsibility of a few business agents; they promised high returns, with the risk in each case of losing only the capital advanced (limited liability). This led to the formation of the joint-stock company in the seventeenth century,[3] but many additional rules had to be introduced before the practice became widespread.

- *Insurance.* The first steps toward insurance were taken in the twelfth century in the maritime Republic of Venice to address the high risk of shipowners who carried goods by sea. Insurance significantly lowered their business risk.

- *Banks.* The term "bank" originates from the Lombard term *banka*, or "bench", which was the cloth covered board on which financial trans-actions took place in fairs and town squares. Lending practices existed everywhere, but the bank that was created in the medieval cities was linked to merchants' activities, so much so that frequently there were merchant–bankers, which only later separated. The banking practices that were developed – such as letters of credit or bills of exchange – did not have the goal of obtaining a fixed return for property owners, as had happened until then, but of enabling credit flows to finance commerce over vast areas.[4]

This credit for productive and commercial activity made cities wealthy, beyond just the merchants, because it increased the work available and provided better living conditions for all. This is why the Catholic Church, particularly following Franciscan teaching as previously mentioned, slowly abandoned condemning usury for such practices as credit for productive purposes, making them morally acceptable. However, there was not always a clear separation between these new forms of investment credit and more traditional credit, such as loans to reigning families for fighting wars; that could lead to serious difficulties, and even failure, for banking houses. Conversely, credit for consumption was made available by special institutions with donated capital – the *Monti di Pietà*[5]

---

3. See Felloni, *Profilo di storia economica dell'Europa dal medioevo all'età contemporanea*, 127–30.
4. See Malanima, *Economia preindustriale*, 451 ff.
5. Literally "Piety Fund", the historical origin of the contemporary pawn shop. These were operated as charities, in which the "mount", or capital fund contributed by the wealthy, was lent at low interest rates to those in need, for the benefit of the borrower rather than the profit of the lender.

– that loaned them at moderate interest rates; these were the first form of "microcredit".[6] Ultimately public banks emerged, which specialized in loans to states in the form of "public debt" bonds, in order to support a war, address famine or public health crises or construct public infrastructure. This ultimately limited the types of credit considered as usury to marginal cases, against which the Church's condemnation remained unchanged, and the purposes and practices of finance radically changed.

- *Double entry accounting.* This was a way of keeping track of accounts by writing all expenses and income in ledger books in order to be able to compare them and precisely understand how well the business was operating. This method was already known in the Islamic world; it was perfected by European merchants, beginning with Leonardo Fibonacci in Pisa, who applied it in 1202.[7]
- *The "ius mercatorum" or "lex mercatoria"* (commercial law). The expansion of commerce increased the disputes between economic agents. To resolve these disputes the merchants' guild, which had its own statutes, imposed a normative system of regulations that was also binding on third parties not belonging to the guild, creating a jurisdiction administered by merchant–judges. The *ius mercatorum* was therefore an international commercial law directly created by the merchant class; all were bound by it, which demonstrated the privileged position merchants held in the cities.[8]

The necessity of recording an ever increasing number of contracts led to the emergence of a new profession, the notary or notary public; such a figure had previously existed with various duties, although in a private role. Beginning in the twelfth century, the notary had the recognized role as the guarantor of the legitimacy of a legal transaction concluded in his presence, which took on the value of a public act. In the middle of the thirteenth century in Bologna around four hundred notaries were already practicing; in Pisa 1183 notaries were attested. During the thirteenth century notarial practice became part of the Guild of Jurisconsults and was included as a subject taught in law schools, particularly in Bologna and Padua.

The concentration of a large part of this dynamic in Italian cities led to their incredible economic prosperity, as Table 2.1 clearly shows. In 1300 the

---

6. See Muzzarelli, *Il denaro e la salvezza.*
7. Felloni, *Profilo di storia economica,* 116. The double entry method was later theorized in an essay by Fra Luca Pacioli in 1494.
8. Galgano, *Lex Mercatoria.*

Table 2.1 Gross domestic product per capita (in 1990 dollars).

Region	1300	1400	1500	1570	1650	1700	1750	1820	1850
England/Britain	742	1,099	1,058	1,111	925	1,515	1,695	2,074	2,774†
The Netherlands	876	1,195	1,454	1,432	2,691	2,105	2,355	1,874	2,355
North–central Italy	1,620	1,751	1,533	1,459	1,398	1,476	1,533	1,511	1,481
Spain	864	819	846	910	687	814	783	–	1,079
Germany	–	–	1146	–	948	939	1,050	1,077*	1,428
France	–	–	727*	–	860*	910*	–	1,135	1,597

Notes: *From Maddison's old database, see Table 1.1; †1849, because in 1850 the series moved to the UK, including Ireland, which lowered the average income level.

Source: Bolt & van Zanden, *The First Update to the Maddison Project.*

cities in north-central Italy had already attained a per capita income double that of the most prosperous areas in Europe in Holland and Spain. England was far behind. A century later the Italian cities were still solidly in first place, but Holland and England were catching up. The Italian cities regressed in the sixteenth century, although their level of income was only attained by Holland, which in the seventeenth century surpassed all others and remained at the top until the beginning of the nineteenth century. By then the British industrial revolution had reached its maturity, but Holland remained wealthy even afterward. The wealth of the Italian cities was surpassed by Britain only in the eighteenth century, while all other European areas lagged behind until the middle of the nineteenth century; this included Spain, where a temporary slight improvement was recorded only in the sixteenth century.

The institutional innovations initiated in the Italian cities continued even when they were in crisis, but it is clear that these were refinements of already existing practices.[9] Among the main ones were these:

- *The stock exchange*, as a site of commercial and financial operations. The first stock exchange opened in Antwerp in 1531, but it only formalized practices that had existed for some time in various commercial European cities;
- *The postal service*, which was introduced in the fifteenth century when Emperor Maximilian entrusted the imperial postal service to Francesco Tasso, a Lombard;
- *The patent*, which protected the commercial exploitation of new inventions. It was first introduced in England in 1624, with a fourteen year duration;
- *Commercial codes*, which slowly took shape in many European countries under the various courts for trade affairs until they were formally codified in the Napoleonic era, with the emergence of the Chambers of Commerce.

---

9. Avner Greif recognized this in the conclusion of his 2006 work: "the late medieval institutional development had direct impact on later institutions. The modern business corporation grew out of the legal form of the corporation, as developed for medieval guilds, municipalities, monasteries and universities. The operation of the late medieval corporations led to the development of particular knowledge, laws, and other institutional elements that manifested in current practices such as trading in shares, limited liability, auditing, apprenticeship, and double entry bookkeeping. European commercial law, insurance markets, patent systems, public debt, business associations, and central banks were developed in the context of medieval institutions" (394).

This lengthy preparation of the institutional ground suited for expanding and improving the functioning of markets, as well as preparing for manufacturing on a larger scale and with increasingly automated systems driven by mechanical (largely hydraulic) power, created the incentives for the strategic inventions that brought about the birth of the industrial revolution in Europe.[10] However, before arriving there we should take a look at the long-term effects of the geographic explorations during the Age of Discovery.

2.2   *The Age of Discovery and commercial companies*

European sea explorations in the fifteenth and sixteenth centuries sparked a true spatial revolution because the world's boundaries became defined and measurable, resulting in both an expansion of opportunities and a compression of space. Movement toward an effectively global narrative accelerated, and the process of globally integrating economics, politics and culture began, which has since continued to intensify. However, the new geographic discoveries first altered the balances Europe had achieved.

Italy was cut out of the colonial exploitation of the newly discovered lands, not because it lacked skilled navigators (all the early explorers were Italian, but they were funded by other governments and companies) or because the Italian ports were on the Mediterranean (the way out of the Mediterranean was well-known, and Genoa and Venice had long established sea routes to Holland and Flanders) but for two basic reasons: the economic positions acquired by the Italian maritime republics were so comfortable (as we saw in Table 2.1) that there was no incentive to change and the Italian city-states were too small to be able to support expeditions on the scale required to cross oceans without stable alliances, which they did not want to establish.[11] Furthermore, the loss of its position in Mediterranean commerce was slow. This was partly due to resistance by the Islamic world; it too was interested in maintaining its routes, which it long defended, but it eventually lost, along with the Italians.

For Portugal, however, it was a unique opportunity. Its location had set it apart from the European traffic flows, and its kings were keen to find a way to escape the marginalization in which they were confined. As for Spain, during

---

10. See Hicks, *A Theory of Economic History*. Hicks, a Nobel laureate in economics, placed the emergence of the European market system at the centre of his work, identifying the institutional and political elements that made it possible.

11. For further information on the decline of Italy see Malanima, *L'economia italiana*.

its long war with the Arabs it had become accustomed to a constant state of war, which had not allowed a prosperous economic state organization to emerge. So they tried their luck with Christopher Columbus, and when they saw the initial results they dedicated themselves to the colonial venture with an approach of military conquest. However, the first colonizing European countries were not the ones that most benefited from the new routes to the Indies and the discovery of the New World. The exploration baton passed from Portugal and Spain to Holland and then to England. Portugal declined because it was incorporated into the Spanish kingdom in 1578 and could no longer act autonomously. The rise of Holland was mainly due to their fierce resistance to Spanish domination, which was possible primarily because of the wealth they had accumulated through commerce (see Table 2.1) The premature Spanish decline was in turn explained by the fact that the wealth sourced from their colonies led them to embark on too many power-seeking military ventures without sufficiently improving their national economic infrastructure. The rise of Britain was the result of a distinctive approach to how they used their colonies, which we will analyze in depth in Chapter 3.

In addition to bringing about profound changes in the balance of power in Europe, the geographic explorations brought to the fore the continent that came to be called America, which until then had been completely isolated from the world, and they brought an end to Asia's semi-isolation. Indeed, although important trade flows had existed since ancient times between Europe and Asia, transportation had always been highly demanding, which had not allowed close relationships. With the arrival of European ships directly in the Indian Ocean that isolation came to an end. This was partly due to the European conquest of Asian territories, but also due to the decline of the Chinese empire and the re-emergence of the Japanese empire.

However, before continuing to examine the economic and political implications of the geographic explorations, we should answer a crucial question: why was it not China that explored and colonized the world? Indeed, while the Islamic world did not measure up to this challenge, as we have seen, we cannot assume the same of China, bounded as it was by an ocean, as was Europe. According to the historian Daniel Headrick five seafaring traditions existed in the fifteenth century, and without doubt the Chinese tradition was the most advanced of all.[12] The Chinese had built formidable ships, called "junks", that were watertight, with multiple bridges and between three and twelve masts; they were capable of carrying up to a thousand men and a thousand tons of cargo. They had used the magnetic compass and the stern

---

12. Headrick, *Power over Peoples*.

rudder since the eleventh century; they were the most advanced ships in the world, and they could have easily crossed the Pacific. A historical episode bears witness to China's abilities in naval technology. In 1405 the Chinese emperor decided to send a flotilla of 317 ships with 37,000 men, under the command of Admiral Zheng He, to Southeast Asia and the Indian Ocean. The largest ships were about five times as long as Columbus's largest ship, the *Santa Maria*. Other expeditions followed until 1423, but successive emperors did not think it necessary to continue to push in that direction. After the last voyage in 1432 foreign trade was sharply curtailed, and the "treasure fleets", as they were called, were destroyed or left to rot, and a ban was issued against building new ones.

Why did this happen? As an explanation scholars argue that the construction of internal canals made coastal navigation less pressing and that the threat of new invasions from the north diverted resources to the construction of the Great Wall.[13] But certainly what counted above all were the size of the Chinese empire, which favoured a mindset of self-sufficiency and a notion of stability that they did not want to undermine by venturing outside the territory, and the lack of political power by the merchant class,[14] which could not oppose imperial decisions. After all, Zheng He's expeditions were desired by the emperor, not the merchant class.

There were two European maritime traditions. The first was the Mediterranean tradition, which because of the generally limited and unpredictable winds preferred a sailing ship with oarsmen to be used as needed. The "galley", of carvel construction, was the type of ship used by the Venetian and Genoese sailors to reach Belgium and England. They were poorly adapted to heavy seas and could not carry more than a few days' provisions for the oarsmen. The second tradition was the Northern European, which developed the "cocca" type ship. These were strong, tall ships of clinker or lapstrake construction (which required much more wood), without oarsmen, and with a load capacity of up to three hundred tons, although they were not easily manoeuvrable. Portugal was the first European country to develop boats suitable for navigation on the open ocean. These were the "caravels", a cross between the galley and the cocca, without oarsmen, with lateen and square sails, a bridge, a castle and a stern helm. The caravels were fast, manoeuvrable and could remain at sea for long periods, but they were not adapted for carrying heavy cargo. Towards the end of the fifteenth century larger ships with deeper hulls were built, called "carracks" (*nao* in Spanish). These two types of ships, equipped

13. *Ibid.*
14. On this theme see Acemoglu & Robinson, *Why Nations Fail* and Hubbard & Kane, *Balance*.

with magnetic compasses, were used for geographic exploration. After the Portuguese circumnavigation of Africa and Columbus's ocean crossing in the fifteenth century, the certainty of being able to face long voyages and win skirmishes with the indigenous peoples in the lands discovered led to a long series of explorations by Europeans, who ultimately left no corner of the world unexplored. Ships were further refined, and the most widespread model became the *galleon*, so called because it was an evolution of the galley (although without oarsmen). Compared to the carrack, the galleon was larger, the prow and the stern became quite tall to accommodate more bridge levels, and it had a highly complex sail system. It was equipped with cannons (even non-military galleons), and boasted a tonnage of between five hundred and two thousand tonnes, so it could stay at sea for months.

For the first time the known world did not stop at the Pillars of Hercules, the African desert where *"hic sunt leones"*, or in the far-off exotic lands of China; rather, it was seen in all its completeness as a globe with many oceans and many scattered lands. Those who had opened this unexpected perspective were products of the most advanced European civilizations, and it was therefore natural that the first thing they sought to derive from them was what produced wealth at that time: commerce. In the first place, new routes were opened to import known products: spices, silk, sugar and other products from the East that until then had traversed the Mediterranean routes controlled by Italian cities, after having navigated across the Indian Ocean and through the Islamic lands, particularly Asia Minor. Not only did the Italian cities see their trade drop drastically, but also the Ottoman Empire, through which goods had passed when not transported by sea, suffered a drop in trade and in state revenue. Not knowing how to respond, it began to decline. In the second place, trade began in new products. The Americas were found to be rich in plants unknown in Europe, or which were known but difficult to cultivate. A partial list includes corn, avocados, pumpkins, potatoes, tomatoes, peppers, vanilla, peanuts, cocoa, sunflowers, pineapples, strawberries, mangoes, papayas and tobacco.

The story of corn is one of the most interesting. This was a staple product in Central America, where some peoples also made popcorn. When it came to Europe it grew successfully in southern Europe in rotation with wheat and in many areas it came to be one of the staple foods for farmers (as polenta) and the main feed for many kinds of animals. The potato, originally from Haiti, spread widely across Europe, particularly in Ireland. Cocoa, which was not transplantable to Europe, was cultivated by the Aztecs and provided one of their favourite beverages, usually reserved for dignitaries. Coffee arrived in Europe from the Islamic world, which in turn had brought it from Africa; it made the reverse voyage and became one of Brazil's main products. Sugarcane was planted by the Spanish in Central America and by the Portuguese in Brazil. Tea was a Chinese beverage that, when the new trade routes were opened, came to Europe from Asia and particularly from the Indian peninsula.

Finally, we should recall the large quantities of gold, silver and other precious metals that came to Europe from the Americas and Africa. Between the end of the fifteenth century and the beginning of the seventeenth century there was a long period of price increases, or inflation, throughout Europe, but predominantly in Spain and Portugal, the countries that imported precious metals, and in the countries from which they purchased their goods (countries in northern Europe, Holland and Italy). The idea that this inflation was due to the increased flow of precious metals (the abundance of which led to a devaluation of the coins made from them with respect to other goods) was already corroborated by contemporary commentators. Along with the monetary cause, the price hikes of the sixteenth century can be attributed to increased demand for food, ships, armaments and construction caused by a robust increase in population and trade.

In addition to the trade in old and new products on the new routes, another trade began that was of crucial importance in the development of the new world: the African slave trade. The demographic catastrophe provoked by the Europeans in the Americas, primarily as a result of the spread of epidemics against which indigenous populations had no resistance, and the specific labour needs of the plantation system,[15] gave rise to a triangular trade that began in Europe, made a stop on the coast of west-central Africa, exchanged European products for African slaves, proceeded to the Americas where the slaves were sold and American products and precious metals were bought, which in turn were taken to Europe and sold. Importing black slaves to America began immediately after its discovery, but over the course of the sixteenth century the practice was intermittent; it is estimated that 266,000 slaves were shipped to America during the entire century. In the seventeenth century the practice increased by a factor of five, but the majority of slaves were transported in the eighteenth century, until the practice was banned during the first half of the nineteenth century.

The large joint-stock companies – as previously noted, an institutional form that originated in the *commenda* – took significant commercial advan-

---

15. The monocultures that spread through Central America, Brazil and the southern states of the United States did not attract European labour due to the gruelling work and modest pay.

tage from the opening up of the entire world to navigation. All colonizing countries set up commercial companies; at various times there were dozens of them. But the two countries that had the most success in using this type of company were Holland and Britain; both supported their companies through legislation as well as military ships. We should recall that Britain's limited resources (as evidenced in Table 2.1) meant that for a long time its geographic explorations were left in the hands of privateers; this is evidenced by the corsairs, or pirates who acted on behalf of and with the authorization of the British government, which issued them a "Letter of Marque" as official consent to their activity. This was the case for Richard Hawkins, his cousin Francis Drake and Walter Raleigh, who were all active between the late sixteenth and early seventeenth centuries. Between 1577 and 1580 Drake circumnavigated the globe following Magellan's route; in 1585 Raleigh founded the first English colony in North America, called Virginia in honour of the English Queen Elizabeth, the "Virgin Queen". The corsairs, bypassing the Spanish and Portuguese monopoly, dedicated themselves to arms smuggling and illegally selling slaves to the American colonies, which needed manual labour. Moreover, the disruption caused by Drake's ships proved decisive when in 1588 he defeated the Spanish *Invencible Armada*.

Among the official companies then created was the East India Company, founded in London in 1600. It was granted a commercial monopoly in the territories east of the Cape of Good Hope, and in the second half of the seventeenth century it was granted the authority to exercise sovereign power over the occupied territories.[16] In 1647 the Company already had twenty-three branches in India, an immense country over which Britain gained complete control after winning a long struggle with France. In the eighteenth century it extended the range of its trade to coastal China, where it founded Hong Kong and Singapore. In 1784 a decree by the British parliament placed the Company under the control of the British government to limit its autonomy and counter the corruption of its agents. All of the Company's commercial privileges were abolished in 1833; it was dissolved in 1857, and the British government assumed all administrative functions over the Indian and Asian territories.

The Dutch "twin" company to the British East India Company, the *Vereenigde Oost Indie Compagnie (VOC)*, operated between 1602 and 1799. Within a few years it had wrested control of the Cape of Good Hope and the Indian Ocean from the Portuguese, establishing commercial bases in Ceylon, Indonesia, Taiwan, China, Japan, and even New Zealand. The Dutch heavily

---

16. See Erikson, *Between Monopoly and Free Trade*.

exploited the peoples in the lands under their domination, levying heavy taxes and employing slavery on the plantations. The VOC was dissolved in 1800 following Holland's loss of independence due to the invasion of Napoleon's armies.

This then is how the large colonial empires came to be built: they provided an outlet for the European nations' empire-building aspirations, which could not be fulfilled within European territories because of the relative parity of nations. The colonial empires were very different from those in the East because they were inhabited by non-homogeneous and geographically distant populations who were markedly different among themselves.[17] Portugal was the first country to build a colonial empire, with a model based on building trading posts. As mentioned above, this was initially its unique characteristic, but when Portugal was united with Spain in 1578 its originality was no longer relevant. Spain instead developed an approach of military conquest over the areas it wanted to colonize, which were all densely populated by native peoples. The Spanish government organized governments in each that were dominated by viceroys and a Spanish elite that employed local labour in the mines to export primarily precious metals to the homeland, while agricultural income accumulated in the hands of owners who were always Spanish. The Spanish political and economic elite that lived in the colonies were wealthy, and hardly inclined to entrepreneurial activity because they were not merchants; in Spain the imports were not utilized for productive activity, but rather to finance wars and ostentatious ways of life. This Spanish style of colonialism explains the ephemeral economic impact of the colonies on the homeland.

The colonial approach developed by the Dutch was similar to that of the Portuguese, in that it was fully focused on trade, but it had a much greater success due to Holland's enduring political autonomy and their cultural advancement. They strove to improve their naval technologies and organizational systems, and they became by far the wealthiest European country in the seventeenth century (Table 2.1). This commercial success was probably the root cause of their delayed industrialization; manufacturing was not wholly absent in Holland, but the intense competition it had to endure from the British cannot be underestimated. England's economy during the fifteenth and sixteenth centuries did not grow much. However, it strengthened politically and culturally during those years, especially during Elizabeth's long reign in the sixteenth century and increasingly leveraged its representative

---

17. Since this work focuses on Europe we will not discuss the economic impact of colonialism on the colonized countries.

government, which in the seventeenth century developed supportive policies that strengthened the country's productivity through mercantilism.

In conclusion, European initiated international commerce played a significant role in improving transportation, diversifying consumption, making strategic raw materials available and making many technological and institutional innovations profitable; these supported the incomes of the countries that most put the "commercial revolution" into practice. It was a sustained process across a span of around seven hundred years, between the eleventh and seventeenth centuries, in which Europe, and in particular the Italian maritime cities, first absorbed what the other more advanced areas of Eurasia had already attained and then leaped ahead. Since the decisive step forward happened in Britain, Chapter 3 is dedicated to its development.

3

Britain: the first European industrial nation

3.1 *The birth of an exception: English parliamentary monarchy and mercantilism*

We are now in a position to ask ourselves why, among all the European countries that were involved in the social, political, economic and cultural transformation of Europe from the Middle Ages onward, Britain was where the industrial revolution first happened.[1] In general, the answer is not particularly difficult. Over the course of several centuries Britain had in fact brought together the greatest number of those conditions conducive to growth that we have sketched in the previous chapters. Not only did it have a temperate climate with plenty of water, as well as being strategically positioned geographically to participate in the geographic explorations, it was also able to evolve its culture and its political and institutional system in a way that best supported the conditions for innovation and investment. It was also fortunate to have significant reserves of reasonably shallow coal, but we can also easily speculate that without that energy resource it would have found other sources. That happened in the cotton industry, which was not a domestic raw material, but Britain replaced that by importing it.[2]

From a political standpoint the English monarchy had continually become less absolute since the Magna Carta in 1215, which contained a long series of

---

1. (Great) Britain is made up of three regions that were long independent: England, Wales and Scotland, which have modernized together. However, in the literature England is frequently used to refer to the whole, a convention we try not to follow here. The term "United Kingdom" includes Ireland: until 1921, all of it, and since 1922 (and the formation of the independent Republic of Ireland), only Ulster (Northern Ireland). Since Ireland's economic development has been quite different from that of Britain we have tried to avoid including it, although that has not always been possible in some of the tables.
2. Clark, O'Rourke & Taylor, "Made in America?".

clauses limiting the power of the monarch over the clergy, the barons and even the common people. While it is true that not all English monarchs behaved accordingly, it is also true that the consultation of the barons and clergy, with the later addition of the "commons", particularly on questions of public finance, was increasingly strengthened, although in a constant tug-of-war between the monarch and the Parliament. In the seventeenth century there was heavy conflict that culminated in Cromwell's brief republican period;[3] there were skirmishes even after that until the Glorious Revolution of 1688, when Parliament assumed direct control of public finance, established a public debt separate from that of the monarch, and founded the Bank of England in 1694. From then on the monarchy remained a symbol of the unity of the nation, but it no longer governed. The representative government progressively became stronger, finally becoming a true democracy. England was the first, and for a long time the only, parliamentary monarchy in Europe. Its government did not directly source from the merchants, as in the city-states, but it was a government that was willing to listen and support the commercial sector's requests. Since it was a kingdom it had greater military resources than the city-states to oppose foreign powers and support its own businesses with the strength of its navy, but it also did so primarily through what were called "mercantilist" economic policies.[4]

The main ones included banning exports of raw wool to incentivize processing it in England, allowing specialized craftsmen to emigrate and allowing machinery exports, all for the purpose of fully utlilizing the country's productive capacity. The most important provisions, however, were the Navigation Acts. The first was enacted by Cromwell's republican government in 1651, which prescribed that trade to and from Britain had to be on British ships and had to avoid using foreign ports as waypoints. This is how England wrested dominance in maritime trade from Holland, while also promoting the growth of the shipbuilding industry in Britain. Another important Act that supported the growth of English manufacturing was the so-called Calico Act, enacted in 1701 and 1721. At first restricting, and then prohibiting, the importation of Indian printed cotton fabrics was a powerful stimulus for the national cotton industry based on importing raw cotton

---

3. After 1630 Charles I tried to rule without Parliament and to collect taxes without authorization; an armed insurrection broke out against the king, who was deposed and ultimately executed.

4. Other scholars have used the expression "Parliamentary Colbertism", referring back to similar provisions by Jean-Baptiste Colbert in France, which did not have the same effects; see Cameron & Neal, *A Concise Economic History of the World*.

from the colonies; it was one of the leading industries in the British industrial revolution.

3.2 Other explanations why the industrial revolution was local to Britain

From a legal point of view Britain developed the so-called Common Law, which demonstrated a high degree of adaptability to changes happening in society; it legislated and administered justice on the basis of changed customs identified by the cases examined, which then became models for subsequent applications, rather than on the basis of conformity to a corpus of laws that could only be changed at sometimes lengthy intervals.[5] This increasingly protected private interests against other private parties as well as against encroachments by the state. The case of the "enclosures" (fencing land to permit its privatizing and its rational exploitation by crop rotation) illustrates better than any other the progressive privatization of resources in Britain for the purpose of using them more effectively, which was capable of increasing the productivity of the entire system.[6]

At the same time, to prevent expanding property rights from irreparably harming those who were unable to take advantage of them, the solidarity provisions that particularly proliferated due to the social teachings of the Catholic Church were standardized after the Reformation in the universal Poor Law. The Poor Relief Act of 1601 levied a tax on the wealthy for redistributive purposes, intended for financing subsidies and workhouses for unemployment and disability relief; it had the stated goal of maximally employing the productive forces of the country, assuring public order so as not to hinder the orderly development of economic activities, and supporting consumption. The universal and impersonal role of the Poor Laws has recently been re-evaluated by Avner Grief and others, even comparing them to the solidarity of China's family-based social institutions, which strengthened the communal approach to economic activity.[7] According to the most recent arguments, the certainty of having a social safety net in case one were to fall into poverty increased the propensity for risk, lowered the rate of violence, reduced the number of revolts, supported internal consumption and

---

5. Hartwell, *The Industrial Revolution and Economic Growth*.
6. See Hudson, *The Industrial Revolution 1760–1830*.
7. Grief & IyIgun, "Social Organization, Violence and Modern Growth".

offered work and apprenticeship opportunities to those who were not able to independently obtain work.

Britain enthusiastically embraced the adventures of geographic exploration, international trade and improving sea transportation; these led it to create commercial companies that specialized in particular routes, colonize all over the world, overtake the early colonial powers (Portugal, Spain and Holland) and defeat France, with the result that it accumulated considerable capital. The so-called "merchant banks" developed in London that, true to their name, provided capital for trade and other international activities.[8] There was no lack of banks (the so-called "country banks") that financed the growing business affairs throughout the country, but as many have shown these banks financed more working capital than long-term capital, which was largely provided directly by investors. As Pomeranz well noted, the colonies enabled Britain to relocate elsewhere the most land intensive activities, not simply cultivation, but other activities such as mining (except coal), in order to specialize in activities that produced greater wealth.[9]

To all this we must add the development of British philosophical empiricism, the birth of political economy with Adam Smith, and the dissemination of culture through newspapers, academia and clubs. Joel Mokyr has gone so far as to argue that the British Enlightenment was crucial in launching and maintaining the industrial revolution.[10] While it is true that only half of the British populace could read and write in the second half of the eighteenth century, we should also note that only Sweden had a greater diffusion of literacy. The technology of the early industrial revolution did not in fact require particularly advanced study, but rather a curious mindset, an ability to learn from experience thorough a process of trial and error, and above all a great incentive to employ one's talents to productive ends (what Mokyr calls "useful knowledge").

Another factor historians have cited as strategic was the widespread practice in Britain of the Western European marriage pattern, or the "nuclear family". According to the most recent work the nuclear family spread in England after

---

8. Today the expression "merchant bank" refers to financial institutions that provide long-term risk capital; it has therefore become synonymous with "investment bank", which is an American term for a long-term financial institution more linked to industrial investments than its British counterpart.

9. Pomeranz (in *The Great Divergence*) maintains that the "great divergence" between China and Britain was determined precisely by this relocation, which enabled Britain to take advantage of many "ghost acres" outside its own territory. What Pomeranz did not emphasize was the long process that led Britain to that outcome.

10. Mokyr, *The Enlightened Economy*.

the Black Death more than in any other European country; and in contrast with the rest of the world, which remained modelled on the extended family.[11] The nuclear family marries later, and women in it tend to work more outside the home, particularly prior to marriage. It practices a more equal relationship between the spouses; the woman is asked to consent to the marriage, and her dowry guarantees her a certain degree of autonomy. It has fewer children and educates them so they can be more autonomous. Since it is fragile it is more open to outside bonds, hence the emergence of associations with monasteries, universities, trade associations, craft guilds, fraternal organizations, hospitals, and, later on, mutual aid societies. The nuclear family is what develops the "bourgeois" virtues of doing one's work well, promoting individual talents, health and personal initiative that McCloskey maintains were crucial to explain economic progress, and in the final analysis the British industrial revolution.[12]

Among the most recent contributions that have tried to explain why the industrial revolution occurred in Britain we should also mention the work of Allen and Kelly, Mokyr and O'Grada.[13] Allen maintains that higher wages resulting from the Black Death pushed Britain towards innovations, particularly labour saving innovations, that could sustain them. Kelly *et al.* argue that few British innovations were directed towards saving labour, and that in the Netherlands where wages were also high, there was no link between high wages and industrial revolution, and high wages could even be a negative factor.[14] Kelly *et al.* insist instead on the productivity of British labour, which was the basic reason for higher wages, but it would explain why higher wages did not become a higher cost per unit produced, guaranteeing the competitiveness of British manufacturing. The authors trace the higher productivity of British workers back to various institutional factors, among them the apprenticeship system, originally created by the medieval craft guilds but which survived in Britain when the guilds were abolished, and better food provisions (linked to agricultural improvements introduced by the enclosures), which made the British taller, stronger, and longer-lived.

---

11. Voigtländer & Voth, "How the West Invented Fertility Restriction".

12. McCloskey, *Bourgeois Dignity*.

13. Allen, *The British Industrial Revolution in Global Perspective*; Kelly, Mokyr & O'Grada, "Precocious Albion".

14. This is why, for example, it has been argued that the loss of the European markets by manufacturing interests in the Italian city-states after the sixteenth century was due to excessively high wages imposed by guilds, which had become closed and self-referential. See Malanima, "When Did England Overtake Italy?", in which the author maintains that wages in Italy were higher or comparable to wages in Britain until the end of the eighteenth century.

3.3   Characteristics of the industrial revolution

An event as complex and unexpected as the industrial revolution cannot be explained by a single factor, but by interwoven causes linked together in such a way that each supported the others. What is abundantly clear is that the preparatory process was slow. It began with the assimilation of many institutional elements that originated elsewhere in Europe, but which were transplanted and refined in Britain in such a way that it could best take advantage of its geographic characteristic of being an island facing both the Atlantic and the North Sea and having coal as a natural resource. Britain accomplished its complete industrial transformation in the two centuries between the mid-seventeenth century and the mid-nineteenth century.[15] New and increasingly mechanized production processes were introduced in various industrial branches, particularly in spinning and weaving cotton.[16] Coke was the innovation in ironworking, first used by Abraham Darby in 1709 at Coalbrookdale, that through successive refinements enabled the production of pig iron, and later steel, by the puddling process; coke freed ironworking from its dependence on increasingly scarce charcoal, as well as producing a more reliable and durable product.

Without doubt, however, the innovation that signalled the definitive break with the past was the development of the steam boiler, a process perfected over nearly a century. In 1698 Thomas Savery built the first steam pump, christened by its inventor as the "miner's friend" because it was primarily used in mines. In 1782 James Watt and Matthew Boulton succeeded in producing their first steam engine (there were countless successive refinements to

---

15. Many scholars today reject the view of the industrial revolution that limits it to the second half of the eighteenth century. Rather, it was a complex process that involved all sectors of the economy, beginning with agriculture and services, that continued without interruption over two centuries.

16. The Italian silk industry created the first automatic water powered spinning machines – the most famous were those in Bologna, which could simultaneously operate many dozens of spindles – and it is possible that the idea that led to the mechanization of British cotton spinning was imported from Italy; see Poni, "Espansione e declino di una grande industria". The principal British inventions in the cotton textile industry were as follows: John Kay invented the flying shuttle in 1733, which allowed a weaver to do the work of two. In 1764 James Hargreaves invented the spinning jenny, a machine that operated several spindles at once. In 1769 Richard Arkwright invented the water frame spinning machine, and subsequently a steam powered version. Following this there were many refinements in spinning, such as Samuel Crompton's spinning mule in 1785, but Edmund Cartwright's mechanical loom of 1784 only really became functional in the 1820s.

it);[17] it too was used in mining, given the serious problems mines had with water accumulation and the abundant availability of coal on site. It was then used in cotton spinning mills in 1785 in place of water power, then in the iron industry and other industries, and finally in transportation when in 1801 Richard Trevithick, a mining engineer, built the first working locomotive. Here too the first application was in mines by George Stephenson, an engine technician, in 1813; even the first railway line, the Stockton–Darlington line in 1825, linked two mines.[18]

Wrigley has very effectively demonstrated that with the steam engine mankind wholly changed how it could extract value from the earth.[19] From working the earth's crust for the most basic resources for human life – food, heating and housing, motive power – mankind then began working the underground resources – coal, then oil, gas, uranium and many other elements – freeing up the soil for cultivation for food and some important raw materials, such as cotton that no longer had to compete for space with the production of other goods, particularly wood. This was the transition from an advanced organic economy (AOE) to a mineral energy based economy (MEBE).

The transition from primarily working the soil to the intensive use of the ground below it had the effect of raising productivity as never before. In contrast to agriculture, the underground reserves were very large stocks unaffected by the size of the land and seasonal variations. By perfecting the machines one could increase the extraction and use of those stocks at will, making possible very rapid productivity increases. Furthermore, with such an abundant energy source there was significant incentive to constantly increase the power of the machines, to the point of driving colossal industrial complexes and infrastructure that were able to produce unheard of quantities of products that had never been seen before. Where poverty was previously unavoidable, given the limited resources the soil could make available every year for a variety of alternate purposes, after the industrial revolution poverty became a social responsibility linked to how products were distributed rather than to their absolute scarcity.

This energy-centric view of the industrial revolution is more meaningful than the view, which holds that the industrial revolution was a consequence

---

17. James Watt was a laboratory technician in the University of Glasgow who was initially called on to repair one of the many existing models of steam boilers used for demonstration purposes for a course on natural philosophy.
18. The Liverpool–Manchester route was the first true rail line for general transportation, which opened in 1830.
19. Wrigley, *Energy and the English Industrial Revolution*.

of science and modern technology. None of the important inventions of the British industrial revolution required different scientific fundamentals than those that had existed in the Roman Empire. Even the steam boiler was known, although its practical utility was not appreciated; it was used only for recreational activities, just as gunpowder was used in China. In any event, even this energy-centric view hearkens back to more important prior causes, such as seeing opportunities in markets to make profits by selling more at lower prices, which provided a strong incentive to seek increasingly powerful energy sources and increasingly automated machines to increase the output of available products and control their cost. Markets in turn expanded in Europe, and in Britain in particular, due to such products and process; in this way we can understand that this is a self-reinforcing and self-perpetuating process.

Table 3.1   Gross domestic product per capita in Britain 1700–1850.

Date	1990 US$ per capita	Annual growth rates
1700	1,513	
1750	1,695	0.23
1775	1,815	0.27
1800	2,097	0.59
1820	2,074	–
1830	2,227	0.68
1840	2,521	1.22
1849	2,774	1.06
1700–1850		0.36

Source: Maddison database.

There have been numerous studies of the results of the British industrial revolution in terms of increased incomes, beginning with the quantitative estimates of national income by Deane and Cole published in 1962.[20] Those initial estimates had already made it clear that this was a very slow process through the mid-nineteenth century, when the industrial revolution is conventionally considered to have ended and its mature phase begun (and when, paradoxically, relative income began to decline, as we will see in Chapter 6).

20. Deane & Cole, *British Economic Growth 1688–1959.*

Table 3.2   Comparison of gross domestic product per capita in 1850.

Region	1990 US$	Index (GB = 100)
Britain*	2,774	100
Belgium	1,847	67
France	1,597	58
Germany	1,428	51
Holland	2,355	85
North-Central Italy	1,481	53
Spain	1,079	39
United States	1,849	67
Japan	681	25
China	600	22
India†	533	19
Ottoman Empire†	825	30

Notes: *1849; †1870.

Source: Maddison database.

The Maddison estimates listed in Table 3.1 confirm the incremental view of British development, especially until the second half of the eighteenth century.[21] Beyond the unavoidable approximation of these quantitative estimates, what emerges is that Britain's achievements were due to the continuity and acceleration of the process rather than to some dramatic initial launch, as the word "revolution" has often suggested.[22] Table 3.2 gives an account of the exceptional nature of this development better than any argument. At the time of the first great international exhibition of modern technology, which was held in London at the Crystal Palace in 1851 and attracted millions

---

21. The highly detailed and refined quantitative analysis in Broadberry *et al.*, *British Economic Growth 1270–1870* confirms this, though there are differences with the series employed by Maddison. In this book, preference has been given to the Maddison data bank, for reasons of comparability.

22. The standard of living also rose slowly, to the point that a "pessimistic" view exists (tracing back to Marx and Engels) that holds that the conditions of British workers actually declined until the mid-nineteenth century. For the entire debate see chapter 2 of Hudson, *Industrial Revolution*.

of visitors, Britain was without doubt the most productive country in the world, the "workshop of the world". In Europe, Holland and Belgium were the closest, but all the countries listed in Table 3.2 had above-subsistence levels, as did the United States. Asia and the Ottoman Empire were clearly far behind. The impact of the British industrial revolution on the entire world will be discussed in Chapters 4 and 5. As we will see, there is a sharp dividing line between the areas that set a goal of industrializing following the British model, and which modernized more or less successfully, and those that either did not want or were not able to set in motion a process of imitation.

3.4   Regional aspects of the British industrial revolution

The general historiographic trend has been to treat the British industrial revolution as a whole, nationally, which stems from the vigorous involvement of all of Britain during the decades of its transformation. Indeed, the developments were such that they involved almost all areas of Britain (but only Ulster in Ireland, which is why we cannot discuss the United Kingdom). However, in his authoritative 1981 work Sidney Pollard explains that it is more correct to use the "region" as the unit for analysing development themes; by "region" he intends an area, more or less large, of economic activity interconnected around a centre that determines the operation of the whole.[23] For statistical reasons however such an area must also be coextensive with some local administrative unit (a metropolitan area, province, region, or a state within a federal nation). The dense regional historiography developed subsequent to Pollard's proposal has shown that the administrative regions defined by nations' administrative structures in general actually show a greater homogeneity as Pollard indicated, although unfortunately not always, which has given rise to a flourishing literature on regional economic history.[24]

Pollard maintains that expansions, contractions, and even stagnations are more consistently interpreted by regions, while the national trends are the result of synthesizing events in the various regions that make up each nation.

---

23. Pollard, *Peaceful Conquest*.
24. History has left a legacy of administrative territories internal to larger nations that could have previously been autonomous nations, and which maintain a less homogeneous economic composition than the "regions" Pollard's definition had hoped for. This is a problem still lived out today in the European Union, which is composed of 274 highly diversified "regions", some larger than nations, others smaller than most of the EU's cities.

There are nations formed from regions that begin to develop at the same time but then demonstrate different capacities for sustaining the development process (and which have different destinies). Some nations instead show a deep dualism, with regions that expand, sometimes at different times, and others that remain backward and passive. Pollard quite appropriately stressed that, the more that dynamic regions are "drowned" in static contexts, any aggregated national analysis loses effectiveness and accuracy in delineating the characteristics of the industrialization process and of subsequent events as well. A regional analysis that compares the dynamic regions among themselves and that explains why others are stagnant or declining leads to much more meaningful generalized results.

As noted, in the case of Britain, as chance would have it, all the regions expanded more or less simultaneously, making regional analysis less important, but it proved useful for later history when some of the areas declined. Scotland, which remained an independent kingdom (although at times united in the person of the English monarch) until 1707, was well endowed with heavy industry, especially metallurgy, shipbuilding and chemicals as well as finance and the production of beer, whisky and non-cotton textiles. All this was supported by a strong presence of distinguished thinkers who formed the famous school of the Scottish Enlightenment (David Hume, Adam Smith, Adam Ferguson and James Hutton). Wales and Cornwall specialized in mining and metalworking, while in Lancashire and Manchester the cotton industry flourished, the Midlands specialized in ironmaking and East Anglia in the wool industry. London developed primarily in services, banking, insurance, logistics, transportation, international trade and the military; many other ports became prosperous as well, among them Bristol, Liverpool and Glasgow.[25]

The contemporary flourishing of all of Britain was certainly favoured by the shared cultural and institutional characteristics sketched above, but also because Britain was an island. In fact, the territorial contiguity among continental European nations paradoxically made it easier for economic links to develop between more developed regions that belonged to different nations, which had negative competitive effects on less well-endowed areas belonging to the same nation. Still, the distribution of natural resources in Britain was such that many areas developed simultaneously, particularly with the availability of internal transportation, which only became efficient in the final phase of the industrial revolution with the railways. We should also recall, as we will revisit in Chapter 8, that the British economy operated under the shadow of

---

25. For further information, see Hudson, *Regions and Industries*.

mercantilist policies, which were not repealed until the 1840s. Ultimately the Napoleonic wars even further isolated Britain, while they made the continent more interconnected. The imitators of the British industrial revolution therefore had to act in an international setting that was far more competitive than that for the British industrial revolution.[26]

---

26. Britain's relative isolation during its industrialization phase also explains the slowness of the process; see O'Brien, "Deconstructing the British Industrial Revolution" and Horn, Roseband & Smith, *Reconceptualizing the Industrial Revolution.*

4

The British model: imitation
and the role of the state

4.1 *Reasons for imitation*

There are three factors that led many European countries to a process that imitated the British industrial revolution. Without doubt the first is the fact that they shared with Britain many of the elements that had led to its industrial revolution, although with considerable diversity from country to country, and, as we will see, from region to region. The second lies in the rapid transmission of information in a space accustomed to the exchange of ideas, people and things. What had happened to Britain demonstrated to those who lagged behind the feasibility of certain advances (the "demonstration effect"). The third consists of the competitive spirit that has always animated European nations, even before its citizens, and that has always impeded a nation accepting a relative loss of power with respect to another (the "balance of power" effect). Now, nothing was more disruptive in changing the balance of power than the industrial revolution. It provided Britain with income and wealth that increased more rapidly than in other countries, which made the divide between them grow exponentially, and for the first time without the need for wars to conquer new colonies or new territories.[1]

The Napoleonic wars, the continental system or continental blockade, and the Restoration were all events that hindered the initiative of those on

---

1. Note that in an agrarian civilization the income and wealth divide between states was determined by the extent of land available and the proportion of the population that could work it, because the per capita and per hectare surplus that could be produced was generally very low and grew only marginally. The per capita income divide was thus not large, precisely because they had only modest capacities for accumulation.

the European continent who wanted to imitate Britain; the process began nonetheless, accelerating when peace prevailed and the absolutist rigours of the Restoration were relaxed, either by the spontaneous decisions of public powers or after popular revolts. This chapter shows how this process of imitation was realized, a subject that has attracted the interest of many scholars. It was long thought that the British model must have been imitated completely, but important differences later came to light that have driven scholars to find more complex explanations.[2]

4.2 A theory of imitation without differences

Marx wrote that "The country that is more developed industrially only shows, to the less developed, the image of its own future."[3] Many believed in "imitation without variants", treating any difference as a deviation that delayed successful imitation and judging the various governments by the standard of their ability – or lack of it – to recreate conditions similar to those in Britain in their own countries. Of course, this position was based on a model of the British case that removed the many local characteristics that could not be considered essential in the process of imitation by the "latecomers", as the continental European countries were called.

The most famous and significant theory was that of W. W. Rostow, who in his 1960 work outlines five stages that an agrarian society must go through in order to transform into an industrial society, and a process applicable to any industrializing country.[4]

Stage 1: traditional society. The starting point prior to transformation: an economic system in stagnation due to the low yield of the natural resources of the soil, population increase and catastrophic natural events (such as recurring plague and famine).

Stage 2: the preconditions for take-off. At a certain point – and here Rostow's research into triggering mechanisms was not exhaustive – society begins to abandon tradition and seek change. This gives rise to entrepreneurial figures who accumulate their own and others' capital to risk in new activities, without however having a significant impact at the aggregate level.

---

2. See O'Brien, "Do We Have a Typology for the Study of European Industrialization in the Nineteenth Century?".
3. Marx, *Capital*, II.
4. Rostow, *The Stages of Economic Growth*.

Stage 3: the take-off. A sufficiently large group of dynamic entrepreneurs forms, from a macroeconomic point of view there are repeated new investments and the system accelerates (the take-off), launching a course of capital accumulation and self-sustaining productivity growth, with a level of production and income growth never experienced before. In general, an economic system does not uniformly innovate; rather, it begins first in certain leading sectors that precede others; this generates a typical process of unbalanced sectoral growth that only over time pulls the entire system ahead to new technological frontiers.

Stage 4: the drive to maturity. Once the entire system is modernized it enters a phase of slower growth due to fewer investment opportunities and a slowdown in the creation of new technologies. Investment stagnates and more resources are dedicated to consumption, entering the final phase of the process.

Stage 5: the age of mass consumption. We should emphasize that the period from take-off to maturity is a time of restrained consumption necessary to make a place for the large investments needed to modernize the entire economic system.[5] Only after this period has ended can the rate of accumulation in the economy be reduced and more purchasing power distributed for consumption.[6] This incentivizes the firms producing consumption goods to invest in processes to standardize their production in order to lower costs and enlarge the market for consumption goods further, which becomes crucial for maintaining a systemic rate of growth.

Rostow's theory was useful in refining important concepts, such as the take-off and the age of mass consumption, as well as describing the more general steps of an industrializing system, but it is unable to explain how one stage transitions to another, or what the mechanisms are for forming the right entrepreneurship at the right moment. Additionally it ignores the role of the state and the effects of interactions between countries, or the international dimension of the economy.

---

5. We saw in Chapter 3 that the debate on the standard of living in Britain highlighted that living standards even in the first industrial nation grew very slowly.

6. See Morris, "How Fast and Why Did Early Capitalism Benefit the Majority?", in which he argues with copious examples that it can take at least five decades before growth brings general benefits.

4.3   *A theory of imitation with differences*

We are indebted to a scholar of great historical depth for a profoundly innovative vision of this process of imitation: imitation with variants. Alexander
Gerschenkron, whose most significant works were published during the same
period as Rostow's, was of Russian origin. He emigrated to Austria after the
October Revolution, then landed in the United States after the Nazi invasion,
where he became a professor at Harvard. His first-hand knowledge of European
languages and realities led him to emphasize the differences among European
countries more than their similarities and he formulated an explanation of
the processes of imitation based on these differences. Gerschenkron's theory
is not a theory of the whole process; rather, it focused on two of Rostow's
stages – transition and take-off – and sought to identify the mechanisms that
allow various countries to begin the process of development even though they
were latecomers.[7]

Gerschenkron opened his reflection by advancing the concept of "relative
backwardness", with which he positioned the various European countries at a
distance from Britain – the leader country – commensurate with the importance and number of prerequisites for the development in Britain that were
lacking elsewhere.[8] The country closest to Britain had the greater probability
of imitating Britain without delays and without major variations. The greater
the distance from conditions of British society, the more difficult it was to
imitate and delays were increasingly more likely; this naturally aggravated the
latecomer's position, as the divide increasingly widened.

However, Gerschenkron saw the possibility of upswing or resilience by the
countries that showed themselves able to put substitutable factors into practice in place of the missing original British prerequisites; these substitutable
factors were able to play the same role as the British prerequisites, albeit in

---

7. Gerschenkron, *Economic Backwardness in Historical Perspective*. A reconsideration of
    Gerschenkron's theory can be found in Sylla & Toniolo, *Patterns of Industrialization in
    Nineteenth-Century Europe*.
8. Gerschenkron did not formalize his analysis of the prerequisites. Others subsequently did
    so, among them Crafts, "Patterns of Development in Nineteenth-Century Europe", 36.
    Later interesting attempts were made to divide reasons for backwardness between polit-
    ical and cultural factors and "objective" factors, such as climate and soil conditions. See
    Tortella, "Patterns of Economic Retardation and Recovery in South-Western Europe in the
    Nineteenth and Twentieth Centuries" and Foreman Peck, "A Model of Later Nineteenth
    Century European Economic Development". Leandro Prados de la Escosura has con-
    firmed the importance of the differences with econometric estimates in his "Gerschenkron
    Revisited".

different ways. According to Gerschenkron, this was the source of the differences between the processes imitating the British model on the European continent. Since not all countries are able to identify these substitutable factors, not all are actually capable of industrializing, or they do so at very different times when they finally can put them into practice. We will illustrate this process in the next two chapters when we consider the cases of various countries, and we will refer back to applying Gerschenkron's theory and the discussions resulting from them.

To this fundamental concept Gerschenkron added another important observation that, if and when a country succeeds in taking off by means of substitutable factors, its take-off can be more rapid than that of the leader because of the so-called "advantages of backwardness". But are there really advantages to backwardness? However paradoxical it may seem, it is true that an imitator country does not need to create inventions or the complex work to perfect them, which requires time and resources. Rather, it can introduce technologies already refined by others, producing a "big spurt" of productivity much more rapidly than what was possible for the leader, which was forced to proceed by the unavoidably more gradual process of trial and error. In this way latecomer countries can not only take off, but also have the possibility of catching up with or even surpassing the leader, if the difference in growth rates in favour of the latecomers lasts long enough.

This final outcome of "catching up" has been much studied by economists,[9] who have sought to generalize the conditions that must be present in a country in order for it to successfully implement this "chase".[10] Thus it is not inevitable that those who start first always remain in the lead; this was certainly true for Britain as the first industrial nation, as we will see. This was true as well in pre-industrial Europe where the Italian cities had flourished during the late Middle Ages and Renaissance but had yielded first before the short-lived but intense expansion by Spain and Portugal, and then before the Netherlands' enduring efforts in the seventeenth century, which in turn was displaced by Britain's overpowering development. The driving force of competition and the capacity for imitation by those who are not too far behind the leader make no leadership position permanently secure; they allow those who have fallen behind to try again and become an imitator country, with a good chance of success.

---

9. Abramovitz, "Catching up, Forging Ahead and Falling Behind"; Baumol, Nelson & Wolf, *Convergence and Productivity*.

10. Among these conditions, widespread education and the dissemination of knowledge seem to increasingly take priority; see Landes, "Does it Pay to be Late?".

Finally, Gerschenkron also noted the fact that taking off at later times, and with profoundly changed technology, the leading sectors in the latecomer countries were not the same as those of the British industrial revolution. This was an important point, but Gerschenkron did not fully develop its implications in depth because he focused his interpretive efforts on the take-off stage and the conditions that made it possible, which overshadowed the paths for ongoing development. In reality those paths have shown enduring diversity over time; various configurations of industrial capitalism have shown they can compete not only on price, quality and the types of products and services, but also on the different institutions that govern production processes.

What emerges from Gerschenkron's conceptualization is particularly the fundamental difference between imitation and innovation. While imitation requires primarily a well-organized society that allows for entrepreneurship, education and international relations, which are goals that even dictatorial governments can pursue (consider Hitler's Germany, Mussolini's Italy or China today), with sometimes amazing growth rates, innovation requires a propensity for risk and a creative capacity that so far has been realized in societies where liberty and participation in managing public affairs are in force. Thus from a historical point of view it is not true that democracy is a luxury that developing countries cannot allow, or that dictatorial governments are more efficient for growth. In reality, the leadership role in economic development until now has always been played by free societies, in which there is bottom-up participation in the government (the Italian city-states, the Dutch Republic, the British parliamentary monarchy, the United States). Only a few imitative processes began in absolutist governments, and many of these have proved to have poor sustainability; in most cases the imitative processes could be fully realized only after the absolutist governments were eliminated, as we will see in the next chapter.

With Gerschenkron's theoretical work, understanding the differences in the courses of development for European countries became an intellectually rewarding exercise. Many scholars have been engaged in case studies of different countries and in qualifying and refining Gerschenkron's generalizations, to the point of denying that there was just one model of industrial revolution – the British[11] – or even claiming that the British model was an

---

11. Cameron writes in "A New View of European Industrialisation": "There was not one model for industrialisation in the nineteenth century – the British – but several ... The customary depiction of an 'industrial revolution' in Great Britain and its repetition in continental Europe and elsewhere distorts the historical record. It also conceals the distinctive varieties of industrialisation" (23).

inimitable exception.[12] While we will defer the discussion of some country case studies until the next chapter, we will consider here some of the more interesting qualifications and additions made by subsequent scholars to Gerschenkron's conceptualization.

As discussed in Chapter 3, Pollard drew attention to the greater logical consistency in using regions rather than the nation when conducting comparative analyses of the process of imitating the British industrial revolution.[13] In the same text Pollard developed another important idea, calling attention to what we might define as "interference" factors. Gerschenkron's analysis was wholly focused on a country's internal prerequisites and on its autonomous capacity to find solutions to its own development problems. The international economy was kept in the background as a powerful incentive to act and as a reserve of technologies to imitate; all things considered, it was an unrestricted environment if a latecomer country knew how to organize itself to adequately exploit the advantages of backwardness. With his concept of "differential of contemporaneousness" Pollard emphasized that there are events of such international resonance that they interfere with the courses prepared by individual countries' decisions, sometimes diverting them negatively from their internally formed directions, which makes considering and analyzing international economic developments important if we are to fully understand the diversity in countries' courses.

Pollard offered railways as an example. Among the innovations of the British industrial revolution that made the most stir abroad, without doubt the railways were foremost in the popular imagination as well as in the concerns of government officials of the time. It seemed that no country could do without railways, but the challenge they posed to the various national economic settings produced not only different but sometimes inconsistent results with the development directions of the various nations. In Britain the railways were not the cause of development, but rather a product of its maturity, and they appeared when the country certainly had no problem collecting the necessary finances or resolving inter-sectoral dependencies (they already had adequate mechanical and metallurgical industries). In Belgium, France, Germany and the United States the railways were a powerful development trigger, which led first to constructing a national metalworking industry, establishing adequate funding channels, and, in the case of the United States (due to the colossal size of the rail network, as we will see), setting up large scale management systems, where for the first time the scientific management

12. Crafts, "Patterns of Development in Nineteenth Century Europe".
13. Pollard, *Peaceful Conquest*.

of labour was applied, through which the United States became powerful and famous.

In the most backward countries like Italy, the railway constructions initiated after the unification by the new government were seen as a powerful means of modernizing the country. These required substantial imports of foreign materials without leading to the creation of a national metalworking industry, except towards the end; they were not a great commercial success, and they ended up putting a burden on the public finances. Gerschenkron was the first to wonder why the Italian rulers had wanted the railways before the country was ready to draw all the economic benefits from them.[14] Pollard offered a highly persuasive response: a typical interference factor, or precisely a "differential of contemporaneousness". Things went even worse for Turkey and other even more backward countries, where the railways were a useless luxury purchased entirely from abroad and paid (when they were paid) with the collapse of already shaky public finances.

Pollard's concept of differential contemporaneousness is applicable to other interference factors, particularly the First World War, which greatly diverted many European countries' development trends (as we will see in Chapters 9 and 10), or the 1929 economic crisis, which we will consider in Chapters 11 and 12. It is also applicable to international commerce, which happens between countries at different stages of development. Regarding the latter point, Pollard uncritically embraced classical liberalism and branded any form of protectionism as an episode of economic war, but things are more complicated than that. We will postpone discussion on this issue to Chapter 8.

4.4 The role of the state

A predominantly liberal-inspired historiography has frequently obscured the role of the state in development. Following Gerschenkron, in some cases the state has been seen as a substitutable factor for take-off; we will see a few examples in subsequent chapters. Otherwise its presence is generally noted only when it has acted badly, even to the point of Pollard's extreme paradox,

---

14. Gerschenkron's suggestion that the impact of the railways would have been greater in Italy had they been built nearer the end of the century when industrialization took off as well, has been further analyzed at an industrial level by Fenoaltea (see "Le ferrovie e lo sviluppo industriale italiano 1861–1913") and on a commercial level by Zamagni (see "Ferrovie e integrazione del mercato nazionale nell'Italia post-unitaria").

which considered that the less the state is present the more development will occur. Even a quick glance at Table 4.1 is sufficient to suggest that the importance of public expenditures has notably increased over time,[15] especially in the twentieth century due to the general expansion of the welfare state (with a tendency after the 1970s to stop or even slightly contract in a few countries). It has also been noted that other interventions – such as monetary and exchange rate controls, protectionism, subsidies, bailouts, direct management of companies and banks, counter-cyclical manoeuvres, and social and regional policies – have not always had upward impact, but they have comprehensively and increasingly engaged public policies to support development and employment.

Thus the role of the state cannot be ignored, which had already proven itself crucial in the pre-industrial period as a foundational element of a progressive capitalism, as we have seen in previous chapters. The following tripartite typology can be a useful basis for discussing the role of the state and the quantity and quality of its presence:

The minimal state. Industrial capitalist systems cannot adequately function without a minimal state to guarantee defence and law and order (or legislation that establishes the rules of the market, foremost among them the defence of competition, and that sees that they are observed through the administration of justice) and to provide some public goods.[16] A public good that has a very broad consensus is money and a central bank to administer it. Another public good has been a postal service.[17] Education has generally been considered a public good, although in certain countries it is accompanied by a sizeable sector of private education. Faced with these roles, the state implements public spending financed through taxation.

The mixed economy state. Beyond the indispensable roles identified above, in a mixed economy the state produces many other public goods (typically welfare and infrastructure, including public housing) while taking on supplementary roles in many areas of intervention: public companies in sectors deemed strategic or inherited following bailouts, and development in depressed areas with so-called regional policies. This follows from "market

---

15. Even in the two non-European countries listed in the table, in which there was a much stronger containment of state growth (for reasons explained in Chapter 6) spending still grew.
16. A public good is a good that, for various reasons, is not in the interest of the private sector to produce, but one that is held to be strategic for growth.
17. An interesting question is whether or not a postal service should be considered a public good today.

Table 4.1   Impact of public expenditure on gross domestic product, 1880–2011.

Country	1880	1913	1929	1938	1950	1960	1973	1982	1996	2011
Britain	9.9	13.3	23.8	28.8	34.2	32.6	41.5	47.4	41.9	46.5
France	11.2	8.9	12.0	23.2	27.6	34.6	38.8	50.7	54.5	55.9
Germany	10.0	17.7	30.6	42.4	30.4	32.5	42.2	49.4	49.0	44.6
Italy	13.7	17.2	19.5	29.2	30.3	37.4	50.2	54.7	49.2	49.1
The Netherlands	–	8.2	11.2	21.7	26.8	33.7	45.5	63.7	49.9	47.0
United States	–	8.0	10.1	19.8	21.4	27.6	31.1	37.6	33.3	39.7
Japan	9.0	14.2	18.8	30.3	19.8	18.3	22.9	34.2	36.2	42.2

Source: Brosio & Marchese, Il potere di spendere; OECD (1986 and 2011).

failures"[18], as in the case of externalities, merit goods or natural monopolies,[19] or from imperfect markets that do not give rise to a sufficient quantity or quality of entrepreneurs. Thus part of the capitalist economy is managed by the state in the form of monopolies or competitive businesses, with different degrees of efficiency and with outcomes that are not always positive.[20] The mixed economy state can implement greater or lesser planning schemes to coordinate its interventions, which however never deny the market.

The maximal state. In this case the state takes on full responsibility for production. In reality this is an extreme model that denies the roots of capitalism, eliminating both the market and freedom of enterprise. This model is recalled only because it existed in history in the centrally planned Soviet economy, which ultimately proved unsuccessful (we will discuss this in detail in Chapters 10 and 16).

The dominant historical model of the state in advanced Western countries is that of the mixed economy, as the American scholar Richard Nelson has recently recognized.[21] Nelson goes so far as to say that there are sectors in the economy that are better administered by public authorities (defence, police, education, health, some research, air traffic control, infrastructure, environmental control, and others), just as other sectors are better administered by non-profit organizations in the civil economy (culture, aid, non-professional sports, and volunteer work), leaving only a slice of economic activity to so-called "private" companies.[22] There are also many areas in which private and public are called to collaborate (in finance, for example, in which the public Central Bank plays an absolutely fundamental role).

However, it is true that the United States has a mixed economy that is

---

18. See Stiglitz, *The Economic Role of the State.*
19. A natural monopoly is defined as a productive sector in which, for technological or market size reasons, it is not efficient to have more than one company. The typical examples are networks such as rail tracks or electrical grids. Public management of natural monopolies prevents a few private individuals from exploiting a monopolistic position. However, public management is not the inevitable solution; an alternative is to leave it in private hands and regulate the industry (as generally happens in the United States). We need also to remember that technologies change over time, and a sector that was originally a natural monopoly can subsequently reconfigure itself very differently, as mobile telephony has illustrated.
20. Note that there are in turn "government failures" – largely due to excessive bureaucracy and corruption – that can encourage the privatization of state-run enterprises.
21. Nelson, "The Complex Economic Organization of Capitalist Economies".
22. Nelson's argument is different than the one that assigns a role to the state due to market failures: "This is not a 'market failure' argument. It is an argument that markets should be fenced off from certain kinds of activities because they are operated much better under communal governance, in one or another of its forms" (*ibid.,*19).

closer to the minimal state, while other states have more or less greater degrees of a mixed economy, as we will see over the course of this work.[23] Europe in particular is noted for having pushed the welfare state much further than the American model, the sustainability of which is in question today[24], and for having enacted various industrial policies in different historical periods, first by protectionism[25] and then by subsidies, for a vast array of public companies – which subsequently have largely been privatized (see Chapter 7) – and at times even by some sort of planning. The reasons for such different character-izations of the role of the state in the United States and Europe will become clear after reviewing the characteristics of development of various countries, illustrated in the following chapters.

---

23. On this whole discussion, see Sheldrake & Webb, *State and Market.*
24. For a spirited comparison between the American and continental European models, which he calls the "Rhine" model, see Albert, *Capitalism Against Capitalism.*
25. Frederich List was the great German theoretician of protectionism as a means for industri-alization, who took inspiration from Alexander Hamilton, secretary of state under George Washington and an advocate of state interventionism. Note that the United States, although it greatly limited state interventions, was always protectionist until after the Second World War.

5

European industrialization

This chapter presents several country case studies, continuing an interpretive thread based on the conceptualizations laid out in Chapter 4, although with no pretence of exhausting Europe's diversity. Accordingly, the factual framework will not be very detailed; it will include only enough to have an idea of the principal developments and to be able to situate each case within a comparative context. The period considered ends with the advent of the First World War and considers "the long nineteenth century",[1] encompassing the initial years of the twentieth century up to the Great War, which is an obvious case of a "differential of contemporaneousness". The war heavily disrupted the development of all the economies that participated in it, and, albeit to a lesser extent, those that did not participate. Although they had developed to different stages, all countries had to respond to the war, which generated a "chain" of reactions that are more easily studied as effects of the First World War (considered in Chapter 9). The war was therefore a watershed.

We will first consider the three main successful economies, giving particular attention to note differences and similarities with the British model.[2] We will then turn to states that, for various reasons, were not able to complete the process of industrialization prior to the First World War, but that had areas that were engaging in it. Modernization was partial in such countries, which left room for serious imbalances that came to light during and just

---

1. A term coined by Eric Hobsbawm to indicate the period spanning from 1789, the beginning of the French Revolution, to 1914, the beginning of the First World War.
2. For brevity we omit the cases of other successful small countries, which are also interesting, such as Switzerland (3.9 million inhabitants in 1913), Denmark (3 million inhabitants), Holland (6.2 million inhabitants), and Sweden (5.6 million inhabitants), which by 1913 had all exceeded 60 per cent of the British per capita income level.

after the war, without however impeding the continuation of the industrial take-off that had begun in the nineteenth century.[3] Tables 5.1–5.5 accompany the national case studies. The first three tables present the data for per capita income from 1820 to 2007 to give a long-term view of the countries considered, while Tables 5.4 and 5.5 offer a few quantitative data of specific interest on the topic of nineteenth century industrialization. Note that in Table 5.2 the levels refer first to Britain/UK until 1938, and then to the United States, which had replaced Britain as the leading country.

5.1 Belgium

We begin with Belgium, which was the country with a resource endowment most similar to that of Britain, with a long maritime tradition (especially the port of Antwerp), pre-industrial commerce and manufacturing in Flanders, and a significant immigration of entrepreneurs, particularly from Britain. It is a small country – 7.7 million inhabitants in 1913 – that in practice consists of two regions: Dutch speaking Flanders and French speaking Wallonia, united by Brussels, the capital. Belgium went through difficult political upheavals, first under the Spanish, then under the Hapsburgs; it was then incorporated into the French empire, and after the Bourbon Restoration it was annexed to Holland. It finally became an independent kingdom after a fairly bloodless revolution in 1830. However, all this had not prevented the development of industry on the British model, which shows just how deeply the development mechanism is *regionally* rooted. Belgium had belonged to different "nations", from which it had not taken on either economic directives or incentives; rather, under various non-oppressive political settings it continued to independently cultivate its own economic interests.

Wool came first, established in Verviers at the beginning of the eighteenth century. The mines came next, particularly coal mines, which were equipped with steam boilers from several entrepreneurs. Spinning machines followed, which were introduced by William Cockerill, a mechanic originally from

---

3. Here too for brevity we omit other small European countries that had only very partially modernized prior to 1913, and in 1913 had a per capita income less than 50 per cent of the British level: Norway (2.4 million inhabitants in 1913); Finland (3 million inhabitants); Portugal (6 million inhabitants); Greece (5.4 million inhabitants). Poland did not yet exist as a nation; after various events during the Napoleonic period it was divided into three parts that were annexed to Russia, Germany and the Hapsburg Empire.

Table 5.1 Income per capita (1990 US dollars).

Country	1820	1850	1913	1938	1950	1973	1992	2007
UK	2,074‡	2,774‡	4,921	6,266	6,939	12,025	16,133	25,002
Austria	1,218	1,650	3,465	3,559	3,706	11,235	17,409	24,235
Belgium	–	1,847	4,220	4,832	5,462	12,170	17,615	23,701
France	1,135	1,597	3,485	4,466	5,186	12,824	17,880	22,202
Germany	–	1,428	3,648	4,994	3,881	11,966	16,891	20,547
Italy	1,511*	1,505*	2,305	2,830	3,172	10,414	16,634	19,842
Spain	–	1,079	2,056	1,790	2,189	7,661	–	17,849
Russia**	–	–	1,414	2,150	2,841	6,059	5,474	7,493
Japan	1,2413	737†	1,387	2,449	1,921	11,434	19,440	22,410
United States	1,361	1,849	5,233	6,126	9,561	16,689	23,285	31,655

Notes: *Only the north–central; **in the area of the former Soviet Union; †1870; ‡Britain alone.

Source: Maddison database.

Leeds, who subsequently built a large metalworking factory near Liège, which became the largest Belgian company in 1830 and was imitated by other entre-preneurs. There was already a cotton industry located around Ghent at the end of the eighteenth century, which in 1810 employed 10,000 people; mech-anization was then extended to linen, which was traditionally hand-worked in Belgium. Later there were sugar refining plants, glassworks, shipyards, and then railway and tram manufacturing. The chemical industry also developed, beginning with a highly innovative approach to sodium carbonate production introduced in 1862 by Ernest Solvay, who set up one of the first and most important Belgian multinationals, which is still active today.

Table 5.2 Per capita income levels, with UK = 100 until 1938, and then USA = 100.

Country	1820	1850	1913	1938	1950	1973	1992	2007
UK	100	100	100	100	73	72	69	79
Austria	59	59	70	57	39	67	75	77
Belgium	–	67	86	77	57	73	–	75
France	55	58	71	71	54	77	77	70
Germany	–	51	74	80	41	72	–	65
Italy	73	54	47	45	33	62	71	63
Spain	–	39	42	29	23	46	–	56
Russia*	–	–	29	34	30	36	–	–
Japan	–	27	28	39	20	69	83	71
United States	66	67	106	98	100	100	100	100

Note: *and former Soviet Union.

Source: Maddison database.

To support and coordinate this intense entrepreneurial activity, banks were created, which quickly showed a remarkable dynamism. In 1822, with the support of King William I, the *Société générale pour favoriser l'industrie nationale des Pays Bas* was founded as a joint-stock company in Brussels; after 1830 it was known as the *Société générale de Belgique*. It was a unique and peculiar investment bank that not only had holdings in industrial companies, but it also directly created companies and followed their interests closely. It gave Belgium an original and distinct financial instrument not available in

Table 5.3 Annual growth rates of income per capita.

Country	1820–50	1850–1913	1913–38	1938–50	1950–73	1973–92	1992–2007
UK	0.98	1.10	0.95	0.87	2.40	1.72	2.90
Austria	1.00	1.20	0.08	0.28	4.70	2.35	2.15
Belgium	–	1.35	0.56	0.87	3.50	2.25	1.90
France	1.15	1.28	1.00	1.06	3.90	1.75	1.44
Germany	–	1.58	1.25	-1.66	4.75	1.80	1.34
Italy	0.00	0.70	0.82	0.94	5.20	2.45	1.10
Spain	–	1.07	-0.50	1.66	5.45	2.50	2.30
Russia*	–	–	1.55	2.31	3.35	-0.50	2.11
Japan	–	1.46	2.30	-1.66	7.80	2.75	0.90
United States	1.05	1.70	0.58	3.71	2.45	1.81	2.10

Note: *and former Soviet Union.

Source: Maddison database.

Britain, emerging as the ancestor of modern financial holding companies. Such was the success of this "bank" that another similar bank was created in 1835, the *Banque de Belgique*, that in less than four years founded or took over twenty-four industrial firms, some of considerable size. Moreover, after independence the new government financed the construction of an extensive railway network, which provided more work to the metalworking and coal industries. This then is how by 1840 Belgium was certainly the most industrialized country on the Continent, and in relative terms it remained so at least until the end of the First World War (see Tables 5.1, 5.2 and 5.3).[4]

5.2   France

While Belgium emerged, although with some original features, as an extension of the British model to the Continent, France instead differed from the British model. At a time when deviations from the British model were considered aberrations, precisely these differences led to a negative view of French development; it was long considered slow and delayed by historians, partly because Gerschenkron did not directly study it, preferring to focus on Germany, Russia and Italy.[5] It was only with the work of O'Brien and Keyder in the late 1970s that this traditional view was revised, which prompted many other important works, such that France is now counted among the cases of successful industrialization, although *sui generis*.[6]

First and foremost, there is the interesting question: why was France not the first to industrialize? Indeed, in the eighteenth century France was far more populous than Britain,[7] with a large internal market that had been unified since the Middle Ages, a reasonably prosperous agriculture (although

---

4. On subsequent developments see Van der Wee & Blomme, *An Economic Development of Belgium since 1870*.

5. Kindleberger, *Economic Growth in France and Britain, 1851–1950*.

6. O'Brien & Keyder, *Economic Growth in Britain and France 1780–1914*. See the bibliography in Grantham, "The French Cliometric Revolution" and also in Dormois, *The French Economy in the Twentieth Century*.

7. In 1701 Britain had fewer than 7 million inhabitants, while France had 20 million; at the end of the century they were at 11 million and 28 million respectively. It was over the course of the nineteenth century that Britain had a true demographic explosion, overtaking France at the dawn of the First World War (41 million to 40 million), despite having continued to deport migrants.

not as dynamic as Britain's and with a poor and institutionally backward area around the Mediterranean), a good pre-industrial manufacturing tradition, and economic growth in the eighteenth century of some significance. Indeed, there are those who have even admitted that France had all the prerequisites for industrializing, if not prior to, at least simultaneously with Britain.[8]

However, the levels of cultural diffusion were lower, income distribution was more polarized, the aristocracy was less business-oriented, and the monarchy was more absolutist than in Britain. It is not generally noted that the beginnings of the French Revolution were determined precisely by a sharp contrast between the monarchy and the bourgeoisie over the issue of who had the authority to introduce new taxes, a question the English had definitively resolved a century earlier in favour of Parliament.[9] The French Revolution with its extremes, and finally Napoleon's rise to power, dragged France into permanent conflict for twenty-five years (1790–1815); while this provided stimulus for certain industries, it cut off France from the British innovations and distorted its use of resources.[10]

All this clarifies why France was not the first industrial nation. Essentially the institutional factors proved less favourable than those of Britain; additionally, France did not have Britain's abundant, high grade and shallow coal mines.[11] After the Bourbon Restoration, France found itself behind Britain, without the hegemony in continental Europe for which it had long fought, and with an incomparably lesser presence in global commerce with respect to Britain. This probably strengthened the attachment of the French to the land, 64 per cent of whom were still active in agriculture in 1851, compared to just 22 per cent in Britain. The slow French demographic growth during the

---

8. Crafts, "Industrial Revolution in England and France", in which the author concludes by evoking the role of chance factors. See also Price, *An Economic History of Modern France, 1730–1914.*

9. See Wallerstein, *The Modern World System*, vol. III.

10. Nevertheless, the Napoleonic era saw some important institutional advances, among them the abolition of serfdom (1789), which obstructed people's mobility out of agriculture, the adoption of the metric system (1790), the abolition of the guilds (1791), the abolition of internal duties and the founding of the *Banque de France* – the central bank – (1800), and the adoption of the Commercial Code (1807).

11. Note that in 1913 France produced 41 million tons of coal, while Britain produced 290 million tons, Germany 279 million tons, tiny Belgium 23 million tons, and the United States 513 million tons. Even in per capita consumption, during the same year France was at 1.6 tons per capita, while Britain was at 4.2, Germany at 3.9, Belgium at 3.9, and the United States at 5 tons per capita. Italy, which did not produce coal, had a still lower per capita consumption at 0.3 tons.

nineteenth century was probably due largely to agricultural families' attempts to limit subdividing the land by having fewer children.

But there was industrial development, and if calculated per capita to account for the effect of slower demographic growth it was respectable. It allowed France to keep pace with, although from behind, Britain's development, as can be seen in Tables 5.1–5.3, but progress was cyclical and without periods of particular acceleration that could be identified as a more rapid take-off.[12] The traditional silk cloth industry, located around Lyon, and the fashion industry, of which France was the leader, remained very important.[13] The mechanized cotton industry grew, which during the 1840s consumed around 60,000 tons of raw cotton, compared to 240,000 tons in Britain. The modern steel industry was established; the Le Creusot complex, which opened in 1785 with the financial aid of Louis XVI, was the most famous. By 1827 there were already more than 100 sugar refineries; gas illumination was introduced, and the glass, ceramic,[14] paper and rubber industries modernized. The era of the railroads then began (see Table 5.4), followed by the electrical and automotive industries. France was in the front line as the leader of Europe with its famous car manufacturers Panhard (1885), Peugeot (1895), and Renault (1898), which however did not make the switch to mass production until later, as imitators of the United States. The *belle époque*, the time immediately prior to the First World War, was particularly prosperous, when France's image was increasingly projected on an international scale[15] (see Table 5.4).

French industry was much more diversified than British industry. It was spread throughout the countryside (when not located around Paris),[16] generally smaller in size because it was more frequently engaged in handicraft work with high value added, for consumers with high purchasing power; even more

---

12. When France did reach parity with Britain, after the Second World War, Britain had notably declined, as we shall see in Chapter 6. See Caron, *An Economic History of Modern France*.

13. In 1801 the French silk weaver Joseph-Marie Jacquard invented the first programmable loom for executing a design.

14. Note that the most important of these industries, Saint Gobain, which later became a chemical industry, was established as a *manufacture royale* in 1665 at the time of Jean Baptiste Colbert, the Finance Minister to Louis XIV, known for having financed the creation of many manufacturing plants and for having experimented with state interventions that were not always beneficial.

15. See Levy-Leboyer & Bourguignon, *L'économie française au XIX siècle*.

16. The process of urbanization was much less pronounced in France than in Britain, both because of agriculture's greater importance and for the lesser requirement for French manufactures to centre around conurbations.

Table 5.4   Kilometres of railways in service.

Region	1870	1913
Belgium	2,897	4,676
France	15,544	40,770
Germany	18,876	63,378
Italy	6,429	18,873
Britain	21,500	32,623
Spain	5,295	15,088
Habsburg Empire	6,112	44,800
Russia	10,731	70,156
United States	85,170	401,977
Japan	0	10,570

Sources: Mitchell, *European Historical Statistics*; *International Historical Statistics: Africa and Asia*; *International Historical Statistics: the Americas and Australasia.*

than Britain, France focused on producing consumer goods in light indus-try, largely financed by the owners themselves through profit reinvestment. The *Haute banque parisienne*, which included the Rothschild bank,[17] primar-ily financed international trade and investments, particularly public bonds, which made up 78 per cent of France's foreign investments in 1850 and 52 per cent in 1880. It was only during the Second Empire that Napoleon incen-tivized the creation of new financial institutions. The most famous was the *Société générale de crédit mobilier*, known as the *Credit mobilier*, founded in 1852 by the Pereire brothers (who had been employees of the Rothschilds). The *Credit mobilier* gave much financial support to the industrial companies that would become crucial in Germany, but in a different economic setting it was not successful, and it failed in 1867. Subsequently the *Banque de Paris et des Pays Bas* was established in 1872, also known as the Paribas, as well as other investment banks, but the bank never played an important role in financing French industry.

---

17. The Rothschild fortunes began with the German Jew Meyer Amschel Rothschild in Frank-furt during the second half of the eighteenth century. He had five sons, four of whom were sent to open branches in the most important European markets of that time: Vienna, Paris, London and Naples, while one remained in Frankfurt.

Table 5.5 Comparative production indicators around 1911.

Region	Population (millions)	Steel produced (millions of tonnes)	Electricity produced (billions of kWh)	Sulphuric acid (thousands of tonnes)
Britain	41	7.8	3.0	1082†
France*	39	4.7	2.1	900†
Germany	65	17.6	8.8	1500
Hapsburg Empire	65	2.6	1.0	350
Italy	35	0.9	2.2	596
Russia	122**	4.9	2.0	275
United States	98	30.0	43.4	2500‡
Japan	52	–	1.5	–

Notes: *excluding Alsace and Lorraine; **with the Asian provinces 165 million; †1913; ‡1914.

Sources: Mitchell, *European Historical Statistics*; *International Historical Statistics: Africa and Asia*; *International Historical Statistics: the Americas and Australasia*.

The state was far less interventionist than in the pre-revolutionary period, limiting itself to supporting infrastructure construction (especially railways), maintaining a certain level of protectionism (a topic to which we shall return later for comparison) and to supporting a series of important advanced technical and professional schools. The first was the *École des ponts et chaussées* in 1747. The revolutionary period saw the founding of the *École des Mines*, the very famous *École polytechnique* in 1794,[18] the *Conservatoire des Arts et Métiers* and the *Ecole Normale supérieure* in 1798. The *École central des arts et manufactures* was established in 1828. French colonialism was far less significant economically than that of the British; the question of the influence of the colonies on the economies of the colonizing countries will be taken up in comparative terms in Chapter 8.

5.3 *Germany*

Just the opposite of France, which had very quickly formed a national state, Germany long retained its local traditions. In the eighteenth century it was fragmented into over four hundred "statelets". Hohenzollern Prussia alone stood out for its size and power. It was a dynasty that came to power in the sixteenth century and grew by inheritance; it implemented an efficient state apparatus and a powerful army, but it failed to modernize its economy. Even after the Napoleonic era, which had seen the abolition of serfdom in 1807, the elimination of the guilds and the privatization of the land, and after the Congress of Vienna had simplified the political geography of Germany into thirty-nine states, the area did not take off, in spite of the availability of abundant coal deposits, particularly in the Ruhr.

In 1818 Prussia began to open up to international trade by lowering and simplifying tariffs, which placed it at the centre of a process of aggregating the other states into a customs union (the *Zollverein*) – formally introduced in 1833 – that abolished internal tariffs and adopted the moderate foreign tariffs of Prussia. This was a major accomplishment, which immediately revealed its full strategic impact with an initial period of expansion during the 1840s and

---

18. This institution inspired the founding of similar technical schools across continental Europe and the United States. As we shall see, the developments by the German polytechnic schools – more applied and less mathematical than the French schools – were particularly important.

1850s; in any event after unification in 1871[19] Germany had its real, rapid and sustained take-off.[20]

To understand the distinctive characteristics of the German case, we should immediately note that the German take-off took place between the era of the railways and large steel mills and the second industrial revolution, which was based on electricity, organic chemistry and the internal combustion engine (a topic we will explore in Chapter 7). All these were capital intensive heavy industry sectors that required large-scale enterprises and financial assets that exceeded the capacity of individual families. As we will see, Germany succeeded in taking full advantage of the potential of these new industrial sectors. It became the largest European steel producer and the European and world leader in electricity and chemicals, setting up numerous joint-stock banks (the *Kreditbanken*) that generously financed the new industrial initiatives. The first of these banks – the *Schaaffhausen'scher Bankverein* in Cologne in 1848 – did not become particularly well known, unlike the successive *Disconto Gesellschaft* of Berlin in 1851, the *Darmstädter* in 1853, the *Berliner Handelsgesellschaft* in 1856, and above all the *Deutsche Bank* in 1870,[21] the *Commerz Bank* of the same year, and the *Dresdner Bank* in 1882.

These were banks with completely innovative ways of operating compared to the British banks. They were both normal commercial banks, which collected deposits from a broad customer base and issued short-term credit, *and* investment banks, which channelled not only its own capital but also that of its customers into long-term credit, surpassing the specialized credit of the British banks. This is why they were called *mixed* or *universal* banks, not only because they were not specialized, but because they offered their corporate customers other services such as share placement, capital restructuring and bailouts, assisting firms "from cradle to grave".

These banks became very powerful in Germany, such that their dominance was already recognized by the beginning of the twentieth century.[22] They frequently held a small equity stake in firms, primarily to place a few of their men on the boards of directors so they could closely follow their operations, but in general they avoided holding a controlling interest (the mixed bank was not, and did not want to become, a Belgian style holding company that managed companies and was bound to them alone). Since the representatives

---

19. Germany maintained a much higher degree of autonomy of the Länder (the German federal states) than any other European nation, a legacy of its tradition of political fragmentation.
20. See Pierenkemper & Tilly, *The German Economy During the Nineteenth Century*.
21. See Gall, *The Deutsche Bank 1870–1995*.
22. See Hilferding, *Das Finanzkapital*; Riesser, *The German Great Banks and their Concentration*.

of each bank held seats on many boards of directors they found themselves in possession of first-hand information on industrial complexes, and at times entire industries, favouring forms of organization of the market, like cartels, that reduced their risk.[23] In 1914 there were nearly a thousand of these, complemented by a moderate form of external protectionism[24] that could be reinforced by dumping.[25] Yet, to face temporary crises these banks required a much more interventionist central bank than the Bank of England or the *Banque de France*, which is just how the Reichsbank acted. In general, the type of economic system that emerged from the institutional innovation of the mixed bank is a much more cohesive system that is coordinated *ex ante*, which Chandler defined as "cooperative"[26] and the German scholars preferred to define as "organized".[27] It was very different from the quasi-competitive system with small companies typical of Britain and from the United States' system (for which see Chapter 6).

The importance of the mixed bank was first remarked by Gerschenkron, who made it his preferred example of a substitutable factor (that is, of a factor which substituted financing by the family or English merchant banks). Since then much has been written on the mixed bank, with still unresolved disputes over the degree of direct involvement by the mixed bank in controlling or directing the affairs of the firms entrusted to it, but particularly on the comparative validity of an economic system based on mixed banking versus that of the Anglo-American model based on the stock exchange.[28] We will consider this topic in Chapter 8.

We can clearly see the success of the German system from the data in Tables 5.1–5.5. Steel, electricity and chemicals, as well as a solid machine industry, were the mainstay sectors of German industry. In chemicals the three famous firms of Bayer, Basf and Hoechst systematically built the coal-

---

23. This is the well-known problem of "interlocking directorates", which has received significant attention in the theory of networks; see Baccini & Vasta, "Una tecnica ritrovata".
24. Germany was home to Frederich List, the pre-eminent theoretician of the necessity of protecting nascent industries; he also supported the *Zollverein*.
25. "Dumping" is defined as the practice of holding internal prices of a product higher than international prices in order to favour exports and recoup the margins lost on the international market from the internal market. Dumping is generally a short-term policy, but may alter permanently the flow of international trade, and as such it is opposed and fought.
26. Chandler, *Scale and Scope*.
27. See Herrigel, *Industrial Constructions*.
28. Wixforth & Ziegler, "*Bankenmacht*: Universal Banking and German Industry in Historical Perspective"; Fohlin, "Capital Mobilisation and Utilisation in Latecomer Economies"; Edwards & Ogilvie, "Universal Banks and German Industrialization". See also the comprehensive review, Tilly, "German Economic History and Cliometrics".

based chemical industry that processed coal to produce intermediates from which artificial colours, explosives, and a surprising number of pharmaceuticals (among them aspirin, which Bayer patented in 1899) could be derived. At the dawn of the First World War Germany accounted for more than half of the chemical exports in the world and was without rivals, even in the United States (which was subsequently quicker in developing the petrochemical industry). In electricity the two large firms Siemens and AEG invested all over Europe and globally rivalled the two large American firms General Electric and Westinghouse. In steel the names of Krupp and Thyssen became legendary.

These were large companies, all within "heavy industry", which can easily be converted into a war industry; this favoured nationalist policies by the Hohenzollern, who thought themselves able to win a hegemony in Europe by force of arms, to the point of leading Germany into the First World War.[29] The science used in these firms was more advanced than that required in textile and engineering firms in the first industrial revolution, and required greater research efforts and expanding secondary and higher education. Germany set up an efficient public system of technical secondary schools and higher polytechnic institutes that produced a significant number of engineers who acquired high status positions in society. Furthermore, the research laboratories in the universities and large companies exchanged senior technical people in a cross-fertilization imitated on a large scale only by the United States. Most of the industrial firms were in Western Germany, while the Eastern part remained extensively agrarian with not very advanced technology; this created an East–West dualism that has impacted the country's destiny until today.[30] This fact is responsible for the not very high *average* per capita income attained by the country in 1913 (74 per cent of that of Britain and only just higher than that of France at 71 per cent; see Table 5.2), which validates Pollard's regional approach. Germany as a nation in fact had many highly advanced areas, more advanced than the corresponding British areas, but many others that were quite backward, which markedly lowered the average national data.

One final aspect should be considered. Germany was the first European nation to introduce a state-run social welfare system extended to all workers, introduced by Bismarck during the 1880s. Between 1883 and 1889 mandatory

29. Note however that Germany's colonial policies were never particularly committed, and the German colonies never had any economic importance for Germany.
30. After the Second World War Eastern Germany became an independent state under Soviet hegemony, which certainly did not improve its fate, such that when the country was reunited in 1990 the East was even more greatly at a disadvantage.

Figure 5.1 Regions of the Hapsburg Empire.

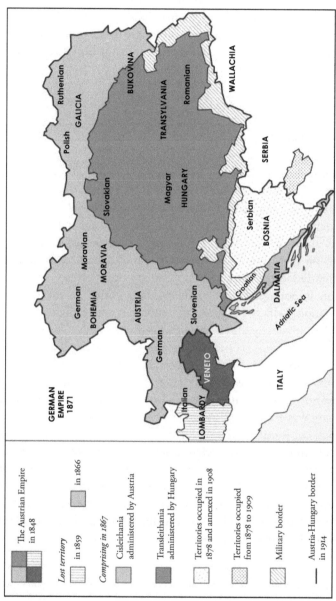

insurance managed under public control was introduced against work-related accidents, health problems and old age, for the purpose of guaranteeing social peace and holding the trade unions in check to allow for an orderly process of industrialization. Germany was the first country in the world to implement such generalized insurance coverage, although it was not universal because it was based on employment relationships and not on citizenship rights, as happened in Sweden a couple of decades later.[31]

5.4 The Hapsburg Empire

The Hapsburg Empire built up over time, clustering diverse territories for varying lengths of time around Austria and its capital Vienna. In the nineteenth century it encompassed eleven different nationalities, each with its respective language (see Figure 5.1).[32] The territory was not very suitable for agriculture, since two-thirds of it consisted of mountains and hills. Its only seaport was on the Adriatic, at Trieste. The coal deposits were not abundant or conveniently located.

It was an important and powerful political entity (in reality one cannot call it a "nation"). In the eighteenth century it was economically relatively advanced, but it subsequently failed to keep pace with others, although the wholly negative view of its performance in the nineteenth century has been extensively revised. First, it should be said that it greatly delayed abolishing serfdom, which happened only after the 1848 revolution. Also, internal tariffs were not abolished until 1850, when a customs union modelled after the *Zollverein* was established. Another negative element was its protectionist policy which cut it out of international trade (consider that at the beginning of the twentieth century tiny Belgium had a greater international trade than that of the entire Empire); moreover, of what little trade there was about half was narrowly concentrated with Germany. Furthermore, the policy of administrative centralization was tempered only by the autonomy conceded to Hungary in 1867 (for which it also became known as the Austro-Hungarian Empire, with the union of the two crowns).

---

31. Ritter, *Storia dello stato sociale*. Universalism did not arrive until the Swedish experiments in the 1930s and the Beveridge Report in 1942; see Zamagni, "Funzioni e strumenti del welfare state in prospettiva storica" and also Zamagni, "L'economia sociale di mercato nella storia".
32. Recall that part of the Italian possessions were lost in mid-century, Lombardy in 1859 and Venetia in 1866.

From a sectoral point of view, the industrial development that did happen privileged light industry, such as food (particularly in Hungary), wool and cotton textiles, glass and paper; the metalworking, railways and electrical industries developed as well, but at a level that was comparatively unsatisfactory. The financial system imitated the German approach with the creation of numerous mixed banks, of which the most famous were the *Creditanstalt* (1885) and the *Wiener Bankverein*.[33] On the eve of the Second World War, these two Viennese banks held controlling interests in 43 per cent of the total share capital of the Empire. The *Creditanstalt*, which remained the most important bank, had interests in armaments, steel, metalworking (including the Czech automobile company Skoda), oil, sugar and other food industries. Even the formation of cartels followed the German example, with nearly 200 cartels in existence on the eve of the war.[34]

In reality, the Empire's main problem was that it had areas with vastly different prerequisites for growth (agricultural conditions, the dissemination of education, and infrastructure) at the beginning of the nineteenth century, and it was not able to bring the most backward areas to make a qualitative leap forward. In the second half of the nineteenth century all the areas grew economically, some more, such as Hungary, some less, such as Lower Austria, but since they all had different starting points that were much lower than those of the more advanced European countries, on the eve of the First World War the result remained unimpressive[35] (see Table 5.6).

Observing the regional differences, we see that only Austria had a reasonable level of development, while the other regions were more or less undeveloped, revealing a deep regional gap in the Empire. Were we to use regional estimates available for Spain and Russia, these too would reveal strong regional imbalances, typical of nations whose history left very different legacies from region to region in regard to infrastructure, cultural development, the spread of education and capital accumulation. By using Maddison's data we are unable to go into further detail on the regional differences.[36]

Gerschenkron dedicated a book to an event that he held to be indicative of the paralysis that characterized the Empire's political economy toward the

33. See Rudolph, *Banking and Industrialization in Austria–Hungary*.
34. Good, *The Economic Rise of the Hapsburg Empire 1750–1914*. See also Berend & Ranki, *Economic Development in East-Central Europe in the Nineteenth and Twentieth Centuries*.
35. See Schulze, "Origins of Catch up Failure".
36. The regional differences have been further developed in other publications, which are not always comparable. See Good & Ma, "The Economic Growth of Central and Eastern Europe in Comparative Perspective, 1870–1989".

Table 5.6 Economic indicators of the Hapsburg Empire regions forming the successor states (post-1945 borders).

Country	1913 income per capita (Austria = 100)	1913 income per capita (UK = 100)
Austria	100	70
Czechoslovakia	60	43
Hungary	60	43
Poland	50	35
Romania	50	35
Yugoslavia	28	20

Source: Maddison database.

end of its existence:[37] at the beginning of the twentieth century it was not able to decide on the construction of a canal between the Danube and the Oder that would have improved internal transportation and attenuated nationalist conflicts within the Empire, gathering broad consensus around a common economic program. Prime Minister Ernest von Koerber, the architect of the project, ended up resigning in 1904 due to the continual sabotage by the Ministry of Finance. Gershenkron ended his work by stressing that Koerber's economic approach would have been capable of shaping a different destiny for the Empire, but since it was not successful it condemned it to dissolution.

5.5   Russia

On the eve of the First World War Russia remained a very backward nation with a per capita income less than a third of that of Britain; 75 per cent of the workforce was still engaged in agriculture (compared to 59 per cent in Italy and 62 per cent in Japan), 72 per cent of the population was illiterate (compared to 48 per cent in Italy), and only 15 per cent of the population settled in urban areas. And yet, if we look at Tables 5.4 and 5.5 we see that it produced as much steel and electricity as France and double that of the Hapsburg Empire, and it boasted more miles of railway than any other European country. So how was this possible? Of course, the key to this discrepancy lay in the fact that Russia was huge; although having an industrial base of some importance

37. Gerschenkron, *An Economic Spurt that Failed.*

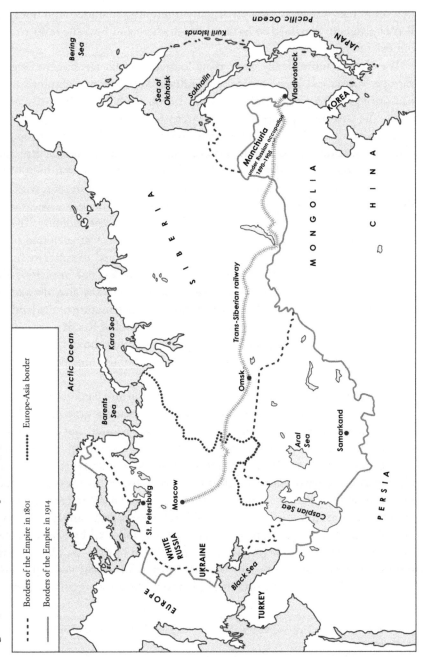

Figure 5.2 The Russian Empire in 1913.

in absolute terms, in relative and per capita terms the effects were submerged in a sea of backwardness. It is particularly interesting to understand both why Russia generally remained so backward and where and how the industry that did exist developed.

We should immediately note that, located on the far Eastern edge of Europe, Russia had been considerably influenced by oriental absolutism and had opened up to greater influence from Europe only at the initiative of the czars. The first attempts to import Western technology were in the time of Peter the Great (1696–1725), but these prompted no effort to change the country's institutions to enable a modernization of its economic structure. The loss of the Crimean War (1855) brought to light the backwardness of the country, and Czar Alexander II decided to abolish serfdom in 1861, which by then had remained in force only in Russia. However, the way it was carried out in no way freed up either land cultivation or peasant mobility. In fact, decisions on land distribution and the control of labour were deferred to the village community (the *mir*), such that those who wanted to emigrate had to continue to pay taxes and redemption payments. It was not until 1907 that Minister Stolypin abolished residual redemption payments and allowed the actual privatization of land.[38] While this institutional structure of the land was long considered the cause of the low productivity level of Russian agriculture, we now have a revised version of this negative view that shows that there was a moderate productivity increase in the second half of the nineteenth century, but it began from very low levels.[39]

Alexander II also encouraged railway construction and bank reorganization. Beginning in the 1880s Russian industrialization made a great leap forward growing at a rapid pace during the 1890s; it was centred not only around Moscow and Saint Petersburg, but also in the Urals, Ukraine and in the Polish regions (see Figure 5.2). The heavy industries linked to railways (coal, steel and machinery), and particularly the arms industry, took off. The textile and food industries were not absent from this growth, but, given the restricted internal market for consumption goods, they did not have a great impetus. Growth slowed at the beginning of the twentieth century, followed by Russia's defeat in the Russo-Japanese war (1904–5). The revolution of 1905–6 occasioned the introduction of a few weak and less absolutist reforms. Strikes and unions were legalized, but by very restrictive legislation. There was agrarian reform, as

---

38. On the eve of the First World War, however, no more than one-third of the land had been privatized.
39. See Gatrell, *The Tsarist Economy 1850–1917*. See also Gregory, *Before Command* and Gatrell, *Government, Industry and Rearmament in Russia, 1900–1914*.

previously noted, but a true Parliament (a Duma) was not conceded, and the intelligentsia, the cultural elite of the nation, distanced itself more and more from a democratic opposition. There was some recovery, but on the eve of the First World War the Russian economy was far from having found a balanced self-sustaining growth path; there were few Russian entrepreneurs, and they were badly organized and relatively marginalized socially.[40]

Gerschenkron strongly emphasized the particular role of the state in Russian industrialization; in the Russian case he saw another example of the substitutable factor of the private investment channels prevalent in Britain. Where in Germany the mixed banks had channeled capital to industry, in Russia – a country much more backward than Germany with respect to Britain – it was the state. The state financed the railways, introduced the gold standard (see Chapter 8) to attract foreign investments, imposed duties on strategic industries to incentivize the construction of factory plants in the country, ordered arms, and was generous with subsidies for entrepreneurs, especially foreigners. In reality, foreign capital was strategic, so much so that on the eve of the war it financed half of the Russian public debt (largely used for railways) and 40 per cent of the capital of all joint stock companies.[41] To fulfil this role the Russian state taxed incomes that were already low, which contributed to restraining private demand, which made the importance of public demand even more relevant.[42]

Gerschenkron held that, had Russia's participation in the First World War not destabilized the country's economic situation, it might have slowly evolved towards political equilibria more favourable for self-sustaining growth and towards an economy in which private demand would have mattered more.[43] Instead, the war proved fatal for Russian capitalism, as we will see in Chapter 10.

5.6 *Italy*

As we saw in Chapter 2, many of the institutional innovations that anticipated the industrial revolution between the end of the Middle Ages and the Renaissance were introduced in "Italy" – an expression that at the time was

---

40. See the interesting study by Rieber, *Merchants and Entrepreneurs in Imperial Russia*.
41. These capital flows into Russia were compensated by a trade surplus due to massive grain exports.
42. See chapter 2 of Gatrell, *Government, Industry*.
43. For more on this issue, see Sanborn, *Imperial Apocalypse*.

Figure 5.3 The Italian pre-unification states.

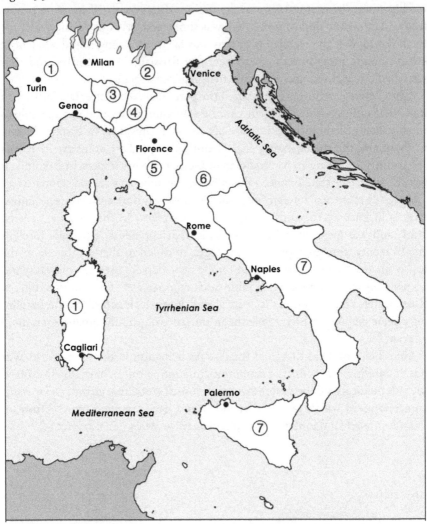

1 Kingdom of Sardinia
2 Lombardy–Venetia
3 Duchy of Parma
4 Duchy of Modena
5 Grand Duchy of Tuscany
6 Papal State
7 Kingdom of the Two Sicilies

merely geographical in meaning, since it was occupied by political entities that were as small as they were unstable. Actually, Italy was home to advanced manufacturing activities that were quite prosperous for their time, as is indicated by the high number of cities that were there, which had no comparison in the rest of Europe. Due partly to political fragmentation and endemic conflict,[44] partly to the excessive insistence on high-priced luxury manufacturing, together with a shift in the trade axis from the Mediterranean to the Atlantic, there was a sharp decline in Italy in the seventeenth century and a persistent backwardness during the eighteenth century, despite the presence of elite thinkers and economists deeply linked to developments in the rest of Europe. Once past the turmoil of the Napoleonic wars, Italy was reorganized by the Congress of Vienna into seven states, two of which were very small and one (Lombardy–Veneto) under direct Austrian domination (see Figure 5.3).

Among these states only the Kingdom of Sardinia proved to be institutionally (it became a constitutional monarchy in 1848) and economically dynamic, with the construction of railways, textile, mechanical and shipbuilding manufacturing, and banks (the *Banca Nazionale degli Stati Sardi*, established in 1849).[45] With Cavour's rise to power, it found a broad-minded politician who knew how to weave international alliances such that it came to support the irredentism of the Italians who wanted primarily to be free of Austria, as well as of other unwanted, obstinately absolutist governments. Cavour's skilfully woven alliances, coupled with Garibaldi's hot-headedness – another Sardinian – who conceived the idea of "liberating" the Kingdom of the Two Sicilies from the Bourbons, led to the political unification of the country in the presence of profound differences in cultural traditions, economic infrastructure, dissemination of education and agricultural productivity.[46]

The new rulers of the unified Italy[47] modernized the country from an institutional point of view, introducing a liberal commercial law and a tax policy aligned with the most advanced European systems.[48] In 1859 it enacted the Casati Act, one of the most advanced European laws on education, and linked

---

44. Conflicts that drove calls for foreigners to bolster the fortunes of certain political parties, with the devastating effects of repeated invasions and foreign rule.

45. See Zamagni, *An Economic History of Italy 1860–1990*. See also Toniolo, *An Economic History of Liberal Italy 1850–1918*; Fenoaltea, *The Reinterpretation of Italian Economic History*; Ciocca, *Ricchi per sempre?* and Felice, *Ascesa e declino*. Note the name of the kingdom as distinct from the name of the island fortuitously acquired from the Kingdom of Savoy after a swap with Sicily in 1720; it was an island that never counted in the kingdom's economy, unlike the Republic of Genoa, annexed by the Congress of Vienna, which played an important role.

46. Only the Po river valley, and particularly Lombardy, had a fairly advanced agriculture.

47. Recall that the Venetia only became part of Italy in 1866, Latium in 1870, and Trento and Trieste only after the First World War, while Savoy and Nice, which were part of the Kingdom of Sardinia, were ceded to France in 1859.

48. Due to serious budget requirements a tax on milled goods was introduced in 1868 – certainly not a "modern" tax – but it was repealed in 1884.

the Italian monetary system to the gold standard.[49] It did not succeed in creating a single central bank, because the issuing banks of several pre-unification states successfully remained in existence, although the *Banca Nazionale degli Stati Sardi* (National Bank of the Sardinian States), renamed as the Banca *Nazionale nel Regno d'Italia* (National Bank in the Kingdom of Italy), was clearly pre-eminent.[50]

However, the country's economy struggled to take off, despite the railway projects launched by the early governments. Traditional activities continued, particularly the production of raw silk for the international market;[51] what we do not see, however, is the introduction of new industrial sectors. We should make clear that Italy had a number of shortcomings: it was devoid of coal and had little iron; public debt was high due to the poor financial conditions of the pre-unification states, many wars, and the time required to get the new fiscal system up to speed; there was no lack of banks (savings banks, cooperative banks, and *Monti di Pietà*), but few were joint stock companies that had the goal of industrial finance. The two most important of these were two French-style commercial banks, the *Credito Mobiliare* (Securitized Credit, 1863) and the *Banca Generale* (General Bank, 1870).

Business picked up a little early in the 1880s, partly due to state initiatives that modernized the Italian navy, financed the creation of Terni, the first important Italian steel mill, and re-introduced some protectionism in 1887, with widely divergent contemporary opinions on its effectiveness. Widespread construction speculation toward the end of the decade precipitated a deep banking system crisis, which saw the failure of the *Credito Mobiliare* and the *Banca Generale*, the liquidation of the *Banca Romana*, and the merger of two other small issuing banks into the *Banca Nazionale* (National Bank), renamed the *Banca d'Italia* in 1893, which continued to share the power of issuing bank notes with two other much less important banks, the *Banco di Napoli* (Bank of Naples) and the *Banco di Sicilia* (Bank of Sicily).[52] The Italian banking system continued to restructure with the founding of German-style mixed banks. The first was the *Banca Commerciale Italiana* (known as the *Comit*)

---

49. The adventures of the lira in the gold standard were indeed troubled. Italy had to leave the gold standard in 1866 due to the third war of independence against Austria, and it was not able to return to it until 1883. It left again in 1894 due to serious economic difficulties, and stayed off, although until the First World War it acted as if it were still part of it.

50. With the *Banca Romana*, inherited along with Latium in 1870, there were six issuing banks in Italy.

51. See Federico, *An Economic History of the Silk Industry 1830–1930* for the important role silk played in Italy's economy and international trade.

52. The *Banca d'Italia* became the sole issuing bank only in 1926.

in 1895, then the *Credito Italiano* (known as the *Credit*) in 1895, while the *Banco di Roma*,[53] a Roman institution created in 1880, converted to mixed bank operations toward the end of the century. In 1898 another Milan bank was restructured into the *Società Bancaria Italiana* (the SBI, or the Italian Banking Company).

Italy's industrial take-off began in the second half of the 1890s, and it continued until the First World War. All the industrial sectors took off, except for chemicals (only phosphate fertilizers). The electrical industry was particularly successful, which partly freed Italy from dependence on coal; on the eve of the First World War Italy produced as much electricity as France and Russia, and double that of the Hapsburg Empire, primarily as hydroelectricity, or "white coal". In the mechanical industry Fiat was founded in 1899; Pirelli (tyres) was founded in 1872 and quickly became the first Italian multinational. At the end of this period, however, from the aggregate data Italy still appeared rather backward, having reached only 47 per cent of the per capita income of Britain, an accomplishment similar to the average of the Hapsburg Empire.

Gerschenkron offered an explanation for this "unsatisfactory" result; he had the merit of re-opening the debate on the post-unification Italian economy at a time – from the late 1950s to the early 1960s – when Italian economic historians were predominately occupied with studies of the Middle Ages and the early modern era. Gerschenkron held that the economic policies of the Italian governments, particularly the ill-conceived protectionism and the haste to build railways, had prevented it from fully benefiting from the "advantages of backwardness", and that neither the state nor the banking system were able to offer powerful substitutable factors as in Russia and Germany. A huge debate followed, which we cannot discuss here.[54]

Furthermore, it is a fact that Italy also suffered, as mentioned previously, from deep regional imbalances, although at that time somewhat less than those of the Hapsburg Empire. In reality, the industrial take-off fully happened in only three regions – Piedmont, Liguria and Lombardy – known as the industrial triangle. There were other regions where industrialization was set in motion, but still only very partially. The entire south of the country progressed very little, to the point that in the early years of the twentieth century it attracted a series of special laws (the 1904 law for Naples was

---

53. Not to be confused with the *Banca Romana* previously mentioned.
54. Along with those texts already cited, see the special issue of the *Journal of Modern Italian Studies*, vol. 15, no. 1 (2010, ed. Malanima & Zamagni), dedicated to 150 years of the Italian economy, and Toniolo, *Oxford Handbook of the Italian Economy Since Unification*.

particularly important, which tried to incentivize some industrial activity in the area), although without appreciable improvements.[55]

5.7 Spain

As we saw in Chapter 2, Spain was never among the countries with the highest per capita income; it reached a peak in the sixteenth century and subsequently declined until it lost its colonies[56] early in the nineteenth century (1824). Agriculture was generally backward, due also to the climate and soil conditions, although it was not without products for export, such as sherry (Andalusia). Education was lacking.[57] In the second half of the nineteenth century things improved, primarily because of the dynamism of two regions, Catalonia and the Basque country, as well as the capital Madrid. Catalonia began developing a cotton industry at the end of the eighteenth century, later developing the mechanical, transportation and electric industries, and some public services. The Basque country founded a steel industry at the end of the nineteenth century, taking advantage of the important iron mines in the area; at first it worked to export the raw material, and later it launched some engineering industries.[58]

So it was that at the dawn of the First World War Spain's level of per capita income was similar to that of Italy (see Table 5.2) with 42 per cent of Britain's per capita income compared to Italy's 47 per cent.[59] Over the course of the long nineteenth century, on the whole, neither of the two nations succeeded in achieving a real improvement with respect to Britain, even though a regional analysis reveals that the aggregate data concealed the take-off of several areas within the country, conceiled by the stagnation in other areas. In the case of Spain, some argue that this was due to Spain's excessively high protectionism, particularly after the tariff increases in 1906,[60] others that it did not belong to the gold standard.[61] Spanish growth subsequently continued at a good pace

55. See Felice, *Perché il Sud è rimasto indietro*.
56. The remaining colonies – Cuba, Puerto Rico and the Philippines – were lost in 1898 after defeat in the Spanish–American war. See Prados de la Escosura, *De imperio a nacion*.
57. On the topic of education, see Nuñez, *La fuente de la riqueza*.
58. See Tortella, *The Development of Modern Spain*.
59. See De la Escosura, "Long Run Economic Growth in Spain Since 1800" and Carreras, "An Annual index of Spanish Industrial Output".
60. Teña, "Proteccion y competitividad en España e Italia, 1890–1960".
61. See Martin-Aceña, "Spain During the Classical Gold Standard Years, 1880–1914".

in the 1920s; it was not seriously disrupted by the Great Depression, but it had a heavy setback with the 1936 civil war and the first two decades of unreasonable autarky by the new Franco regime. These were the real reasons why Spain showed a decline compared to Italy between 1913 and 1938 (Tables 5.1–5.3).

6

British decline and the emergence of the United States and Japan as competitors

In this chapter we will examine the two most successful examples of industrialization outside Europe. The first, the United States, has been directly connected to European history from its beginnings. European emigration created and profoundly shaped the US, and its ties to Europe have always been very close, not just economically, but militarily and politically as well. The second, Japan, shows just how great Europe's influence has been, even in a place so geographically and culturally distant. Furthermore, we should remember that the United States, Europe and Japan were the three great world powers after the Second World War, and it is important to be familiar with their origins to understand their international dynamics. That said, this chapter opens by considering another important question that has given rise to a vast literature, namely the decline of Britain's leadership beginning in the second half of the nineteenth century.

6.1 *British decline*

Over the long term, there has never been a power that has resisted the ravages of history, not even the Roman Empire, which certainly endured much longer than many other powers. In and of itself, then, a story of decline has always been part of the historical dimension. The large interest in the British decline is due to the fact that it was the first to happen in the industrial age, showing that although the "first mover" in the industrial age has great advantages, these are not sufficient to guarantee maintaining that position. Furthermore, unlike preceding declines, the British decline was due mainly to economic, social and cultural reasons rather than political and military ones. Britain kept its territorial integrity, it always won its wars, and it did not have political revolutions, which is indicative of a different impact of the industrial revolution.

However, leadership was increasingly decided at the economic level rather than at the politico-military level. The story is one of the decline of British leadership, not the disappearance of Britain as an advanced country. Britain continued to grow economically and to deepen its structural transformation: it was the first country in which agriculture was greatly reduced in favour of industry, and it was the first country in which industry was greatly reduced in favour of services. But, on the whole, since the 1870s its rate of income growth has been lower than those of many other industrial countries. This allowed other countries to "catch up" to its levels of per capita income, not only the United States at the end of the nineteenth century, but also most of the more advanced European countries, as well as Japan, after the Second World War (see Tables 5.1–5.3).

No wonder then that the question of British decline has attracted the interest of many scholars who have sought above all to identify its causes. It has long been discussed whether one should even talk about decline, given that the country only slowly lost ground, and if one looks over shorter terms rather than as a century long process it is not easy to grasp it.[1] It is a very complex phenomenon, and the many factors taken into consideration are all important in one way or another. Here we will present a schematic summary, ordering them in three groups for consideration:

- an early start;
- the burden of leadership; and
- institutional rigidity.

We make no attempt to put them in any order of importance.

AN EARLY START

This may seem paradoxical, in that an early start usually gives advantages from a competitive standpoint, but one can also view the question from the other side of the coin of the "advantages of backwardness". Just as backwardness can reveal advantages, having begun early produces disadvantages. The machines and infrastructure adopted were the first, less perfected models, which quickly reached a high degree of economic obsolescence (that is, they were not the most efficient and competitive), even though they still worked perfectly. The temptation was to leave them operating to the end of their physical lives, and thus Britain lost competitiveness in various fields, for example, trains: the first

---

1. See Dormois & Dintenfass, *The British Industrial Decline*.

trains were small and narrow gauge, built for small tunnels and sharp turns, but with the advent of larger and wider trains the entire British rail system became obsolete, and it was a struggle to modernize it.

INSTITUTIONAL RIGIDITY

As we saw in Chapter 3, Britain had evolved internally such as to make it possible for the industrial revolution to happen, but it did not draw inspiration from the institutional innovations of other countries that sought to imitate its success in making its own economic activity more efficient.[2] This aspect has been investigated in relation to four main applications:

- *Finance.* Britain was not successful either in making its stock exchange efficient or in introducing banks more closely linked to industrial financing, leaving its industries without effective financial support.[3] In the case of the stock exchange, the necessary information transparency was not available to the public, which suffered serious losses from share issues of new industries, and people thus preferred to invest in safer securities. In the case of the banks, the merchant banks were too tied to financing international activities (see point three) to be interested in national industry, while the models of French investment banks or German mixed banks were never considered.
- *Education.* Britain did not introduce a public education system, as had all countries on the continent, and in particular it took no interest specifically in technical education.[4] Classical education prevailed in the private schools (which, we should recall, were called *public*[5] schools),

---

2. See Kirby, "Institutional Rigidities and Economic Decline".
3. William Kennedy is the scholar who has most studied this thesis, see his *Industrial Structure, Capital Markets and the Origin of British Economic Decline*. See also von Helten & Cassis, *Capitalism in a Mature Economy*, in which they maintain that the rapid process of consolidating British banks into a few large institutions deprived many areas of local banks able to sustain small-scale activities.
4. There have been many contributions to this field: see, most notably, Wiener, *English Culture and the Decline of the Industrial Spirit*; Locke, *The End of the Practical Man*; Sanderson, *The Universities and British Industry 1850–1970*; Aldcroft, *Education, Training and Economic Performance, 1944 to 1990*.
5. The word "public" is highly ambiguous in the Anglo-American world. Indeed, it expresses both the concept of public in the common sense of the term and the concept of "belonging to the people", thus in a private-collective sense. This is the sense in which the above-mentioned expression "public school" should be understood, as well as the widely used term "public company" in the United States, being a private company owned by shareholders.

AN ECONOMIC HISTORY OF EUROPE SINCE 1700

while, beyond the classical disciplines, purely scientific disciplines were taught in the universities. Technicians were self-taught and did not have a high social status, unlike the engineers in Germany, France, Italy or Japan. The mentality of the entrepreneur was often more focused on business in general (finance and trade) than on the technical side of production,[6] which prevented Britain from doing well in the second industrial revolution, as it required more widespread medium and higher level technical education.

- *The Corporation.* The evolution towards forms of corporate managerial organization was much slower in both Britain and Germany than in the United States. Chandler[7] labelled British capitalism as "personal", meaning that the managerial revolution was not as generalized as it was in the United States. Lazonick[8] noted that the British factory was left in the hands of the shop stewards – the department heads who maintained a master–apprentice relationship with the workers under them – instead of being organized according to Tayloristic principles and a clearly defined functional hierarchy. The productivity of a similar "non-scientific" labour organization could not be competitive with those in the United States or Germany.

- *The state.* The state in Britain was lacking in assuming greater responsibility for the development of the country, preferring to commit many of its resources to the colonies (with dubious effects; see Chapter 8) and to international leadership, the burden of which will be discussed in the next point.

THE BURDEN OF LEADERSHIP

We are accustomed to seeing the international leadership of a country as a supportive factor for its income, which is true, but what we tend to forget is that leadership also imposes burdens, which we will examine in the British case:

- *The colonies.* As this will be discussed in Chapter 8, here we limit ourselves

---

6. Recent studies have revised this view: see Pollard, *British Prime and British Decline*; Rubinstein, *Capitalism, Culture and Economic Decline in Britain, 1750–1990* and, particularly, Edgerton, *Science, Technology and British Industrial "Decline", 1870–1970*.
7. Chandler, *Scale and Scope*.
8. Lazonick, *Business Organization and the Myth of the Market Economy*.

to noting it for completeness. Military and administrative costs, as well as over-commitment in supplying unsophisticated markets, were the chief drawbacks.

- *Support for the gold standard.* The Bank of England administered monetary policy more with the goal of maintaining international stability than of supporting its domestic economy. It long administered the reserves of Japan and the United States until they created their own central banks, as well as India's reserves.
- *The predominance of London's financial centre.* The interests of the City of London, the largest financial centre of its time, were held to be more important than those of British industry. London's demonstrated ability in international activities was such that it attracted investors and the merchant banks towards foreign investments rather than national investments, with the promise of higher rates of return.[9]
- *The role of "policeman of the world".* Britain's involvement in many wars, with the purpose of maintaining a balance of power in Europe (virtually all the European wars from the Napoleonic wars onwards), together with colonialism, led to over-investment in the military and considerable losses of human capital.[10]

The relative decline of Britain was halted during the 1930s and 1940s, as we shall see, but it increased precipitously in the years after the Second World War in a completely unexpected way. The British struggled to become aware of it and failed to set a more realistic policy both with regard to Europe and to diversifying the economy beyond manufacturing.[11]

6.2   *The rise of the United States*

The American model of industrialization originated from Europe, and there was no difference in their ideals and core values. There were however notable differences in the context in which they were situated and in the implemen-

---

9. A promise that on average was not fulfilled, as shown in Pollard, "Capital Exports 1870–1914: Harmful or Beneficial?". But what interested investors were the expected rates, rather than those actually obtained, which were out of their control.
10. Kennedy, *The Rise and Fall of the Great Powers*.
11. Comfort, *The Slow Death of British Industry*.

tation of those ideals; which we will explore in this section.[12] First, we should recall a few basic chronological facts. Although the colonization of the United States had already begun in the first half of the seventeenth century, the European population of the area as a British colony proceeded quite slowly. A century later the population had not reached beyond 250,000 people, and on the eve of the Revolution there were only two and a half million settlers.[13] With the 1776 Declaration of Independence the United States broke its ties with Britain, and after victory in the Revolutionary War in 1789 it established a federal government that regulated the relationships between the states in a (mostly) non-conflictual manner. The only episode of open conflict was the Civil War (1861–5) that set the Northern states against the Southern states; the victory by the North brought about the abolition of slavery.[14]

The United States did not begin its industrial development particularly rapidly. When it established itself as an independent nation at the end of the eighteenth century, 80–90 per cent of its labour force was in agriculture. With abundant land available and good labour productivity, per capita incomes were high. The first industries, already founded in that era, continued to expand during the first half of the nineteenth century. There was a strong tendency towards mechanization, due both to the scarcity and the high cost of manual labour, thus wages were high. After the middle of the century and the end of the Civil War, it was the railways that marked the country's real take-off, unifying its already large market. Growth continued at a rapid rate and without significant interruptions until the great crisis of 1929 (see Tables 5.1–5.5), a period characterized by the growth of the large corporation in the capital intensive sectors of the second industrial revolution.

Why was the large corporation the United States' winning card, and why was it so successful in the United States instead of in Europe, which had inspired American development? The first point to consider is the resource to population ratio. What became the territory of the United States, over a long process of colonization, was an immense area that was very sparsely populated by indigenous peoples in early stages of development. As is known, the European colonizers found no difficulty in marginalizing the local popula-

12. See Hughes & Cain, *American Economic History*, and Engerman & Gallman, *Cambridge Economic History of the United States*.
13. The subsequent progression records 5 million in 1800, 13 million in 1830, 31 million in 1860, and 76 million in 1900.
14. On the economic aspects of slavery, see Fogel & Engerman, *Time on the Cross: The Economics of the American Negro Slavery*. The authors argue that slavery was economically efficient in the short run, but in the long run it would have hindered the diversification of the economy away from agriculture.

tions and in appropriating the immense territory replete with vast valuable resources, particularly arable land, gold, and oil. This abundance of resources left an indelible mark on the mindset of Americans, who always found themselves addressing the problem of managing the process of extracting resources as efficiently as possible, rather than the problem of how to extract a few scarce resources from those who held them by historical legacy and who might not use them efficiently, as in Europe. Scarcity is a typical European phenomenon, one which immediately evokes conflict over distribution. Wars, revolutions, and social conflicts were endemic in European culture; these long marked its destiny, even in the industrial age in which the ability to increase resources without necessarily taking them from someone else – a characteristic of the industrial process – should have recommended a change in attitude. In the United States, however, distributional conflicts were secondary and marginalized because resources were abundant, and thus a constructive attitude prevailed of how to best organize the use of resources.

The second significant element to the success of the corporation follows from the country being a population of emigrants. During the long nineteenth century – until 1914 – over 30 million Europeans emigrated to the United States. An emigrant is by definition mobile and considers it normal to seek work where it is, rather than remaining where one is born, or wherever one finds oneself, to die of hunger. Consequently the United States as a country is made up of people who are not content with what they have (or do not have), but who seek to improve their conditions with an attitude open to mobility and risk in order to build their futures with their own hands (the typical "self-made man"). Furthermore, early on emigrants to the United States came not from one country, but many, with different cultural backgrounds, yet they were ready to find common ground to live together, although with some inevitable friction. They developed "American" values that became shared by all, in a "melting pot" that nullified the risk that different ethnic groups would form as they had in Europe, which were sources of irremediable divisions and conflicts. The declaration of the federal state itself should be seen in this light, even though, as noted previously, it was precipitated by the necessity of facing up to the power of Britain. In reality, there were no fundamental reasons, either economic or cultural, for conflict between the states, and it was relatively easy to decide to coordinate among themselves while maintaining a strong decentralization of powers. That decision subsequently revealed itself to be strategic for establishing a single market of unprecedented size, with the dollar as its single currency, English as its single language, and a single foreign policy.

There is a third point, without which the first two would not have been able to be as effective. The territory was not only devoid of people and culture, but, naturally, of laws as well. To introduce a new law it was not necessary to fight against the interests of those who backed existing laws. Gradually as economic and social developments required, new laws were introduced by consensus in a political environment that organized itself democratically from the outset. These laws had a much greater consistency with regard to the requirements of productivity and efficiency than could be reached in Europe, where numerous compromises with preceding regimes and vested interests were necessary. Even urban planning in the new American cities was more suited to the new industrial era, more so than the medieval urban planning of European cities. The American "can do" mindset, contrasted with a European one that often oscillated between the two extremes of resignation in power-lessness and, conversely, violent revolt.

Now we can more readily see why the large corporation was so successful in the United States. In such a country there were no markets already in operation, as there were in Europe, nor were there professional craftsmen. Most of the emigrants arrived without much education, and so the best way to efficiently extract resources to increase production in order to serve an expanding market was to create enterprises that controlled the production process from top to bottom, through automated, mechanized integration, upstream and downstream, to discipline the work force as needed. The birth of the railways added impetus. The exceptional length of the rail network (see Table 5.4) forced a high degree of coordination, achieved through a mana-gerial structure that combined a line, with operational responsibility, and a staff, with responsibility for planning and overall operation. A capillary-like information system based on reports permitted a detailed analysis of costs.

Telegraph and telephone (Western Union and AT&T) followed, and then steel, in which Andrew Carnegie (who had been a supervisor in the railways) began constructing increasingly colossal factories.[15] After steel came oil, in which David Rockefeller built the largest refineries in the world with Standard Oil, his company, threatening to become a monopoly. Electricity followed with General Electric and Westinghouse, and then the adventure of the automobile began with Henry Ford.[16] In 1913 he was the first to introduce

---

15. In Pittsburgh, in just three factories in 1894, Carnegie produced 1.7 million tonnes of steel, more than had been produced throughout the United States six years earlier.

16. Henry Ford was an engineer, the son of a family of farmers of Irish descent. He became fascinated with building cars, and he founded his company in 1903 with a model that cost $850. With the innovations he introduced that model eventually came to cost between $345 and $360, less than the annual salary of one of his assembly line workers.

a complete assembly line, lowering the production time of his famous black Model T from twelve hours and eight minutes to one hour and thirty-five minutes, which more than halved the cost. Thus it was, as Chandler said, that Henry Ford succeeded in squaring the circle by building the cheapest automobile in the world while paying the highest wages in the world (and becoming one of the wealthiest men in the world). The chemical industry was the only sector unable to immediately rival Germany, even though by 1890 two large corporations had emerged, Dow Chemical and DuPont. With the petrochemical industry during the 1920s the United States finally leaped ahead in this sector as well. In the commercial sector large companies were also established, such as Woolworth; in 1879 it introduced single-price stores in which merchandise for sale was pre-weighed, pre-packaged and sold with standard prices that could easily be added up.

This is how the country emerged with large corporations at the heart of the system. According to Sklar's monumental work, the centrality of the large corporation was preferable to that of the state, in that the corporation was a more direct expression of the "people" (in the United States sovereignty rests with the people).[17] The company has thus tended to take on social responsibilities; this is why its managerial structure was created to ensure stability and continuity. Companies were also quick to call for anti-trust legislation to protect themselves from the perverse consequences of excessively large companies.[18] From this viewpoint we can understand why large companies did not welcome the emergence of other strong, powerful organizations. Banks were thus kept small by restrictive legislation that prevented them from becoming large enough to counterbalance the corporations.[19] During the Civil War a Banking Act was passed that required the national banks to have a single location without any branches, while banks within each state were allowed to have several branches (although this practice was rarely implemented). Furthermore, although American banks were "universal" banks, they could not commit more than 10 per cent of their credit to any single customer. For this reason American banks multiplied, finally reaching a total of nearly 30,000 at the advent of the First World War; they remained weak and marginal, partly because there was no central bank to oversee them until 1913. Instead the stock market was strengthened, in direct service to the companies. The

---

17. Sklar, *The Corporate Reconstruction of American Capitalism, 1890–1916*.
18. The Sherman Act of 1890 was the first of many legislative interventions designed to avoid cartels and large monopolies.
19. In this regard see the interesting work, Roe, *Strong Managers Weak Owners*. On the costs of rejecting the mixed bank, see Calomiris, "The Costs of Rejecting Universal Banking".

powers of the states, and particularly those of the federal government, were constrained as tightly as possible. As has been noted, even the establishment of a central bank – the Federal Reserve – was delayed until 1913. Beyond just anti-trust legislation, protectionism was also demanded from the state in order to take advantage of the national market without worrying about foreign competition.

By the end of the nineteenth century US per capita income had already exceeded that of Britain, while in absolute terms the US economy had become the largest and most powerful in the world. Nonetheless, Europeans had not yet felt intense competition because the United States' foreign trade was modest (as were its foreign investments, since it was more interested in its internal market), nor had they felt the United States' influence in European affairs. It remained turned inward and had not yet thought about global power relations or about replacing British global leadership.[20] Moreover, Germany's competitive capacity was growing, and in many markets it went head-to-head with the United States, when it was not ahead of them. Not even the First World War succeeded in altering this picture, although it gave the United States an awareness of the responsibilities coupled with its power, and it broke the virtuous cycle of growth in Germany. Only the Second World War was to mark a sharp discontinuity in the isolationist attitude of the United States.

6.3 Japan's take-off

Over the course of its long history Japan had been strongly influenced by China, with a sophisticated and complex civilization based on the Confucian culture of loyalty, probity, decorum and harmony, as well as an intense nationalism that had developed to distinguish itself from China. This nation-alism entailed an ethic of a disciplined and productive life, which constituted the cultural background on which subsequent transformations would be grafted. Unlike China, Japan had an emperor who, in Western terms, had already become "constitutional" since the eighth century in that he retained a symbolic role of unifying the nation but did not directly exercise power, which was in the hands of the head of the military aristocracy (the *shogun*). Power tended therefore to be fragmented at the local level, giving rise to a

---

20. In 1823 President Monroe issued the Monroe Doctrine stating that the United States would not interfere in European affairs, in exchange for similar behaviour on the part of Europe regarding the US.

polycentric system similar to the European feudal system (the local governors were called *daimyo*). Pre-industrial Japan had large cities, functioning markets and a fairly well developed credit system.[21] The spread of education among the higher restricted classes (the *samurai*) was excellent, although they could not dedicate themselves to business, which was left in the hands of the people. In any case Japan was closed to Western influence (as was China), prohibiting its citizens to travel outside the country and limiting trade to one Dutch ship per year, which was permitted to dock on a small island in the port of Nagasaki; this was the policy of *sakoku*, or "closed country" and this is why Japan had not been able to keep pace with European and American industrial developments.[22]

Following the Western penetration of China, the American admiral Matthew Perry arrived in the port of Tokyo with his ships in 1853–54, which was a useful docking point for ships travelling from California to Asia. Threatening to bombard the capital if Japan's foreign policy did not change, the emperor ceded and Perry was able to impose "unequal treaties", requiring not only that Japan open itself, but also that it could not impose tariffs greater than 5 per cent. The country initially followed the path of xenophobic revolts, but Mitsuhito, a young and intelligent emperor, ascended the throne and altered Japan's destiny by initiating a series of institutional reforms in 1868 – a movement known as the Meiji Restoration, from the name that Mitsuhito wanted to give to his government ("Meiji" means "enlightened government"). The caste system was abolished. Samurai were no longer salaried, and so they were forced to engage in careers in business. The state bureaucracy was modernized, and the education system was made more efficient and general. Trained young people were sent to the West to study Western institutions and advise the government on what action to take, with reforms modelled after Western inspiration.[23] The feudal system was abolished and the government set up a centralized adminis-

---

21. In the middle of the nineteenth century, Edo (Tokyo) had a population of over 1 million people, Osaka numbered 300,000 inhabitants, and Kyoto 200,000; see MacPherson, *The Economic Development of Japan 1868–1941*.

22. See Morishima, *Why Has Japan Succeeded?* and Minami, *The Economic Development of Japan*.

23. By 1871, 280 people had been sent at state expense to study in Europe and the United States, and upon their return they were placed in key government posts. In a long tour between 1871 and 1873, Prime Minister Okubo himself visited factories, railways and shipyards in Europe and the United States, carrying back to his homeland not only models for armaments, but production chains for civil consumption. The transformation he imprinted on the country was so rapid and all-encompassing that he was assassinated in 1878 by a samurai conspiracy, but that did not succeed in reversing the reform process that had already begun.

tration following the French model. The army was organized on the Prussian model, the navy was modelled after the British, and industry and finance predominately followed the American and German models. Education was also reformed along the lines of the continental European model. In 1882 the central bank was formed and the entire banking system reformed. The constitution was promulgated in 1889.

With a new industrial base, it became possible for Japan to set in motion its industrial ventures. The initial attempt by the Meiji government to create public companies quickly failed. The companies were sold, and from then on the Japanese government did not further attempt to manage companies directly, limiting itself to a promotional and coordinating role. It was not easy for Japan to find a way to take off because it was a small, mountainous country with very few subsoil resources (a little coal and copper), so to produce it had to import, which in turn had to be paid by exports. But what should it export? Fortunately a traditional industry came to the rescue, which provided it with a staple for its early exports: raw silk. Japan strengthened and modernized its production cycle and became a major exporter of raw silk, supplanting even Italy in international markets at the beginning of the twentieth century. Indeed, raw silk comprised between a third and a fifth of all Japanese exports before 1940. Tea was initially an important export as well, but it subsequently declined even more rapidly than silk. Desperately seeking resources, Japan quickly became a colonial power, initially with a war with China in 1894–5, from which it gained Taiwan (renamed Formosa), then with Russia in 1905, acquiring various areas of influence; one of them, Korea, was particularly important.[24]

The textile and heavy industries subsequently took off, although slowly and on a small scale, because the unequal treaties were not abrogated until the end of the nineteenth century, when Japan was able to offer a little more protection to its entrepreneurs. By 1913 11,000 kilometres of railway had been constructed, which was no small amount for a country smaller than California, and electricity expanded. Between 1870 and 1913 per capita income grew at rates comparable to those in Europe (see Tables 5.1–5.5), but by 1913 the per capita income level with respect to Britain remained quite low at 28 per cent, on a par with Russia. The fact is that the relative worsening during the first three quarters of the nineteenth century, given Japan's "closure", had been considerable; the results of the first half-century after opening were good, but not particularly outstanding, and they were not such as to allow it to well and truly catch up. In any event, it was during this early period of Japanese devel-

24. Korea was annexed in 1910.

opment that clusters of companies emerged that act synergistically, which remains a characteristic of the country today. These were called *zaibatsu*, and they were linked primarily by family ties.[25] At the centre of the group was the bank, which breathed financial life into the companies, even in their times of crisis, despite the central bank's propensity to bail them out. The most famous *zaibatsu* were controlled by families with commercial backgrounds and are well-known names even today: Mitsubishi, Sumitomo, Mitsui.

Japan seized the occasions of the First World War and the 1929 crisis (which had limited impact on the country) to allow it to more successfully implement the process of catching up with Europe and the United States. Although its progress was violently interrupted by the Second World War, Japan was able to successfully resume its catch up in the 1950s, to the point of bringing Japan into the ranks of great powers alongside the United States and Europe (see Chapter 16).

No other large Asian country followed in the steps of Japan until after the Second World War. The others, unable to modernize their institutions, took a different path of stagnation and poverty; this was sometimes due to Western domination, at other times – as in China – because they retained the classic imperial model. In Chapter 16 we will have more to say about that and the spectacular take-off of some Asian countries in recent times.[26]

---

25. After the Second World War the Americans dismantled the *zaibatsu*, considering them responsible for Japan's war-mongering policy. However, analogous groups called *keiretsu* were quickly reconstituted; these were no longer held together by familial bonds, but by managerial ties (see Chapter 16). For a comparison between the Japanese and German economies, see Dore, *Stock Market Capitalism*.

26. For an overview of the rest of the world, see Baten, *A History of the Global Economy 1500 to the Present*.

7

Technology, business and socio-economic change

7.1 *The three industrial revolutions*

As the economist Joseph Schumpeter had occasion to remark at the turn of the twentieth century, and which others have reiterated, inventions that are produced gradually tend to cluster around a few core technologies.[1] Fully developing the implications of those technologies generates a powerful development cycle that ultimately saturates the market when all who have sufficient purchasing power are equipped with those technologies, and the process begins afresh with another "swarm" of innovations around different core technologies. The international economic system thus operates in long-term cycles, from a half-century to a century and a half, that are characterized by different technological paradigms.[2]

This is why we talk about not just one industrial revolution, but several. As we saw in Chapter 3, the *first* industrial revolution, which began in the eighteenth century and lasted well past the middle of the nineteenth century, was characterized by the use of the steam boiler from steel-making to railways, as well as increasingly mechanized systems for producing goods, which allowed process innovations. Making use of underground coal stocks made an energy available that was not only much greater, but also qualitatively different, than the past. Inorganic chemistry made available powerful bleaching agents (soda and chlorine), although these were not particularly innovative.

---

1. Schumpeter, *The Theory of Economic Development*. We are also indebted to Schumpeter for the important distinction between invention (the first appearance of an idea), innovation (the first industrial application of the invention) and diffusion. Much time can pass between these three stages, particularly in the early phases of an industrial revolution.
2. See Perez, *Technological Revolutions and Financial Capital*. On the development of capitalism over the very long term see Neal & Williamson, *Cambridge History of Capitalism*.

Based on simple science that was largely already known, this industrial revolution did not require high levels of general education; individuals could invent and innovate by themselves in laboratories that were not particularly well equipped. Goods were no longer processed in the home, as in the pre-industrial era, but in factories where a division of labour, the use of specialized machinery and increasingly powerful steam boilers were possible; this favoured the centralization of people, and it was a potent factor in urbanization.

Another long-term effect was that women were displaced from the work force. Indeed, as long as work remained on the farm or in home workshops, women were always involved. When the distant factory emerged with long, fixed working hours, most married women were confined to the home, which was further reinforced by a demographic transition (see §7.3) that made for large families. This is how the nineteenth century myth emerged of the woman as the "angel of the house" and the man as the "breadwinner", which deepened the cultural and economic divide between men and women; in the twentieth century this resulted in the movement for women's liberation, which is still going on today. Despite all that, companies remained small, scattered and poorly integrated vertically; they were generally run by the owner and did not need much capital. The railways were an exception; for good reason, in many countries they ended up being widely supported by public finance when they were not directly owned and managed by the state.

The *second* industrial revolution began in the second half of the nineteenth century when transportation costs rapidly declined with the expansion of the railways and steam navigation. Information began to travel as never before, initially with the telegraph, then the telephone and radio. It then became possible to develop a technology based on large factories with economies of scale: the larger they were the more they saved on fixed costs. The core technologies of the second industrial revolution were electricity (and its low power version for telephones), the internal combustion engine[3] (which used gasoline, a derivative of oil instead of coal) and was particularly used for automobiles and airplanes, organic chemistry and radio. From a scientific viewpoint, all these innovations were more complex than those of the first industrial revolution; they required higher levels of culture and education not only to create them, but to implement them as well. A systematic dissemination of medium-level technical education, as well as widespread higher education (beginning the era

---

3. The internal combustion engine was invented by Christian Huygens in 1824, but it was not until 1876 that Nicolaus August Otto succeeded in building a four-cycle engine; Gottlieb Daimler and Karl Benz were the first to make it run on gasoline in 1888.

of degreed engineers), were required to be able to utilize this new technology. Universities and companies prepared research laboratories to continuously perfect products and processes.[4]

The most important consequence of the second industrial revolution was the need for high amounts of capital for companies that, from the outset, were much larger than those of the first industrial revolution, due to greater product standardization. On the one hand this created a need to find financing channels – the large mixed banks and the stock exchange – that were more robust than private finance, and on the other it drove companies to increasingly grow in size to both achieve a certain level of control over the market and to increasingly take advantage of economies of scale. This is how the large corporation came to exist in environments favourable to these developments, particularly in the United States and Germany. This event was so significant and loaded with implications that it merits a more thorough discussion in §7.2. The large companies gave a further incentive to concentrate people into great conurbations, and their existence fostered the formation of powerful unions in various sectors.[5] Trade unions had already begun to grow in the first half of the nineteenth century, organized more by individual trade than by business sector. This union organization remained typical in Britain and France even when things changed with the second industrial revolution, but not so in the United States and Germany.

The second industrial revolution was followed by the third industrial revolution, which began around the middle of the twentieth century, and is still ongoing. Based primarily on alternative energy sources to coal, oil and gas – nuclear foremost, followed by solar, biomass, wind and water (which had been used previously, but is now used to produce electricity)[6] – at its centre are artificial materials (such as plastics and synthetic textile fibres), biochemistry (antibiotics, genetic engineering) and electronics. The relationship between new science and technology has become very close, and the education levels

---

4. A vast literature exists on the topic of human capital and its increasing significance for development. Among the most recent summaries, see Prados de la Escosura, "Capitalism and Human Welfare".

5. For an overview of changes in work organization and industrial relations, see Huberman, "Labor Movements".

6. While the total amount of energy necessary for the world's economic activity has increased incredibly, with increases in population and income, the energy density of GDP (the quantity of energy needed to produce a unit of GDP) today tends to decline, due to greater efficiencies in production processes and the industrial maturity of many countries. With the exception of transportation, many services now use little energy; see Stein & Powers, *The Energy Problem* and Bhattacharyya, *Energy Economics*.

necessary to produce innovations are very high, well beyond university level, with invention increasingly the result of work by research teams in highly specialized laboratories. Electronics, without doubt the most distinctive element of this third industrial revolution, has led to substantial changes in the ways we live and work. In particular, the tendency for a population to concentrate around enormous industrial complexes as in the second industrial revolution has stopped; production can now be fragmented in decentralized factories connected together and coordinated by computer, and even in small craft workshops. Assembly lines are more automated with robots programmed to produce a wide variety of customized products. Telecommuting is being introduced for white collar work, making it possible to work from home, or remotely, by computer.

Yet another new aspect of this third revolution – perhaps less appropriately called "industrial" than the others – is the large increase of employment in services, so much so that many already speak of a post-industrial era. With a fragmented work force the large factory unions characteristic of the second industrial revolution are in crisis, as is the employer-employee relationship. Self-employment that was once common in the pre-industrial era is now again on the rise. The large infrastructure projects typical of the first revolution (consider the railways) or the second (consider the vast electric and telephone wiring networks, interstate highways and airports) have no equivalent in the third revolution, which uses increasingly small factories, leading to far less use of raw materials, energy and manual labour.

Finally, the computer and telecommunications revolutions have caused the international economy to leap forward, increasingly becoming a global economy, an economy in which companies no longer operate within national boundaries. When companies organize their production and plan their sales they think on a global scale, with implications for relocating production according to convenience; this sets in motion a production process spread across different nations, with a consequent growing trade in intermediate products. We no longer wonder where a product is made, especially something as complex as a car, because multiple factories and workers in diverse countries contribute to the final product. This has resulted in a number of developing countries, which were previously isolated, being brought into the global economy with workers in advanced countries without sufficient specialized skills losing work to developing countries with much lower labour costs (see Chapter 16). But many implications of this third revolution still escape us.

Having said all this, it is clear that the various technological paradigms not only produce new products and production processes, but also far-reaching social repercussions on how people live, work and organize themselves. In particular there have been unforeseeable impacts on life expectancy and the family, as well as on how companies and consumption are organized, topics that we will consider in the next sections.[7]

7.2 Companies: corporations, cooperatives and clusters

As we have seen, in the first industrial revolution productive activity took place in the factory rather than in workshops attached to homes.[8] Initially the company was generally not large, and it was managed by the capital owner, whose employees worked long hours in an unhealthy environment, with wages capped at subsistence levels. These conditions provoked protests, which resulted in the creation of labour unions and populist political parties, as well as the institution of companies that were not linked to capital ownership, but to an association of persons who practised equality. This was known as the "cooperative", which especially spread in Europe in the mid-nineteenth century, and also in the United States, Japan and elsewhere.[9] In a cooperative the *association* is what counts, rather than capital. An egalitarian governance results from the formula "one head, one vote", profits are distributed equally, and labour and capital are paid at market rates. A number of models for cooperative companies have emerged; the best-known among them are the *consumer cooperative*, of English origin; the *credit cooperative*, of German origin, in which the members are savers and investors; the *labour cooperative*, of French origin, in which the members are the workers themselves; the *agricultural cooperative*, of northern European origin, in which the members are the farmers; and the *social or community cooperative*, of Italian origin, with a mixed social base that includes workers and recipients of services. In 2015 there were nearly a billion members of cooperatives throughout the world, even in sectors of the economy, such as home insurance, public services (electricity, water, telephone), catering and transport.[10]

In §7.1 we saw that corporations were created during the second industrial revolution, and we will now look more closely at their characteristics.

---

7. A slightly different reading of the industrial revolutions, albeit one still in line with the above, is Freeman & Louça, *As Time Goes By*.
8. On the subject of business history, see Jones & Zeitlin, *Oxford Handbook of Business History*.
9. See Zamagni & Zamagni, *Cooperative Enterprise*.
10. Battilani & Schröter, *The Cooperative Business Movement, 1950 to the Present*.

Since the United States, for very specific reasons (see Chapter 6), was the first country to understand the potential of the large corporation and developed its organizational characteristics between 1860 and the First World War, it should come as no surprise that the most notable historian of large corporations was Alfred Chandler, of Harvard University.[11]

Chandler emphasized that the large corporation was created not only to take advantage of economies of scale, but also to benefit from product diversification based on the full use of the same raw materials and intermediate products in one single plant (economies of scope) – a characteristic of the chemical industry in particular – and economies of speed. To achieve the latter, it was necessary to move to a "scientific" organization of work to avoid wasting time during various work stages.[12] This workflow process was carefully studied by American engineers. The best known was Frederick Taylor – hence "Taylorism" – who held that the best solution was to build an assembly line, where all the work steps were done in optimal order. Work pieces were not carried by hand from one worker to another; rather, they were on a production line while workers stood in front of it to perform their specialized work, and the pace of the line was such that there was barely enough time for each step. The assembly line required a significant investment in systems programmed to produce one single model of product, which pushed towards standardization; in return it lowered dramatically the unit costs of production (as happened with Ford's black Model T).

In this way the corporation increased labour productivity by many times, and it lowered unit costs so much that, in the sectors in which products could be standardized, small companies were crowded out. The incentives of economies of scale and scope were such that the large corporation quickly showed a tendency to become increasingly larger, through both horizontal integration (by merging with similar businesses) and vertical integration (by acquiring upstream and downstream companies in its supply chain) to ensure that the flow of its production process was not hampered by imperfect markets.[13] If

---

11. Among the most important of his works are: *Strategy and Structure* and *The Visible Hand*, in addition to the previously cited *Scale and Scope*. See also Colli, *Dynamics of International Business*; Amatori & Colli, *Business History: Complexities and Comparisons*.

12. Chandler reminded us that the production process does not consist only of the two operations summarized by the expression "input-output"; one must also consider the extremely important intermediate "throughput" phase, which acknowledges that for input to arrive efficiently to the output, it must pass through its processing steps in the minimal time.

13. The large corporation lowering transaction costs as an alternative to the market was first theorized by Coase in "The Nature of the Firm" and revived by Williamson in *The Economic Institutions of Capitalism*.

the company produced its raw materials and intermediate products internally, it could be sure of always having a sufficient quantity of the proper quality; if the company then integrated with companies that used its products, or established a network of direct sales offices, it could be assured of having an effective presence in end markets.

With the large corporation becoming ever larger, direct control by the owner was impractical, just as the family finances were not enough to finance it (see the next section). A "scientific" organization emerged for running the company through a complex white-collar hierarchy of managers. The chief executive officer (CEO) is at the top; under that person is a team of senior managers divided by function (the head of the legal department, the head of human resources, the head of technical operations, the head of R&D, and so forth), and then a tier of operations managers, who supervise the various operational areas, or "divisions". Everyone must produce not only decisions, but also written memoranda of them, so that everything that happens can be continually monitored, studied and made more efficient in order to precisely identify operational costs. Over time behavioural routines are established that are codified, which can then be formally taught. As had happened much earlier for engineers, a corpus of ideas was developed for managerial careers that were taught at university level in "business schools".[14]

The ownership of these large corporations therefore became more diffuse; only in a few cases is there a single main shareholder, who might be the founder or a descendent. This then is how the separation between ownership and control came about. The manager in charge of a large enterprise may not own even a single share in the company; nominated by the board of directors – on which sit the representatives of the owners – the manager is usually free to make the business decisions she thinks best, as long as the company does well and profits its shareholders. When that does not happen, she may be fired and replaced. While this is generally true, there are important differences between the ownership structures of large corporations in different countries, depending on different forms of finance and/or on different managerial cultures. The managerialization of corporations makes them more stable and enduring over time, since they do not have to face crises of generational

---

14. The first to use that name was the Harvard Business School, created in 1908, but business and financial schools had been created much earlier, inspired by the European model of the *Scuole Superiori di Commercio* founded on accounting (the first example of which was in Antwerp in 1852); these were then slowly modified with typical American organizational contents. For an exhaustive analysis of these topics see Engwall & Zamagni, *Management Education in Historical Perspective*.

transitions, as in family companies, or run the risk of having incompetent managers just because they are the children of the founder. This is why the company that is created first – the "first mover", as Chandler called it – retains a competitive advantage that is difficult for new entrants to erode, unless the shareholders make an error appointing managers, or some technological innovation radically displaces the first mover from its position.

The economic system that forms in the presence of these large stand-alone corporations (those that do not coordinate with others) is a mix of markets (typically oligopolistic, with strategic moves best studied by game theory) and corporate planning. Their enormous size encourages these companies to disregard all limits, for the purpose of continuing their growth. National boundaries are crossed (becoming multinational); expansion beyond a single sector is accomplished through the formation of conglomerates[15] and the tendency towards monopoly quickly becomes clear. To avoid this outcome, which is held not to be acceptable for either consumers or democracy, the United States quickly enacted antitrust laws (the first was the Sherman Act of 1890, as noted in Chapter 6); Europe was much slower to adopt antitrust legislation, and indeed allowed cartels (because its companies were smaller), and frequently its natural monopolies[16] (as well as others) were placed under public control.[17] As noted above, not all sectors were equally involved in this transformation of the company, but it affected those in which products could be highly standardized (transport, metallurgy, mechanical appliances, oil) and/or those in which the economies of scope (chemicals, food) are high.[18] The case of textiles is interesting; in the United States there seem not to have been large companies, while a certain number appeared in Germany and Britain before 1913. Over time, however, textile companies tended to disappear from the ranks of large business, even in the two European countries.

But the large companies did not remain stand-alone everywhere. There are places where they coordinate in more or less cohesive groups.[19] The best-known example is that of the Japanese economy, with its *zaibatsu*, but networks of

---

15. Companies that engage in very different business activities, even those that differ from each other technologically.

16. A natural monopoly is defined as a situation in which, given the size of the market and/or technological characteristics, it is not efficient to have more than one company.

17. There were many more state controlled enterprises in Europe than those definable as natural monopolies; see Toninelli, *The Rise and Fall of State-Owned Enterprises in the Western World*. For an Italian history, see Zamagni, *Finmeccanica*. There is now an extensive history of the principal Italian state holding company: Castronovo *et al.*, *Storia dell'IRI*.

18. See Sabel & Zeitlin, *World of Possibilities* and Scranton, *Endless Novelty*.

19. See Chandler, Amatori & Hikino, *Big Business and the Wealth of Nations*.

companies exist in many other Asian, Latin American and European countries.[20] With the third industrial revolution, even small and medium-size companies have found ways of coordinating with other companies of the same size in industrial districts, or with large companies (in a cluster[21]), particularly in sectors in which quality and product customization count (fashion, ceramics, mechanical engineering, and niche products). Family management is diffuse in these types of companies.[22]

If we add to the aforementioned company forms (small business, corporation, and cooperative) the social companies, or the non-profits,[23] of which there are many in the world, we have a variety of companies adaptable to different market logics, ethical preferences and political choices.[24]

7.3 A longer life and a smaller family

Changes in the population are among the most striking features of the industrial revolutions, and they deserve mention.[25] As Table 7.1 shows, it is immediately apparent that the rapid growth of the world's population began only with the industrial revolution, which at once allowed more consistent annual rates of economic growth and an increase in life expectancy (or average lifetime), which previously had rather depressingly remained at around thirty years, due mainly to a very high infant mortality rate. Life expectancy had a particularly significant improvement at the global level only after 1950, whereas in more developed countries that improvement had already begun in the nineteenth century; this is further confirmation of the close connection between population and economic development, as can be seen in Table 7.2. We note in passing that the current economic development difficulties in Russia, to which we will return in Chapter 17, are well highlighted by Table 7.2, which shows a slowdown in that country and we do not see a particular advantage for the United States, despite its position as an economic leader.

---

20. Morikawa, *A History of Top Management in Japan*; Granovetter, "Coase Revisited".
21. Belussi & Sammarra, *Business Networks in Clusters and Industrial Districts*; Becattini, Bellandi & De Propis, *A Handbook of Industrial Districts*.
22. Colli, *The History of Family Business 1850–2000*.
23. See Borzaga & Becchetti, *The Economics of Social Responsibility* and Borzaga & Defourny, *The Emergence of Social Enterprises*.
24. See Scranton & Fridenson, *Reimagining Business History*.
25. For further details, see Bacci, *A Concise History of World Population*.

Table 7.1   Long-term world population trends.

	10,000 BCE	0	1750	1950	2000	2014
Population (millions)	6	252	771	2530	6235	7200
Annual % increase	0.008	0.04	0.06	0.6	1.8	0.8
Life expectancy (years)	20	22	27	35	58	69

Source: adapted from Bacci, *A Concise History*; OCSE data for 2014.

This remarkable improvement in life expectancy came about with a lowering of the mortality rate, which fell from annual levels of 3–4 per cent to less than 1 per cent.[26] The birth rate also fell from 3–4.5 per cent to less than 2 per cent; it is precisely this dramatic change in demographics that is called the "demographic transition".[27] In fact, it has been historically shown that the birth rate adapted to the mortality rate only after a delay, which generated large population increases for a brief time. This delay is of particular concern, as it has resulted in highly populated countries such as China and India, in which there have been public campaigns, often to accelerate lowering the fertility rate with ethically dubious implications. In any case, there is no evidence of people having long persisted with a high birth rate once well-being and a falling mortality rate have become widespread. For a graphic representation of the demographic transition, see Figure 7.1.

Let us turn to the fundamental question: why did the industrial revolution and economic development generate such a demographic trend? What were the causes of lower mortality? Three factors have been considered relevant: improvements in medical science, better nutrition and better hygiene. While it is obviously true that all three factors were relevant, it is by now generally agreed that nutrition and hygiene (particularly sewers and proper waste disposal) impacted primarily early on, when the problem was surpassing precarious subsistence levels.[28] Paradoxically, today excessive nutrition is a source of serious illness and even death.[29] Regarding medical science, initially

---

26. Mortality rate is typically expressed in units of deaths per 1,000 individuals per year; so, a mortality rate of 10 (out of 1,000) in a population of 1,000 would mean 10 deaths per year in that entire population, or 1 per cent.
27. The birth rate is the total number of live births per 1,000 of a population in a year.
28. Bacci, *Population and Nutrition*.
29. This paradox of wealth is certainly one of the reasons for the unsatisfactory life expectancy in the United States today.

Table 7.2 Life expectancy trends in advanced countries.

Country	1750–59	1800–09	1850–59	1880	1900	1930	1959	1994	2012
Britain/UK	36.9	37.3	40.0	43.3	48.2	60.8	69.2	76.8	80
France	27.9	33.9	39.8	42.1	47.4	56.7	66.5	77.8	81
Germany				37.9	44.4	61.3	66.6	76.2	80
Italy				35.4	42.8	54.9	65.5	77.9	82
Russia				27.7	32.4	42.9	64.0	64.4	66
United States			40.0	46.5	48.0	59.0	69.4	75.5	78
Japan				35.1	37.7	45.9	59.1	79.4	84

Source: adapted from Bacci, A Concise History; OCSE data for 2014.

Figure 7.1 The demographic transition.

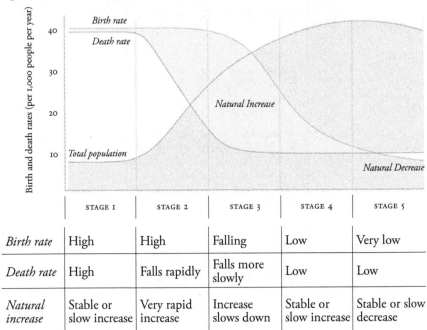

	STAGE 1	STAGE 2	STAGE 3	STAGE 4	STAGE 5
Birth rate	High	High	Falling	Low	Very low
Death rate	High	Falls rapidly	Falls more slowly	Low	Low
Natural increase	Stable or slow increase	Very rapid increase	Increase slows down	Stable or slow increase	Stable or slow decrease

Source: Max Roser; www.OurWorldInData.org/data/population-growth-vital-statistics/world-population-growth

drugs that decreased the incidence of epidemics, such as vaccines, antibiotics (and disinfectants), were what significantly raised life expectancy. Indeed, it has been shown that the largest hecatombs in pre-industrial times were caused by epidemics such as plague, cholera, typhus and smallpox, as well as gastrointestinal and venereal diseases, various poxes and tuberculosis. We can see confirmation of this in many of today's underdeveloped countries which, although poor and often undernourished have the benefit of advanced drugs and have a life expectancy far higher than that of today's developed countries prior to the industrial revolution, despite having comparable poverty levels (or even lower, since today's wealthy countries enjoyed an agricultural civilization frequently more advanced than that of today's poor countries).

A few other important observations on the effects of the demographic transition are worth noting. The longer average lifespan allowed a reduction in the energies required to raise children, increasing people's ability to directly engage in productive activities and allowing longer time for educational study, which raised the technological abilities of a vast part of the population and made it possible for people to plan for the longer term. Population growth has brought the benefits of specialization and economies of scale. Conversely, we must mention the negative effects of the concentration of a large and growing population in unpleasant and polluted cities (particularly in developing countries), unemployment (although this is more tied to the effects of poor economic policies rather than excessive population) and the explosion of welfare costs. Most of these negative effects can be relieved by improved technologies, in addition to the containment of global population growth as developing countries also lower their birth rates. Indeed, world population is expected to taper off by 2050 at a level of little less than 10 billion people.

In recent years, we have reached a point where birth rates are declining in developed countries so much that population is shrinking: fertility rates have fallen below the so-called "replacement" level of two children per couple.[30] In these countries the traditional population age "pyramid" has turned into a "whirligig" with a narrow base, which not only greatly increases the impact of seniors on the total population, with major changes in society and consumption, but also causes serious sustainability problems for welfare systems that are financed by the taxes paid by younger workers, who are now declining in proportion to the older population. Families are becoming increasingly smaller, not only because the tradition of large families has been lost even where it had been strongly rooted in favour of mono-nuclear families, but because there are fewer children; divorce, and alternative concepts of marriage (heterosexual and homosexual) have further challenged the traditional stable family, with more and more dwellings inhabited by single people.[31]

7.4 *Migration*

There has always been migration for reasons such as natural disasters, searching for food, colonization and military conquests; it is certainly true that the sedentary life typical of agrarian civilizations never wholly eliminated it, so we can accept Fisher's statement that "we are all descendants of migrants".[32] However, with the transportation and communications revolutions during the nineteenth century people's mobility took on a dimension that quantitatively cannot be compared to any prior time. Recent research regarding Europe,

---

30. In 2015 Italy had one of the lowest birth rates in the world at 1.3 children per couple.
31. See Hartmann & Unger, *A World of Populations.*
32. Fisher, *Migration: A World History*, xii. See also Bacci, *A Short History of Migrations.*

using an overall indicator of population movements that included emigration, immigration, and internal migrations between rural and urban areas, suggests that since at least the sixteenth century around 10 per cent of the population was mobile. However, over the course of the nineteenth century, European mobility exceeded 20 per cent in the second half of the century, reaching nearly 60 per cent in the first half of the twentieth century, and just under 50 per cent in the second half of the twentieth century.[33] Only during the latter period has Europe seen significant immigration of non-European peoples.[34]

Looking solely at emigration from Europe between 1850 and 1920, we can see from Table 7.3 that from just over two million emigrants during the 1850s, there were 10.5 million emigrants during the first decade of the twentieth century, with a later dip only because of the First World War. Note the absence of France, which had insignificant emigration (due to its low birth rate) and which soon became an immigration destination, as did Belgium and Switzerland. The drop in emigration from Germany after the 1880s stands out clearly, when the country began to industrialize rapidly. Whereas, emigration from Spain, Russia and especially Italy grew decade after decade opening up a split in those countries between areas that developed and those that lagged behind from which population started emigrating.[35] Emigration from Ireland (which is combined with Britain in the table) always remained high, which bore witness on the one hand to the failure to solve the island's economic problems, and on the other hand to the great ease of emigration due to the language and the countless relations between those who were still in the country and the many who had already emigrated. These destinations were partly European countries that had already advanced, but in large measure they were to North and South America, particularly to the United States, and to Australia as well. According to extensive studies by Jeff Williamson, the effects of this emigration were a convergence in wages and income between emigrant and immigrant countries, as well as the abandonment of certain backward areas in Europe by a part of the more entrepreneurial people, with their consequent further decline.[36]

From a qualitative point of view, it should be reiterated that until after the

---

33. Lucassen & Lucassen, "Quantifying and Qualifying Cross-Cultural Migrations in Europe Since 1500".

34. Manning, *Migrations in World History*.

35. For an accurate analysis of the reasons for emigration, see Hatton & Williamson, "What Drove the Mass Migrations from Europe in the Late-Nineteenth Century?" and O'Rourke & Williamson, "Around the European Periphery 1870–1913".

36. Taylor & Williamson, "Convergence in the Age of Mass Migration". See also Hatton & Williamson, *Migration and International Labor Market, 1850–1939*.

Table 7.3 Emigration from Europe for the decades 1851–1920 (thousands).

Region	1851–60	1861–70	1871–80	1881–90	1891–1900	1901–11	1911–20
Hapsburg Empire	31	40	46	248	440	1,111	418
France	27	36	66	119	51	53	32
Germany	671	779	626	1,342	527	274	91
Italy	5	27	168	992	1,580	3,615	2,194
Portugal	45	79	131	185	266	324	402
Russia	–	–	58	288	481	911	420
Spain	3	7	13	572	791	1,091	1,306
Britain	1,313	1,572	1,849	3,259	2,149	3,150	2,587

Source: Mitchell, *International Historical Statistics: Europe 1750–1988.*

Second World War global emigration was comprised of Europeans (with the exception of the forced emigration of African slaves between the sixteenth and nineteenth centuries, and a modest influx into Europe from the colonies). This is because emigrating requires having information and knowledge about one's destination available and some accumulated savings to face the long journey, but above all it requires a culture that encourages individual or family initiative and aspires to improve one's life conditions, a culture that developed only in Europe. An important implication of the emigrants' relative cultural homogeneity was that their "integration" into their destinations, whether other European countries or colonies created and governed by Europeans, was generally smooth, although not without transitory conflicts.

7.5 The revolution in consumption

The category of "consumption" as we know it today did not exist throughout history. In fact, people simply tried to survive, mostly on goods they produced themselves. Only the few cities had a market for products, but even there citizens' purchasing power was so low that the variety of products offered for sale was minimal, and most of it was oriented towards perishable food products. The thin stratum of well-off people and governors paid servants, slaves, and artisans – for whom the wealthy were their "customers" – for goods for the most part made to order, rather than products that were for sale in the market. Even for this well-off section of the populace, the diversification of products was quite limited, and there were few exceptions to this scenario. With the rise of the bourgeoisie in the Middle Ages – the inhabitants of cities, who had become wealthy through trade formed a "middle class" – and a ready market emerged for durable goods – furniture, ceramics, tapestries, sheets and tablecloths, various furnishings, clothing, jewellery, watches, drugs, arms, and carriages – products built by merchants and artisans who worked for the market and were no longer dependent on a patron.[37] It was with the rise of the bourgeoisie that the phenomenon of manufacturing first originated. Real industry emerged when technological improvements succeeded in lowering production costs and making durable goods available not only to the middle class, but also to the working class, particularly with the second industrial revolution (consider the case of Ford, as previously discussed).[38]

---

37. This phenomenon is well described by Goldthwaite, *The Building of Renaissance Florence*.
38. On the topic of standards of living, see the many chapters dedicated to this in Broadberry & O'Rourke, *Cambridge Economic History of Modern Europe*.

Another phenomenon, which has been termed the "industrious revolution", occurred over the course of the eighteenth and nineteenth centuries and sustained and influenced the "consumption revolution".[39] We have mentioned the separation of tasks between the man who worked outside the home and the woman who remained at home, created by the industrial revolution. Not only did the woman in the home have the traditional task of bearing and raising children, but also the additional task of determining what and how the family consumed; she adapted what was produced by industry for the needs of the family, reworking purchased products for domestic work capable of effectively raising the quality and length of life. Entrusting this responsibility to the woman began among the middle classes, and only after the mid-nineteenth century did it spread among the working classes. And so it was that, alongside the male/female dualism resulting from specialization in production, another dualism arose: the woman was entrusted with the task of organizing family consumption, while the man participated only in the major decisions (where to live, and later the means of transportation).

As Jan De Vries wrote:

> During industrialization, the household became more rather than less important as a productive unit because the market economy was rarely able to produce and distribute more than the "raw materials" for a higher standard of living, or, more exactly, for the standard of living to which people aspired. Increased gross national product did not translate into better health and nutrition or greater domestic comfort, unless households converted the purchased raw materials into finished products.[40]

It was only in the second half of the twentieth century in more developed countries that specified roles within the family and the dominant role of women in promoting consumption were abandoned. This led to the triumph of consumerism *tout court*, or the acquisition of all ready-made products, with only a minimal contribution by the family to their production – a contribution no longer primarily entrusted to women.

---

39. De Vries, *The Industrious Revolution*.
40. *Ibid.*, 237.

8

The international economy, 1870–1914: the gold standard, finance and colonialism

Having presented the changes that the industrial revolutions caused in the systems of production of the European countries, the United States and Japan between the end of the eighteenth century and the beginning of the twentieth century, it is now time to consider the changes in international economic relations,[1] which are no less significant and revolutionary. We will cover four topics in this chapter: the enormous increase in mobility of goods, labour and capital; the evolution of finance; the first attempt to establish an international monetary regime through the gold standard; and finally, we will touch on the vast topic of colonialism, which we will develop only in broad synthesis.

8.1 *Mobility of goods*

Industrialization produced an incredible increase in international trade, which previously was held in check by high transportation costs, people's low purchasing power and the lack of product diversification, all barriers that were progressively loosened as economies gradually changed. Britain was of course the first country to significantly expand its international trade, such that in 1913 it was still the world's largest exporter, although closely followed by Germany (in Table 8.1 see the next to last column that shows the index of export values in 1913). The United States was still some distance behind, while the value of French exports was at only one-third that of Britain. Between 1820 and 1913 global exports grew 33-fold (the last column in Table 8.1), and grew by another sixteen times between 1913 and the end of the twentieth

---

1. For further development of this perspective, see Foreman Peck, *History of the World Economy.*

century, reflecting the standstill during the interwar years. The two significant growth periods were 1820–70, when an openness to international trade
predominated in many countries, and after the Second World War, when
there was a consistent process of trade liberalization. The period from 1870 to
1913, despite a rise in protectionism, saw a quite substantial growth rate, but
the interwar period was disastrous, and not only for trade. With the expansion of international trade its impact on GDP increased; smaller countries,
who were able to specialize in a narrow range of products, experienced the
greatest impact. In addition, there was a multilateralization of trade. This
meant that exports and imports needed not to balance out bilaterally, but the
balance could be reached at the aggregate level, allowing a greater flexibility
in the use of global resources.

Since the time of Adam Smith and David Ricardo, economists have always
seen international trade as an important extension of the specialization of
labour already applied at the national level; it increases global economic
productivity and uses resources more efficiently. Furthermore, it is a means
of modernization, in that it allows importing, among other things, strategic
raw materials (such as raw cotton, coal or oil) and advanced machinery, while
it facilitates exporting manufactured goods, even if not all that advanced,
as long as prices are contained; this allows nascent industries to strengthen
operations by broadening their foreign markets.[2]

For these reasons economists have always recommended free trade (trade
without tariffs, quotas or other restrictions) so its beneficial force can fully
deploy. And yet, examining the history of industrial capitalism we notice that
no country of any size has ever industrialized in the presence of complete
freedom of trade; not even Britain, which only became a free trader in the
1840s with the repeal of the Navigation Acts, the Calico Acts and the Corn
Laws, after its industrial revolution had come to an end.[3] Rather, small countries, which are heavily dependent on international trade, were the ones which
were more favourable to free trade, as demonstrated by the low levels of
protection in the Netherlands and Denmark.

---

2. Pollard talked about bifronted (or two-sided) trade by intermediate countries: one side
was *backward*-looking towards more advanced countries from which it imports advanced
products and to which it exports traditional products, and the other side *forward*-looking
towards more backward countries, to which it sends manufactured goods and imports raw
materials and foodstuffs. See Pollard, *Peaceful Conquest*. "Intra-industry" trade is defined
as the trade in raw materials rather than in finished goods. Exchange in finished goods is
defined as "inter-industry", in that specialization happens for specific models within the
same industry.

3. Bairoch, *Economics and World History*.

Table 8.1 Index of exports by volume and growth rates per period 1820–1992 (1913 = 100).

Region	Index by export volume (1913 = 100)					Average annual growth rates				Value in 1913 (GB = 100)	Value in 1992 (USA = 100)
	1820	1870	1913	1950	1992	1820–70	1870–1913	1913–50	1950–92		
Britain/UK	3	31	100	100	494	4.6	2.7	0.0	3.8	100	43
Germany	4	18	100	35	1071	3.0	3.8	-1.3	8.1	97	91
France	4	31	100	149	2090	3.9	2.7	1.1	6.3	29	52
Italy	7	39	100	126	3853	3.4	2.1	0.6	8.1	12	39
Russia	–	–	100	97	612	–	–	-0.1	4.3	–	9
United States	1	13	100	225	2350	5.1	4.7	2.2	5.6	49	100
Japan	–	3	100	210	17784	–	8.1	2.0	10.6	4	66
World	3	24	100	128	1602	4.2	3.3	0.7	6.0	–	–

Source: Maddison, *Monitoring.*

This fact can be verified from Table 8.2, which gives average nominal tariff levels for several years between 1877 and 1926. Among the large countries only Britain was a free trader (it had a few tariffs for tax purposes), while Japan's low level of protection had been imposed by international treaties until the end of the nineteenth century, after which there was a sharp upturn. The largest countries – the United States and Russia – were also the most protectionist, while among small countries only Portugal was an exception. In reality, as suggested by the German economist Frederick List, the largest countries had reason to believe that some protection for nascent industries would allow launching, with a good probability of success, industrial sectors that did not yet exist, given the potential of the internal market of a large country. In any case, as we have seen, until the 1930s the levels of protection were never high enough to have a strongly negative impact on international trade.

It should also be noted that the rise of protectionism in the years 1880-90 was due in large part to defensive duties on grains, which many European countries had introduced to revive agriculture from the crisis that had hit it after cheap American and Russian grain had arrived in European markets with the expansion of steamships. The pros and cons of protectionism are one of the most controversial topics today among both economists and economic historians; however most would agree that too high a level of protectionism has only negative effects, while the most modern theories of strategic trade give some justification to moderate, temporary protection, aimed at strengthening competitive abilities.

One last observation on trade treaties. The very existence of protectionism led countries to have an interest in negotiating mutual advantages from lowering selected tariffs. Such negotiations were always bilateral in the nineteenth century, but countries sought to "multilateralize" its effects through the so-called "most favoured nation" (MFN) clause. If countries X and Y enjoyed this clause and one of them, say Y, later reached a more advantageous deal with country Z, country X would also benefit from this new agreement without the need to renegotiate with Y.

While international trade had the phenomenal expansion we saw previously, the factors of production – labour and capital – became far more internationally mobile. We discussed the topic of migration in the previous chapter, emphasizing that this was not a new phenomenon, but rather an acceleration of mobility never before seen on a global scale. With regard to capital movements, these too were not new. Even in the pre-industrial era bankers had practised international finance, particularly for war, but in the nineteenth century many economies became more dynamic, the stock

Table 8.2   Average levels of nominal protection 1877–1926.

	1877	1889	1897	1913	1926
United States	29.9[a]	30.1[a]	21.0[a]	18.9[a]	13.5[a]
	42.8[b]	45.4[b]	41.6[b]	40.5[b]	38.6[b]
	68.4[c]	66.2[c]	51.2[c]	46.5[c]	34.9[c]
Germany	–	8.8	9.6	6.9	5.2
Russia	14.6	34.5	33.8	30.3	–
Britain/UK	5.3	4.9	4.7	4.5	8.6
France	5.2[d]	8.3[d]	11.6[d]	9.0[d]	5.7[d]
	6.6[f]	8.6[f]	10.6[f]	8.8[f]	–
Austria-Hungary	0.9	6.6	7.7	7.0	7.7*
Italy	8.45[d]	16.8[d]	16.2[d]	7.5[d]	3.1[d]
	7.3[e]	17.6[e]	18.5[e]	9.6[e]	11.9[e]
Japan	4.0[a]	2.5[a]	2.5[a]	10.0[a]	6.5[a]
	4.5[b]	3.0[b]	3.5[b]	19.5[b]	16.0[b]
Spain	13.9[d]	14.7[d]	15.5[d]	13.7[d]	15.7[d]
	12.7[e]	11.0[e]	14.6[e]	14.9[e]	16.0[e]
Belgium	1.3	1.7	2.0	1.4	3.1
Ireland	0.8	0.4	0.5	0.4	2.1
Sweden	8.9	11.3	11.3	8.3	9.0
Switzerland	–	3.2	4.6	4.4	8.7
Denmark	–	–	9.2	4.9	5.2
Portugal	28.3	34.8	31.5	22.8	10.2
Europe	9.2	12.0	11.9	9.3	8.3

Notes: a total trade; *b* only protected goods; *c* protected goods as a % of total trade; *d* data from Mitchell; *e* data from Federico-Tena; *f* estimates from Levy-Leboyer-Bourguignon, 1985, tab. VI; – data not available; *Austria only

Source: Mitchell (1981), tables F.1–H.5 adapted by P. A. Toinelli in *Lo sviluppo economico moderno*; Italy and Spain (Federico & Tena, 1997); United States (US Bureau of Census, 1975, series U.208–1); Japan (Minami, *The Economic Development of Japan*, fig. 7.5)

exchanges expanded, the first multinationals were created, and long-term capital flows substantially increased.[4] There is less quantitative global and comparative information on this phenomenon and the first available global framework described the situation on the eve of the First World War (see Table 8.3). We see clearly that Britain was by far the biggest global investor, followed by France. Several small countries were important, such as Holland, Belgium and Sweden; the United States still had a very modest foreign projection. As for the recipient countries, Table 8.4 has only those in Europe, which counts for a small fraction of total British investment, but it is important for all the other European countries. This difference is due to Britain's significant economic commitment to its colonies and dominions, as we will see later. From other sources,[5] only slightly different from those in Table 8.4, it appears that Latin America attracted just over 19 per cent of the total, Asia 14 per cent, Africa 11 per cent, and the rest went to countries settled by Europeans (the United States, Canada, Australia and so forth). Regarding the breakdown by sector, well over half was committed to the development of natural resources that were essential for the new industries, followed by infrastructure, while only 15 per cent went to manufacturing industries.

With the aggressive expansion of international markets for goods, labour and finance, a true international economy emerges in which each country must attend to its balance of payments, which compares the payments a country makes to foreign countries (imports, foreign labour, overseas capital) with the payments it receives from abroad (for exports, remittances by emigrants, invested capital). If the balance of payments is balanced, the country can continue its economic modernization projects undisturbed.[6] If there is a balance of payments surplus (a country has more revenues from abroad than payments), the imbalance will tend to produce adjustments, but in general internal economic activities are not negatively affected by it. Problems arise however when there is a balance of payments deficit (a country has more payments abroad than revenues), because the country is not receiving enough money from abroad to make its foreign payments. If it has reserves it can use them temporarily, or it may take loans, but in the end it must find a way to set the situation aright by acting on its internal economic variables. This point is essential to understand the operation of the first international system of payments that emerged, which we will discuss in §8.3.

---

4. See Obstfeld & Taylor, *Global Capital Markets*.
5. Maddison, *Monitoring*, 63; Jones, *The Evolution of International Business*.
6. Note that parity can be attained by compensations among its various components. For example, it is possible to have parity with a deficit trade balance but a surplus capital flow.

Table 8.3   Capital stock invested in 1914 (of current US dollar millions).

Region	Total	% in Europe	% composition
UK	20,000	5.2	43.4
France	9,700	55.7	21.0
Germany	5,800	44.0	12.7
Holland	1,200	⎫	2.6
Belgium and Switzerland	4,300	⎬ 43.5	9.3
Sweden and other European countries	1,400	⎭	3.0
Total in Europe	42,400	26.7	92.0
United States	3,500	20.0	7.6
Other countries	200	–	0.4
Grand total	46,100	26.0	100.0

Source: Feinstein, Temin & Toniolo, *The European Economy Between the Wars*, 88.

8.2   *The financial system*

This section will be relatively brief because much has already been interwoven into the previous chapters.[7] Here we will only summarize the evolution of finance during and after industrialization. First, recall that all countries that modernized created a central bank – which sometimes was not an easy process, as in the Italian and American cases – that became the repository of one of the undisputed public goods, the currency. The first was the Bank of Sweden in 1667, then the Bank of England in 1694; the last of the countries considered in this work was the United States, which created the Federal Reserve only in 1914. The central bank had a monopoly on issuing paper money and maintaining reserves of gold and other currencies. It also had other responsibilities. It set the discount rate (the rate at which banks could acquire cash from it), which was the reference point for all bank rates; this rate signalled a restrictive (a rising rate) or expansive (a falling rate) monetary policy. It oversaw exchange rates, when fixed exchange rates were still in force.

---

7. For further information see Kindleberger, *A Financial History of Western Europe* and also Neal, *A Concise History of International Finance*.

It maintained a relationship with the Treasury, a government's economic and finance ministry, which could be more or less close, depending on the degree of autonomy of the central bank. It oversaw the banking system, which could also be more or less close, depending on legislation. Finally, and very importantly, it was the lender of last resort, or LLR.

The latter function was carried out (with greatly varying degrees of readiness according to the traditions and operation of the economic system) in order to avert a crisis and ensuing panic if there were too many failures – particularly of banks – and economic agents desperately sought liquidity. The central bank intervened (when and how remained unknown to avoid speculation) by broadly providing liquidity at a fixed interest rate, halting the tendency to sell off securities (which drove down their prices excessively) and restoring equilibrium.

The organization of the financial system that took shape alongside the stock exchange was a diversification in the types of banks that had come into existence in the pre-industrial era when, alongside private bankers, public banks (the forerunners of the central banks) and the *Monti di Pietà*[8] providing credit for consumption were established.[9] In the second half of the eighteenth century the first savings banks were created; they first appeared in the Hapsburg Empire and then spread to other countries. These were non-profit banks created to collect small deposits for the purpose of making people with modest incomes accustomed to interest-earning savings, while at the same time limiting usury and avoiding hoarding (hiding money under the mattress), which took liquidity (cash) out of the system. These banks were managed very conservatively, and the surplus from bank operations was directed to charity and social works. The savings banks were very successful, and at times became banks of significant size, with important local influence. In several countries the postal service established postal savings banks, which provided even more opportunities to collect small savings.[10]

At the same time, the joint-stock banks expanded, which had two configurations; they were either short-term lenders (commercial banks), which relied on deposits, or long-term lenders (variously called merchant banks in Britain,

---

8. Literally "Compassion Fund", the historical origin of the contemporary pawn shop. These were operated as charities, in which the "mount", or capital fund contributed by the wealthy, was lent at low interest rates to those in need, for the benefit of the borrower rather than the profit of the lender.

9. In the Mediterranean countries there were "grain funds", or "grain banks", that loaned grain in-kind for sowing and were repaid in-kind (including an interest rate) at harvest time.

10. In general these went to finance local public works through a "*Cassa Depositi e Prestiti*", a savings and loan bank.

banques d'affaires in France, and investment banks in the United States) that made loans on the basis of their underwritten capital (they did not take deposits). We previously noted the peculiar characteristic of the German model, where many banks of this type were mixed or universal. Cooperative banks were created in Germany in the mid-nineteenth century in two versions; one was an urban, or popular, bank based on Schulze–Delitzsch's model, and the other was a rural bank, with unlimited liability, based on Raiffeisen's model. These types of bank spread on the European continent; they were more closely connected to small-scale local businesses than the savings banks.

In this way a powerful financial grid for recycling savings was created. On the one hand, as noted above, it eliminated hoarding, and on the other it succeeded in meeting a wide variety of credit needs, such that usury, although never eradicated, was confined within narrow bounds. With regard to corporations, which comprised the most advanced part of the various national economic systems, the relative importance of the stock exchange or the banks in financing them resulted in the existence of two alternative financial systems. The first was the Anglo-American "market-oriented" system, in which the stock exchange has an absolute primacy, and banks play a secondary role in supporting current activity rather than investment activity. In this system the corporations respond only to the stock market, and so to the shareholders, who are private individuals and institutional investors, such as pension funds, but generally not to other companies. They do not have forms of collaboration or information circulation outside of those made available to the stock market. The second is the German "bank oriented" system, in which the mixed bank instead has the role not only of granting loans to companies, but of being partner in all their financial needs (see Chapter 5), and the stock market is smaller and of secondary importance. The connection between the corporations and the banks also translates into an interconnection between companies, which frequently cross-hold blocks of each other's shares, and circulating information reserved for the reference group that is not available either to the stock market or to the public, which encourages greater *ex ante* coordination of decisions.

There are advantages and disadvantages to both these systems, which in any case have shown themselves capable of sustaining very dynamic companies they are able to face up to many challenges, so much so that both systems have remained in existence to this day, even though the shift towards globalization is converging finance towards a hybrid model.[11]

---

11. See a thorough discussion in V. Zamagni, *Finance and the Enterprise.* For a reflection on more recent years, see Reszat, *European Financial Systems in the Global Economy.*

8.3 *The gold standard*

How was it possible for an increasingly complex international economy to function in the absence of international supervisory organizations? The answer is simple: by generally adopting an international monetary system known as the *gold standard*. In order to understand the essential elements of this monetary system, we should recall that from the time of the Middle Ages a mixed standard monetary circulation of precious metals and paper currency had developed in various European countries. Some countries used two metals, silver and gold, which was called a bimetallic standard; others used only silver or gold, which was known as monometallism.[12] Conventionally the gold standard dates back to 1717 in Britain when Isaac Newton, the head of the mint, fixed the price of gold at £3, 17 shillings and 10.5 pence. Since Britain, the leader country, preferred gold, *gold monometallism* became operational internationally during the second half of the nineteenth century.

Originally only metal coins were in circulation, but the spread of promissory notes, drafts, and then bank notes (which were easier to circulate and produce), relegated metal as a reserve in bank safes in the form of ingots; as gold was scarce, to increase liquidity paper money in circulation was not fully covered by the gold held in reserve. One of the core principles of the system was the right of *convertibility* of paper money to precious metal at a predetermined *parity*. This convertibility served to prevent issuing too much paper money, which had to be maintained equal to a multiple of the precious metal reserve; the multiplier was first fixed by tradition, and later by law. To increase the paper money in circulation beyond what was permitted by the existing reserve, it was necessary to acquire more precious metal, which was not easy; vice versa, when there was less precious metal, it was necessary to reduce the paper money in circulation. This was the "discipline" of the system bound to the precious metal, defined by the *rules of the game*.[13]

Since it was a system based on trust, given that there was not enough metal in reserve to convert *all* the bank notes in circulation, it depended on the correct application of the rules of the game. When that did not happen, the loss of trust led to bank runs to convert paper money to gold, which led to the collapse of the entire system and the loss of convertibility. To this point, this is how it worked within each country. What has attracted the atten-

---

12. Bimetallism was abandoned due to complications linked to the relationship between gold and silver; silver monometallism was abandoned primarily because Britain, the leader country, preferred gold.

13. Flandreau & Zumer, *The Making of Global Finance*.

tion of many scholars is the fact that this regime produced a mechanism for correcting international imbalances in the balance of payments. It maintained fixed exchange rates between currencies, maintaining remarkable order and stability in the international economy. It is not by chance that the two most prosperous and expansive periods of industrial capitalism to date, 1870–1914 and 1947–73, were also the two periods in which fixed exchange rates based on the gold standard were in force. The nexus between fixed exchange rates and international expansion has stirred up a lively literature; here we can only give the main conclusions.[14]

Let us examine how the gold standard works on an international level. When things are not going well in a country and a deficit emerges in its balance of payments, the country has difficulty securing sufficient quantities of foreign currency; it will tend to offer more of its own currency to purchase the foreign currency, which leads to a devaluation of its own currency. However, with a convertibility principle operating, anyone paid in a currency that is likely to depreciate would prefer to be paid directly in gold, which maintains a fixed parity with both the depreciating currency and the currency into which the gold will be converted, avoiding any loss on the exchange.[15] As a consequence of this mechanism, a country with a deficit in its balance of payments will see its gold reserves decrease, a gold outflow. This is when the rules of the game come into play. With a lower reserve, the country must reduce its paper money in circulation, tightening credit and raising its interest rate. These measures will in turn restrict internal demand (and thus imports as well), lower prices (which will make its exports more competitive), while higher interest rates will attract foreign capital. All this leads to rebalancing its balance of payments and preventing an effective devaluation of the currency, which, although with minor fluctuations, will essentially remain fixed.

The mechanism also works in reverse to rebalance the balance of payments with a surplus, which sees an influx of gold, and hence an expansion of its paper money in circulation. This leads countries in deficit and countries in surplus to share the burden of readjustment.[16] That said, we should note

---

14. See Gallarotti, *The Anatomy of an International Monetary Regime*. See also Tew, *Evolution of the International Monetary System*.

15. Note that the conversion and transportation operations of gold had a modest cost, such that it allowed small currency fluctuations around parity, because it was not worth converting currency before a devaluation trend had exceeded the transfer costs of the gold (carriage, insurance, commissions and interest). These fluctuations around parity were called *gold points* and were conventionally around 1 to 2 per cent.

16. If a country has a surplus balance of payments there is always one country in deficit, since at a global level there is perfect compensation.

that countries with a surplus sometimes wish to increase their gold reserves, and choose not to play by the rules of the game by expanding their monetary circulation, a process called the *sterilization* of gold. This creates greater difficulties for the country with a deficit, which is constrained to bear all the burden of readjustment by itself. The severity of this burden could force a country to leave the gold standard and let its currency fluctuate, but the disadvantages of not being part of the gold club can be high; governments resorted to this measure only when they could do nothing else, and generally only temporarily. The readjustment mechanism is *automatic*, in the sense that it has an intrinsic logic, but it requires that countries follow the rules of the game, which implies the political will to want to remain in the system.

At this point one might wonder why the world has not always maintained a gold standard. A few observations should suffice to clarify the matter. First and foremost, it requires an international economy that is not disturbed by traumatic events that prevent the system from operating properly. It is no coincidence that in prolonged periods of war the gold standard has always been abolished, because countries needed to print paper money to finance the war, even at the cost of increasing inflation; furthermore, countries with serious internal difficulties could not always comply with the rules of the game. In light of this, some scholars have concluded that periods of high international stability and development were what allowed the gold standard to work, and that the gold standard was not what generated stability, even if it contributed to maintaining it.[17] This remains an open question today.

It has also been noted that a system of fixed exchange rates inextricably links the monetary and fiscal policies of all countries that participate in it to those of the leading nation/currency, through the series of actions and reactions briefly described above[18]. If and when a leading currency is able to bear the burden of this leadership of the entire international monetary system things work, otherwise the mechanism seizes up. The classic gold standard was sustained by the British pound, although not without problems for the Bank of England, which did not always have enough gold on hand. The other successful period of the gold standard was established at the UN Monetary and Financial Conference at Bretton Woods, New Hampshire in 1944, and is therefore known as the Bretton Woods system, and was sustained by the US dollar. It was a diluted version of the classic gold standard, called the *gold*

---

17. See also the essays in Eichengreen, *The Gold Standard in Theory and History* and also by the same author, *Globalizing Capital*.
18. Monetary policies include the fixation of interest rates and of the money supply (liquidity); fiscal policies fix tax rates and public expenditure.

exchange standard, because most countries did not keep gold reserves, but reserves of dollars, and only through exchange with the dollar could they gain access to gold. In this case as well, problems arose, which at the beginning of the 1970s decreed its end.

To understand these problems it is necessary to focus on gold, the load-bearing pillar of the system. Gold has its own market, as does any other commodity. When it is scarce its price tends to rise, and when it is plentiful the price tends to fall. The fact is that there are limited gold mines, and, more importantly, they are discovered in cycles that are not always synchronized with the expansion of economic activity. Accordingly, a gold standard system does not generally maintain fixed price levels. When there is little gold supply, there is little increase in the paper money in circulation, and if economic activity increases at the same time, the price level tends to fall, resulting in *deflation*. When there is a high influx of gold, which in turn means paper money increases disproportionately with economic activity, the price level tends to rise, resulting in *inflation*. However, in a gold standard system inflation and deflation propagate in the same way internationally, and exchange rates can remain fixed.

Over time, two conclusions have been reached:

1 since deflation is not favourable to economic activity, the shortage of gold that would inevitably result from a great increase in economic activity came to be seen as an uneccesary limiting factor that negatively interfered with economic activity;

2 at the same time, the need for an "external" discipline, such as the one provided by the gold standard, to prevent excessive inflation was greatly reduced by the greater awareness and propriety of the monetary authorities of the countries that counted most,[19] such that it became clear that it was possible to maintain stable exchange (and price) conditions even *without gold*.

In any event, when the gold standard was abandoned in 1973, after having learned many lessons on the mechanisms of fixed exchange rates, readjustments of prices and the balance of payments, a system of flexible exchange rates was established that produced great global financial instability. We will take up that topic again in Chapters 14 and 16.

---

19. Other countries, such as those that cannot control runaway inflation today, would not have been able to remain on the gold standard.

8.4 *Colonialism*

It is not possible here to exhaustively consider the topic of colonialism, which would entail an analysis of its impact on an unending number of countries in the Americas, Asia and Africa.[20] We will only offer a few general observations on different styles of colonialism that have left very different political and economic legacies, along the lines of the comparative works by Acemoglu and Robinson.[21] The first distinction to make is between colonialism in which Europeans settled in areas with sparse local populations, such as the United States, Canada, Australia and New Zealand, and areas with already dense indigenous populations. In the first, Europeans were able to create societies deeply rooted in European cultures, with strong incentives towards democratic state organizations, given the absence of existing concentrations of power and the abundant resources that allowed strong social mobility. These areas very quickly became autonomous and began to fully participate in the internationalization of the industrial economy described previously in this chapter.

In the areas where Europeans had to govern a large local population, the style of government established instead reflected more how the conquest happened and the characteristics of the local people. It is not easy to model this, but three types can be identified. The first is the style of Spanish colonization.[22] It was by military conquest, and it was confronted with peoples that were generally accustomed to obeying rulers (the Incas, Aztecs, and Mayas) that dominated agricultural areas (Latin America), and who therefore had little propensity towards initiative and trade. The resultant institutional organization was generally authoritarian and paternalistic, and the Spanish ruling class tended to extract all it could to benefit the colonizer. The advantages for the colonizer were quite short-lived (as noted in Chapter 2, Spain never really flourished), and the disadvantages for the colonies have endured to this day, despite the formal independence that nearly all the colonies attained in the early nineteenth century. Authoritarian governments, a major expansion of monocultures for the benefit of the European countries, very limited spread

---

20. Here we are discussing colonialism, not the more general concept of imperialism, which includes the effects of a global hegemony by a power that is not colonial. For more detailed discussions, see Fieldhouse, *Colonialism 1870–1945*; Reinhard, *A Short History of Colonialism*.

21. In particular, Acemoglu, Johnson & Robinson, "The Colonial Origins of Comparative Development" and "Institutions as the Fundamental Cause of Long-Run Growth".

22. The Portuguese style was partly different, with a greater trade component, but with analogous results.

of education, and a mindset oriented toward rents[23] are the legacies of this style of colonization.[24]

The second model is that of the British Empire, which was the largest in the world.[25] This empire was in large measure conquered by market penetration, and it settled predominately in areas in which trade could be established. India is a paradigm case: it was the East India Company that conquered India (see Chapters 2 and 16), which was an area with strong commercial traditions. It is not surprising therefore that over the longer term the British colonies experienced greater economic success than those of the Spanish, because they were based on exchange rather than rents and on more inclusive governments, although there was no lack of exceptions.[26]

Finally, the third case primarily concerns Africa, where colonialism arrived later due to climate conditions that were prohibitive for Europeans, and where it was faced with fairly populous but stagnant societies that had often stopped at pre-agrarian levels of development, particularly in sub-Saharan Africa. Nearly all European countries sought to colonize Africa: France (which had also attempted a transatlantic venture, with moderate success), Belgium, Germany, Italy, Portugal, Britain and even the Netherlands (which had had much greater successes elsewhere). The result was not just a babel of different and intertwined clashes between European powers, artificially constructed states with boundaries mapped on a drawing board, and cultures that were too distant from each other to allow mediation; it also created a legacy of unsustainability that even today is having serious negative effects not only on Africa itself, but on the whole world. Europe's historical responsibilities in having produced the conditions for Africa's instability are particularly grave.

Finally, we should mention Russia's "colonialism", which it pursued in the areas bordering Russia; some of these areas it wholly absorbed, such as Siberia, while others it dominated but ultimately lost, such as the Nordic areas to the northwest, including Estonia, Lithuania, Latvia, Finland, and even part of Poland. Many other areas such as Belarus, Ukraine, Georgia, Armenia and Azerbaijan, which were of European culture, as well as culturally Islamic areas

---

23. In economics rent is contrasted to profit, the former being the payment for the use of a good owned by someone else (mostly real estate) and the latter the payment to the owners of capital invested in an entrepreneurial way. Rent is a passive revenue, with low risk, while profit is an active revenue, with high risk.
24. See Acemoglu & Robinson, *Why Nations Fail.*
25. The Dutch style was somewhat similar to that of Britain, but far from Britain's scale.
26. See Ferguson, *Empire.*

such as Kazakhstan, Uzbekistan, Turkmenistan and Tajikistan, are formally independent today, but remain under a strong Russian hegemony.

It has long been thought, particularly in Marxist literature, that colonialism could not have had other than a highly positive impact on the colonizers to the detriment of those colonized.[27] The theoretical framework of reference is that of a zero-sum game: what is lost by some in the game is gained by the winners. History however offers countless examples of negative-sum games; the dynamics of some turns of events are linked together in such perverse ways that all players end up losing. This is often the case with devastating wars, as well as economic crises in general. Some recent analyses have revised the prevailing generalizations about colonialism, analysing the impact that colonization has had on the colonizer countries themselves.

First, it is important to clarify that not all advanced countries practised colonialism. As is well known, the United States was never a colonial power. Although many European countries were (and Japan was a colonial power in Taiwan and Korea), not all profited economically. Colonialism was therefore not a necessary component of economic growth. Furthermore, our judgement on this practice, as on many others, depends on the time horizon considered. What may be considered a gain in the short term may turn out to be a loss over the long term, and vice versa. Colonialism typically should be analysed over the long term, and even the very long term. Finally, colonialism was a phenomenon that had many dimensions: a desire to have new lands to settle, a drive for the religious conversion of new populations, the pride of propagating its culture, the necessity of controlling militarily strategic zones, and the need to compete with other powers beyond just economic interests.

Table 8.4   Percentage of exports in the colonies 1894–1934.

Date	Britain	France	Holland	Germany	Italy	Japan
1894–03	30	11	5	0.3	0.3	3
1904–13	33	13	5	0.6	2	8
1919–28	41	15	7	–	2	14
1929–34	44	24	5	–	2	21
Colonial population, c.1900 (millions)	325	36	34	10	–	–

Source: Clark, *The Balance Sheets of Imperialism.*

---

27. Marx himself held that the colonies would cost more than they would yield.

With these caveats we can now attempt a comparative analysis based on an indicator that gives us the extent of the colonizer's involvement in the economy of the colonies: trade. Since information on capital investments is scarce, what information we do have turns out to be closely correlated to the importance of trade, such that we can consider trade to be a full indicator of the economic importance of the colonies for the colonizer. As can be seen in Table 8.4, on the eve of the First World War Britain was the only nation that had strong economic ties with its colonies, while France and Japan strengthened them somewhat during the interwar period. The involvement of other countries was negligible, particularly for Germany (which was stripped of its colonies by the Treaty of Versailles; see Chapter 9).[28] The field for ascertaining a positive economic impact by colonialism is therefore restricted to very few countries, and we have accurate quantitative cost-benefit analyses for Britain alone.[29] Since the colonies had sometimes substantial military and administrative costs, to understand if there were real benefits, these benefits must be calculated net of costs.

This has been done in a work by Davis and Huttenback.[30] The authors take the profit rate of British companies in the empire during the period from 1865 to 1914 as the benefit obtained from being settled there.[31] They then calculated the direct military and administrative costs and subtracted them to obtain a profit rate *net of costs*. Comparing this net profit rate with the profit obtained by British companies in other non-colonial markets, they concluded that there were advantages in the colonies until the 1880s, especially because to that point many British companies operated as monopolies. Subsequently this and other conditions changed, such that the profit rates outside the colonies were greater. Of course, investors earned the nominal profit rate, and so continued to believe that their investments were profitable and put pressure on the British government to remain in the colonies. Those who lost were

---

28. At the end of the nineteenth century, in addition to the countries mentioned above, Portugal alone had a colonial presence of some importance, with 9 per cent of exports and 16 per cent of imports, in an area with a population of around 8 million.

29. For France there are studies that emphasize the substantial costs of the colonies, however without producing a rigorous analysis that can provide conclusive results; see Brunschwig, *French Colonialism 1871–1914*.

30. Davis & Huttenback, *Mammon and the Pursuit of Empire*.

31. An analysis of the preceding period has not yet been made. However, it is known that the colonies played only a marginal market role for British production, but they provided it with strategic imports, such as raw cotton, and the strong incentive to produce ships to control the settlements and international trade.

Britain itself as a country and those who paid the taxes needed to meet the costs of the colonies.[32]

We should note that the costs considered by Davis and Huttenback are only the direct costs. There were also indirect costs, as other studies have shown. This is particularly relevant in the British case, given the deep involvement by Britain in the economic structure of the colonies. Many have noted that the production over-commitments by British industry during the first industrial revolution in textiles, steel and railways, which caused the decline in English leadership (see §6.1), was directly connected to the availability of colonial markets for these products, products that had already been technologically surpassed in more sophisticated European markets prior to the First World War. If we add to this the negative impact of decolonization after the Second World War, we can certainly conclude with Davis and Huttenback that "the British as a whole certainly did not benefit economically from the Empire. On the other hand, individual investors did".[33]

---

32. The interpretation of Davis & Huttenback has caused much discussion, with some dissent: see O'Brien, "The Costs and Benefits of British Imperialism 1846–1914" and Offer, "The British Empire: A Waste of Money?".

33. Davis & Huttenback, *Mammon and the Pursuit of Empire*, 267.

9

The socio-economic consequences
of the First World War

There are many reasons why the First World War broke out, and this is not the place to offer a comprehensive summary; but it's helpful to recall some of the economic background. The Franco-Prussian War of 1870–71 over the territories of Alsace-Lorraine had had significant economic impact – important mines of iron, zinc and coal were located there; the success and expansion of German enterprises was viewed with alarm by the nationalistic milieus of Italy and France; there had been intense economic conflict in the Balkans among all the major powers; and a serious dispute had broken out between Germany and Russia over protectionism (the two shared a common border, since Poland did not then exist). However, none of these factors would have been sufficient to trigger a war had there not been a deeply rooted conviction in Europe that war was a valid means for asserting hegemony, acquiring new territories, and enriching the victor.

This was a legacy of the pre-industrial past, when productivity stagnation and scarce accumulation of capital stock could offer some justification for such a belief.[1] The fact is that in the industrial era not only was such a belief unfounded, because there were other means to become wealthy (investing to increase productivity and thus per capita income), but war became a means of slowing accumulation by destroying fixed and human capital and disrupting markets. Frequently wars concluded with significant losses by all combatants, a negative-sum game. This new awareness spread very slowly through Europe, particularly in certain countries such as Germany, where even major industrialists such as Rathenau of AEG were in favour of war.[2]

The First World War was long and destructive in terms of both human

---

1. We refer to justification because war could be very harmful in the pre-industrial era too, in that famine and epidemics often accompanied it.
2. See the quote in the Introduction to Berghahn, *Quest for Economic Empire*, 9.

and physical capital. Nearly nine million soldiers died in the war, and around forty million people, excluding those killed in the civil war in Russia (see Chapter 10), were cut down by the "Spanish flu" between 1918 and 1919, a deadly influenza that spread because of the war. While it was largely a war of fixed positions, there were air raids and occupations in France, Belgium, Poland and the Veneto. From the published research on the effects of the war, from which Table 9.1 is taken, we can see just how heavy were the human losses and the destruction of capital, to which, as we will see, we should add the breakup of the Austro-Hungarian Empire, the drama of German reparations and the slowdown in the European economies.

Table 9.1   The effects of the First World War.

Parameter	Data
Duration of war (days)	1,564
Number of countries in the conflict	33
Population of those nations in conflict (millions)	1,100
Soldiers mobilized (millions)	70
Soldiers wounded and killed (millions)	20
Soldiers permanently maimed (millions)	15
Soldiers killed (millions)	10
Civilians killed (millions)	10
Loss of human capital as a percentage of the pre-war level	
Britain	3.6
France	7.2
Russia	2.3
Italy	3.8
Germany	6.3
Austro-Hungarian Empire	4.5
Loss of physical capital as a percentage of pre-war capital	
Britain	9.9
France	59.6
Russia	14.3
Italy	15.9
Germany	3.1
Austro-Hungarian Empire	6.5

Source: Broadberry & Harrison, *The Economics of World War I*, 28, 35.

The finances of the warring nations were severely tested because of heavy military expenditure, with effects that were felt a long time afterwards, as we shall see. In some countries, such as France and Italy, the production base for steel, armaments and explosives was insufficient and had to be expanded, which required additional financial commitments by the state. Since it was impossible – with the partial exception of Britain – to meet these commitments just by increasing taxes and expanding the public debt, governments broadly resorted to printing money. This led to inflation, which was partially checked by price controls during the war, but which subsequently exploded (see Table 9.2), resulting in their exit from the gold standard. Inflation; rebalancing the public finances; returning to the gold standard; reintegrating surviving soldiers back into activities assumed by women during the war; converting industry from war production to peacetime production; reparations of material damages: these were all difficult problems that winners and losers had to resolve without any international aid, problems that created social and political tensions, and which in the case of the four principal European economies did not always lead to adequate solutions.

Table 9.2   Consumer price indexes 1913–24, 1913 = 100.

Date	Britain	Germany	France	Italy	United States
1913	100	100	100	100	100
1914	97	103	102	100	103
1915	115	129	118	109	101
1916	139	169	135	136	113
1917	166	252	159	195	147
1918	225	302	206	268	171
1919	261	414	259	273	189
1920	258	1,017	359	359	204
1921	234	1,338	312	427	180
1922	190	15,025	300	423	167
1923	180	15,883	335	423	171
1924	181	128	282	436	171

Source: Mitchell, *European Historical Statistics; International Historical Statistics: Africa and Asia; International Historical Statistics: the Americas and Australasia.*

9.1 *The break-up of the Austro-Hungarian Empire and the territorial reorganization of Europe*

Germany had 13 per cent of its territory taken away; Alsace-Lorraine was restored to France, and the Polish regions, along with those parts held by Russia and the Hapsburgs, were reunited with the rest of Poland and re-established as a nation. From the ashes of the Austro-Hungarian Empire ten new nations were formed, in whole or in part, as well as two free cities (Fiume[3] and Gdansk) and the parts that passed to Italy (see Figure 9.1).[4]

Customs outposts on the borders were increased, money in circulation multiplied (and with them the central banks), and new fiscal systems had to be established, all of which meant the further fragmentation of Europe. That the new nations had to begin their economic life with no international financial aid, further presaged future instability. There was only one small private American aid fund, the ARA (American Relief Administration) that lasted from January to July of 1919. The weak League of Nations formed at Versailles[5] was only capable of organizing a few international conferences[6] and providing consultation for establishing financial and monetary systems in several of the new countries created by the breakup of the Austro-Hungarian Empire, but all the necessary capital had to be raised on international markets at current interest rates, with a resultant debt load on the public finances of the newly established states.

Aside from institutional uncertainties and foreign debt, what were the main challenges the new states confronted?

1 *Agrarian reform.* For both political and economic reasons, the landed estates that largely populated these areas of Eastern Europe were divided up; this required reforms that were both politically difficult and economically disruptive, in the sense that with the estate broken up productivity

---

3. Fiume was incorporated into Italy in 1924.
4. For the Eastern European economies, see Berend & Ranki, *Economic Development*; Kaiser & Radice, *The Economic History of Eastern Europe 1919–1975*; Aldcroft & Morewood, *Economic Change in Eastern Europe Since 1918*; Teichova, *Central Europe in the Twentieth Century*.
5. Recall that in the end the United States did not accept being part of it, thus weakening the only international institution that was successfully created at the end of the First World War.
6. The main conferences were Genoa in 1922, the purpose of which was to restore the gold standard, and Geneva in 1927, which would have led to tariff reductions; it was unsuccessful because its decisions were not ratified.

Figure 9.1 New states formed after the First World War

Source: Feinstein, Temin & Toniolo, *The European Economies Between the Wars* (Oxford: Oxford University Press).

dropped, which was only recovered after the construction of the appropriate infrastructure and by working the land more intensely.

2 *Reorienting trade.* The trade links of areas that hitherto had been part of different national clusters now had to be reorganized to adapt to a new internal market and more diversified foreign markets, a process that took time.

3 *Infrastructure consolidation and reconfiguration.* Often the internal infrastructure had either belonged to a different country (with different standards), or were built according to different directions and dimensions. For example, Vienna, which hitherto had been the capital of the Austro-Hungarian Empire now found itself the capital city of a small country, or Yugoslavia or Poland, which inherited railways with three different gauges.

4 *Industrialization.* With the exception of Czechoslovakia and Austria, few of the new nations had an industrial base of any relative significance, so all of them had to promote industrialization in a setting that was less than favourable. Most immediately thought to increase tariffs, prompting a general trend across Europe of increasing tariffs, which, as we shall see, were raised even more after the 1929 crisis. The success of these attempts to force industrialization was rather disappointing (see Table 9.3, which gives the results until 1929, when the Great Depression worsened the situation everywhere). Only Czechoslovakia had a good rate of growth and, starting from a fairly good base in 1920, nearly doubled its industrial production index. Per rate of growth Yugoslavia was second, but its level of per capita income in 1929 placed it just above Romania and Bulgaria. Poland and Bulgaria showed truly disappointing results. Poland, primarily due to the particularly negative effects of the war (industrial production in 1920 had fallen to one-third that of the pre-war level), and Bulgaria due to the country's complete disorganization. If we bear in mind that the per capita income level of Austria in 1929 was just over half that of the United States, we can grasp just how poor these countries were.

In conclusion, the territorial reorganization of Eastern Europe required a long period of international prosperity and peace if it was to consolidate and evolve towards a more prosperous state. That did not happen, in the first place because of the onset of the Great Depression (see Chapter 11), and then because world war broke out once more, which produced a political setting that set back strengthening the economies of that area by at least fifty years. The poverty and hardships of Eastern Europe made it unstable and weak, and

Table 9.3 Industrial production index and per capita income, 1913–29, in the countries of the former Austro-Hungarian Empire.

Country	Industrial production				Per capita income		
	Growth rate 1913–29	Indexes (1913 = 100)			Growth rate 1913–29	1929 index (1913 = 100)	1929 index (Austria = 100)
		1920	1924	1929			
Austria	1.0	47	80	118	1.1	123	100
Hungary	0.2	48	67	103	-0.1	97	57
Czechoslovakia	3.9	87	124	186	1.1	122	82
Poland	-0.8	35	57	87	1.2	125	57
Yugoslavia					-0.5	90	37
Romania					-1.5	69	31
Bulgaria					-1.0	81	32

Source: Feinstein, Temin & Toniolo, *The European Economy Between the Wars*; Good & Ma, "The Economic Growth of Central and Eastern Europe in Comparative Perspective, 1870–1989".

easy prey to the convulsions that gripped Western Europe, as we will see in Chapter 12.

9.2 *German reparations and the German economy in the 1920s*

The new Weimar Republic began its economic life with the worst of portents. Not only had the human losses of the war been high (two million soldiers killed), but the country had lost 13 per cent of its territory, which included 75 per cent of its iron ore mines, 68 per cent of its zinc mines, and 26 per cent of its coal mines. All its colonies had been confiscated, as had its navy and all remaining arms, as well as commercial ships in excess of 1600 tons, one-quarter of its fishing fleet and several thousand locomotives, rail cars and trucks. Nor did the requisition of goods stop there; Germany was forced to send the allies various in-kind products as part of reparations until 1923.

We come then to the question of reparations. Of the fourteen points set out by United States President Woodrow Wilson, that came to constitute the basis of the Treaty of Versailles one provided that Germany, which was held responsible for the war, pay a "reparation" sum for damages suffered by the Allies. The point in question, Article 232, stated: "Germany undertakes, that she will make compensation for all damage done to the civilian population of the Allied and Associated Powers and to their property during the period of the belligerency of each as an Allied or Associated Power against Germany by such aggression by land, by sea and from the air". As can be seen no quantitative parameters were set, and the damage could be interpreted more or less extensively, for example, one might think that Germany should also pay the costs of the occupation troops and the war pensions of the allied countries. To arrive at an operational proposal a reparations commission was appointed, based in Berlin, and in the meantime requisitions were made of in-kind materials.[7]

Before following the intricate events that determined the value of the reparations, let us pause a moment to reflect on the process itself. In the past the losing party in a war was sometimes requested to pay a compensatory fine, but in general it was a *one-time* sum, in some cases paid in several instalments. At the end of the Franco-Prussian War in 1871, France was asked to pay a sum in gold to Germany, which was made quickly, increasing Germany's gold

---

7. Ongoing supplies of various products were requested, among them coal, which represented between 4 and 5 per cent of German GDP during 1919–22.

reserves and causing – under the gold standard – an inflationary period unfavourable to German exports. We know that Bismarck regretted having asked for the fine, saying that the next time he won a war he would pay compensation to the loser (in order to bring about its economic ruin). What emerges from this episode is that a compensation payment can destabilize the existing economic balance, besides being odious to the loser as well as problematic if its gold reserves had also been lost, as was the case for Germany after the First World War (but not for the case of France cited above).

At this point we understand why as fine a mind as Keynes, in one of his earliest writings that was widely circulated, recommended prudence and moderation in requesting reparations if one did not want to incite the oppressed countries' revenge.[8] Since, as we shall see, the German reparations were also linked to the payment of allied war debts, Keynes suggested that both of these be cancelled, believing that neither the reparations nor the war debts would be paid for more than a few years because "they do not square with human nature or agree with the spirit of the time".[9] Keynes's recommendations ended with an exhortation to the United States, which he already clearly saw as the emerging hegemonic power, to be generous in aid for European reconstruction.

None of Keynes's suggestions were received, and the reality surpassed his most tragic predictions, culminating in the second great global conflict. The fact that the United States was unyielding in requesting payment of the loans made to its allies during the conflict (see the estimate in Table 9.4) made the victorious European countries even more unbending in demanding that Germany pay at least sufficient reparations to repay the debt to the United States.

This link between war debts and reparations led to a vicious cycle that ended up causing considerable damage and we need to understand how these events were interconnected. The Berlin Commission's first proposal regarding the reparations was set out at the Conference of Boulogne on 20 June 1920 in the sum of 269 billion gold marks. To understand the order of magnitude of this figure we can compare it to German GDP of that time: it was equal

---

8. Keynes, *The Economic Consequences of the Peace*. Keynes's prophetic passage is worth quoting in full: "If we aim deliberately at the impoverishment of Central Europe, Vengeance, I dare predict, will not limp. Nothing can then delay for very long that final civil war between the forces of Reaction and the despairing convulsions of Revolution, before which the horrors of the late German war will fade into nothing and which will destroy, whoever the victor, the civilization and the progress of our generation" (*ibid.*, 251).

9. *Ibid.*, 264.

Table 9.4 War debts and German reparations.

	German reparations (gold marks billions)			War debts (US$ billions)			
	Reparation Commission	German government	from/to	USA	Britain	France	Other
Up to 31 August 1921	8.1	51.7	USA	–	4.7	4.0	3.2
Dawes Plan	7.6	8.0	Britain	–	–	3.0	8.1
Young Plan	2.8	3.1	France	–	–	–	3.0
Other	4.5	5.0	Other	–	–	–	–
Total	23.0	67.8	Total	–	4.7	7.0	14.3

Note: the conversion of gold marks into dollars was 4.2 marks per dollar, so 23 billion gold marks are equal to 5.5 billion dollars.

Source: Sauvy, *Histoire économique de la France entre les deux guerres*, vol. I; Holtfrerich, *German Inflation 1914–1923*.

to about six times German GDP. It is not surprising that the Germans did not deem the figure realistic and requested a revision. At the Paris Conference in January 1921, the Commission set a lesser sum of 226 billion gold marks, but it added a levy of 12 per cent on German exports for forty-two years, in addition to the payments in kind previously discussed. Germany responded that those conditions were still unacceptable, to which the Allies responded in May 1921 with the "London Ultimatum", in which the reparations were set at 132 billion marks, to be paid in instalments with 6 per cent interest. To ensure the flow of payments, the Commission identified a series of fiscal sources that were to be dedicated to that purpose. This amount was still three times larger than the figure Keynes had deemed the maximum possible.

This time Germany had no choice, but since its internal economic situation was chaotic (as we shall see in the next chapter), it requested a moratorium on the monetary payments, while it continued the in-kind payments. Controversy broke out over these in-kind payments (shipments of telegraph poles and coal) that ended up with French and Belgian troops invading the Ruhr in January 1923 to direct the product supply operations themselves. The local German population responded by ceasing production, which needed to be supported by government subsidies. Germany's monetary situation, already precarious, began to deteriorate drastically. While in 1921 tax revenues covered 47 per cent of expenses, and 40 per cent in 1922, over the course of 1923 that coverage fell to 7 per cent of expenses, and by October just 1 per cent. The balance was made up by printing paper money, inflation turned into hyper-inflation, and the German monetary system was destroyed.

In November 1923, after hyperinflation had rendered the mark unusable,[10] a new mark, the Rentenmark, was introduced that was loosely based on the value of the country's land, industry and developed infrastructure. In December the task of setting a reasonable payment plan for the reparations was entrusted to a commission chaired by Charles Dawes, a senior US official. The Dawes Plan, which went into operation in 1924, provided for annual payments that increased with an index of prosperity of the German economy, without setting a timeline. Moreover, to facilitate launching the plan it provided for a commercial loan to be floated on the New York Stock Exchange; this met with considerable success, allowing the German economy to not only begin paying reparations with the proceeds of this loan, but also to cover a few other shortfalls in its balance of payments. It was only in August 1924, after the Dawes Plan was applied, that the currency circulation was at last stabilized with the Reichsmark (see Table 9.5).

---

10. One dollar was worth 4,200 billion marks!

Table 9.5   Postwar monetary stabilizations 1922–8.

Country	Year of stabilization	% of new parity with respect to pre-war parity
Sweden	1922	100
The Netherlands	1924	100
Britain	1925	100
Denmark	1926	100
Italy	1926	27.3
France	1926	20.3
Czechoslovakia	1923	14.6
Belgium	1926	14.5
Yugoslavia	1915	8.9
Greece	1927	6.7
Portugal	1929	4.1
Hungary	1924	0.0069
Austria	1922	0.00007
Poland	1926	0.000026
Germany	1923	0.0000000001

Source: Feinstein, Temin & Toniolo, *The European Economy Between the Wars.*

Since an inflow of foreign capital was what allowed this stabilization, the German economy became highly dependent on this capital, which financed one-third of internal investments during 1925–7 (two-thirds of which was from the United States), and the influx of foreign currencies more than financed the reparations instalments, keeping the balance of payments in equilibrium. As Costigliola writes, it is true that "The Dawes Plan was the cornerstone of American efforts in the 1920s to help build a prosperous and stable Europe. That structure, however, rested on shaky grounds" for many reasons.[11] Germany had to maintain high interest rates to attract private – not public – capital. But since municipalities borrowed most of these loans for public infrastructure projects and for the agricultural sector, these could not be expected to be sufficiently profitable to cover such high interest rates. The

11. Costigliola, "The United States and the Reconstruction of Germany in the 1920s", 497.

interest rate declined, making investment in Germany less attractive.[12] The attractiveness of the German market for foreign investors waned, particularly for American capitalists, who saw the US stock exchange expand throughout 1928. When the German economy began to cool at the end of 1927,[13] the withdrawal of American capital became inevitable; this caused the German economy to worsen, which became a crisis towards the end of 1928, a year prior to the US Great Depression. In 1928, the best postwar year for Germany, per capita income was only 13 per cent higher than before the war; nevertheless, Germany was not the worst among the economies we are analysing, as can be seen in Table 9.6.

Again in 1928 a new plan was sought with a definitive method for reparations; it was entrusted to a new commission chaired by the American banker Owen Young, which produced the Young Plan the following year. This plan set a lower annual payment, with a provision for increasing the payments later, and set a payment timeline of thirty-seven years. By the time the agreement was reached the German economy was in crisis, and the global crash began soon after with the American crisis. The reparations and war debt payments were suspended in June 1931 at the height of the international financial crisis (discussed in Chapter 11) and were never resumed.

The consequences of reparations kept the German economy depressed and weak, to the point of making it one of the originators of the Great Depression. We should mention here another aspect of these consequences, the question of "revaluation". Hyperinflation had wiped out all liquid capital (bank deposits, state bonds, etc.) as well as the money in circulation; this caused enormous losses to the middle class, the largest holder of such capital. After stabilization, an interminable discussion dragged on about possible ways to at least partially compensate these losses, but in the end nothing was done. This increased middle-class disaffection with the Weimar Republic and pushed the country towards political extremism; this was further reinforced by the disastrous consequences of the Great Depression (about which we will say more in Chapter 11).[14]

In conclusion, if one accepts the estimate by the Berlin Commission, the reparations actually paid by Germany comprised only a very modest sum

---

12. Schuker, in *American "Reparations" to Germany*, argues that most of the American capital that flowed into Germany was never repaid.

13. Temin argues that this cooling off was initially an internal phenomenon, and only later was it aggravated by the withdrawal of American capital; see Temin, "The Beginning of the Depression in Germany".

14. See Taylor, *The Downfall of Money*.

(Table 9.4); its estimate excluded most of the payments in-kind and the value of confiscated foreign German assets (included in the German government's estimate). To obtain such a poor result ($5.5 billion in reparations paid against net war debts of $18.3 billion) the Allies adopted a determination that would have been better placed elsewhere. And the perverse effects Keynes had anticipated occurred, as will be seen in Chapter 12. The responsibility for this senseless policy must be equally divided between the United States, which was still too isolationist to think of shouldering the burden of balancing the world's economy and polity,[15] and the European countries that won the war, which had not yet understood that it was necessary to abandon a nationalist logic (and revenge) and embrace a new logic of European integration. Finally, we should note that the German reparations affair was not just an enormous political mistake. From an economic point of view the flow of international transfers was poorly conceived. Indeed, the United States, which wanted to be repaid for their loans, should have had a deficit balance of payments to absorb foreign capital. Instead it continued to carry a surplus balance of payments, and thus found itself in the position of having to finance the transfers sent to it, which in fact made its demands of being reimbursed impossible.

Table 9.6   Economic indicators relative to 1929 (1913 = 100).

Parameter	France	Germany	Italy	Britain	United States
Per capita income	135	111	121	112	130
Industrial production	142	120	158	128	193
Exports	147	92	123	101	158

Sources: Maddison, *Monitoring*; Feinstein, Temin & Toniolo, *The European Economy Between the Wars*; Maddison database for per capita income.

9.3   *Britain, France and Italy in the 1920s*

The 1920s saw a Europe incapable of breathing life into a new development cycle, due fundamentally to structural reasons and the international relations we've described in the preceding section. In addition to these reasons some countries added difficulties of their own, which led to various devel-

---

15. At most they accepted bilateral negotiations or, in the worst moments of the crisis, "bankers' diplomacy", which did not directly expose them officially.

opments and outcomes that were at times unexpected and paradoxical. Of the three largest economies discussed in this section, Britain, the pre-war leader, showed the most unsatisfactory progress. The economic weakness of the two European countries that had been the most solid prior to the war – Britain and Germany – was the cause of the slowdown throughout the whole of Europe during the 1920s. In this economically depressed setting both France and Italy, despite the turmoil of their political affairs, had less negative economic outcomes, for very different reasons. A comparative analysis will serve to compare internal political economies and international influences in order to draw a few conclusions.[16]

BRITAIN: THE PRIMACY OF THE POUND AT ALL COSTS

While Germany's difficulties were predictable, given the unreasonable conditions placed on it by the Treaty of Versailles, it is certainly more surprising to see that Britain, the victorious power, spiralled downward during the 1920s so that in 1929 its per capita income (see Table 9.6) was just barely above its pre-war level. Unemployment remained high (Table 9.7), fluctuating between 7 and 11 per cent during the entire decade, a rate similar only to that of Denmark, while exports stagnated. It is very curious indeed what produced such disastrous results. The Great War had weakened Britain financially as well as industrially and commercially. Its factories had not been renovated and its traditional exports had been displaced by other countries; in the meantime it had accumulated a debt of $4.7 billion to the United States, and its loans to its European allies were largely non-performing (Table 9.4). Inflation, although more under control than in other European countries, was higher than in the US, making a devaluation of the pound inevitable, but this was a move it wanted to avoid at all costs. Politicians and economists broadly shared the belief that the problems of the British economy would be resolved if the pre-war conditions were restored, one of which was monetary stability. When the Europeans returned to the gold standard, under American pressure from the Dawes Plan, Britain's decision in April 1925 was to return to the pre-war exchange rate with the dollar, $4.86 = £1.00 (see Table 9.5).

Moggridge has described in detail the British government's superficial analysis of the pre-war gold standard and their confidence that Britain remained a leading nation, and thus did not have to suffer the negative backlash of unco-operative decisions eventually made by other countries.[17] They referred to the

---

16. For an overview of the events of the 1920s, see Meier, *Recasting Bourgeois Europe*.
17. Moggridge, *British Monetary Policy 1924–31*.

Table 9.7   Incidence of industrial unemployment.

Date	France	Germany	Britain	United States
1920	–	3.8	3.2	8.6
1921	5.0	2.8	17.0	19.5
1922	2.0	1.5	14.3	11.4
1923	2.0	10.2	11.7	4.1
1924	3.0	13.1	10.3	8.3
1925	3.0	6.8	11.3	5.4
1926	3.0	18.0	12.5	2.9
1927	11.0	8.8	9.7	5.4
1928	4.0	8.6	10.8	6.9
1929	1.0	13.3	10.4	5.3
1930	2.0	22.7	16.1	14.2
1931	6.5	34.3	21.3	25.2
1932	15.4	43.5	22.1	36.3
1933	14.1	36.2	19.9	37.6
1934	13.8	20.5	16.7	32.6
1935	14.5	16.2	15.5	30.2
1936	10.4	12.0	13.1	25.4
1937	7.4	36.9	10.8	21.3
1938	7.8	3.2	12.9	27.9

Source: Oliver & Aldcroft, *Economic Disasters of the Twentieth Century*, 52 (Italy is not included).

traditional economic theory by which equilibrium would be restored through the flexibility of prices and wages, the proper application of the rules of the game, and the use of reserves. The British government's decision was not only supported by the City, which could not but see the strengthening of the pound as positive, but surprisingly even by the Federation of British Industries, which did not seem worried about the loss of competitiveness for exports.

Keynes was the only one who raised his voice – which was unfortunately unheard – against the Chancellor of the Exchequer, Winston Churchill's

decision in an impassioned article published immediately after the stabilization of the pound. He railed against the use of an obsolete theory that did not
correspond to actual behaviours,[18] foreseeing that the decision would keep the
British economy in a "chronic position of spurious equilibrium" by a policy
which acted to "hamper without hitting, to injure without killing and so to
get the worst of both possible worlds, overvaluation and deflation".[19] In fact,
to sustain the overvalued pound the government had to resort to a restrictive
monetary policy with high interest rates that discouraged investments, while
exports fell, also as a result of a prolonged miners' strike in 1926. The balance
of payments became negative and reserves ran low, creating significant problems for the Bank of England, which did not wish to resort to loans. The
situation only began to improve at the end of the decade, only to quickly
reverse again after the Great Depression.

FRANCE: A REALISTIC MONETARY STABILIZATION

There were many paradoxes in the French economy in the 1920s. The first was
that France, which had suffered huge losses in the war,[20] considered it essential to obtain the means for reconstruction through reparations, and it based
its peacetime diplomacy on doing this, but in reality it ended up rebuilding
with its own means, given the slowness and paucity of the payments made.
The recovery of Alsace-Lorraine, industrialized regions rich in raw materials
certainly played a positive role, as did the increased productive capacity of
heavy industry made during the war. But another paradox that should be
mentioned was the great political instability that afflicted the country, which
peaked between March 1924 and July 1926 with eleven different governments
in the space of 29 months, without ending in a dictatorship. As we shall see,
in a similar situation, Italian democracy did not hold out. France instead
found Raymond Poincaré,[21] a credible and capable gentleman, who was to
stabilize the franc on 23 July 1926 (although legally only in June 1928), which

18. He wrote "We ... are stupid ... if we continue to apply the principles of an economics
    which was worked out on the hypotheses of *laissez faire* and free competition to a soci-
    ety which is rapidly abandoning these hypotheses" in "The Economic Consequences of
    Mr. Churchill", cited by Pollard, *The Gold Standard and Employment Policies Between the
    Wars*, 38.
19. Quoted in Moggridge, *Maynard Keynes*, 490.
20. 1.3 million soldiers died plus 1.1 million seriously wounded, in addition to more than
    300,000 civilians; ten provinces destroyed; see also Table 9.1.
21. Raymond Poincaré (1860–1934) was one of the most respected men in French politics at
    the time.

restored order to the public finances and monetary policy without damaging French democracy.

A further paradox is related to the type of stabilization that was put in place. Counter to British suggestions, the franc was stabilized at the rate of 25.53 francs per dollar, in contrast with the pre-war rate of 5.18 francs; France simply acknowledged the devaluation that had happened between the war and postwar period, without attempting the recovery of the pre-war exchange rate. France's success was the flip side of Britain's failure, even though the British did not want to admit it; Britain continued to berate the *Banque de France* for having accumulated gold, and the French government for having permitted the devaluation for the purpose of taking foreign markets away from British exports. The fact is that in a world like that of the 1920s, which lacked multi-lateral international economic institutions, there was no way to coordinate decisions, nor was it legitimate to criticize unilateral decisions as imprudent and selfish when everyone acted from that view (including Britain!).

The French economy was the best performing of the three analysed here, even though Italy surpassed it in industrial production. In particular, exports, which increased around 50 per cent, and a significant increase in per capita income of about one-third, were its bright spots.

ITALY: FROM DEMOCRACY TO DICTATORSHIP

While France experienced great political turmoil, Italy's troubles were definitely dramatic, sliding it into a dictatorship that lasted twenty years. Many factors drove the country to leave democracy, something unthinkable in the pre-war years. We will list some of them quickly here:[22]

- The difficult process of converting industries from war-time to peace-time production, which could not be supported by the state because its finances were deeply in deficit, with the subsequent bankruptcy of companies and banks.
- The social conflict exacerbated by unemployment and inflation, which led to the occupation of lands and factories in the "Red Biennial" of 1919–20.
- Political developments, which saw, in 1919, the electoral system change from majority to proportional representation, heralding a period of minority governments that lacked the necessary authority.

---

22. See V. Zamagni, *An Economic History of Italy* for the details and bibliographic data, as well as Toniolo, *L'economia dell'Italia fascista*.

- The birth of Benito Mussolini's fascist movement in 1919, which began perpetrating illegal acts that the police did not adequately counter.
- King Victor Emmanuel's poor attitude towards liberalism – he did not want to use the army to block the march on Rome in 1922, instead handing power over to Mussolini, who was waiting in Milan. Mussolini arrived in Rome in a railway sleeping car to form his first government.

It is not easy to judge which of these factors carried the most weight in leading to the final outcome of Mussolini's rise to power. Certainly the impact of the war and the lack of any international aid for reconstruction were the initial causes that triggered the entire process, while the very limited practice of mass democracy (universal male suffrage had been introduced only in 1913) is the other underlying reason. Still, Mussolini's rise to power did not immediately break with previous policies. Indeed, he nominated Alberto De Stefani – a liberal academic economist, although close to fascism – as finance minister. De Stefani continued the previously begun process of rebalancing the public finances, to the point of having a balanced budget. Strikes were forbidden (unions were not abolished until 1925) and the economy rebounded, but with too high an inflationary trend, which prompted Mussolini to replace De Stefani with Giuseppe Volpi at the end of 1924; Volpi was a great Venetian financier and entrepreneur who had established the SADE electric company and CIGA, a company of grand hotels. Volpi had to face the problem of debt payments to Britain and the United States, which he managed to have almost entirely written off; he then had to stabilize the lira to rejoin the gold standard (Table 9.5).

At that juncture his desire to stabilize the lira at the market's current exchange rate, as had the French, was overruled by Mussolini; in a famous speech at Pesaro on 18 August 1926 he imposed "Quota 90", which was an exchange rate overvalued at ninety lire per pound sterling, roughly the same exchange rate in force when Mussolini came to power.[23] No one could say that Mussolini had let the lira "lose value"![24] At the same time, the public debt was consolidated, and the banking system was reformed such that the *Banca d'Italia* became for the first time the sole issuing bank.

As a result of these measures many economists, Keynes among them,

---

23. In any event this was a lesser rate than the pre-war rate of 25.5 lire.
24. There have been many interpretations of the "Quota 90", among them that of Cohen, "La rivalutazione della lira del 1927", in which the author maintains that, after closing down the Parliament at the end of 1925, Mussolini wanted to impose his will even on people in business.

expected a crisis due to the fall in exports and investments. In the event, the consolidation of the dictatorial regime, which allowed the government to manipulate prices and wages downwards without much difficulty, avoided a crisis of serious proportions, such that by 1928 recovery in the Italian economy had begun. The government devoted itself to organizing an "integral land reclamation" policy to structurally improve Italian agriculture, and conditions in the country seemed to return to normal. Overall, the 1920s were fairly positive for the Italian economy, which saw its industrial production increase in all sectors; this was particularly true in chemicals, where for the first time important new enterprises such as Montecatini and Snia Viscosa emerged (see Table 9.6 for an aggregate picture of the results). The traditional interpretation that the Italian economy stagnated under fascism cannot be accepted, although the fascist government's response to the 1929 crisis put the country on a very different track than one might have expected from a democratic government.

9.4 *The "Roaring '20s" in the United States*

In the United States the 1920s were a decade of rapid economic growth, and particularly of profound socio-cultural changes based on the emergence of a mass consumer society. Republican governments reduced taxation on the wealthiest classes, which had been heavily taxed during the war years even though American participation was mostly indirect. This move, along with an expansive monetary policy, created a favourable investment climate. Consumption was promoted by a policy of rising wages, due to the welfare capitalism Henry Ford had inaugurated immediately after the war,[25] which especially came into practice in the 1920s. However, the leading role of the large American firms in politics and society marginalized the unions, which contributed to the growing inequalities that gained ground in the United States during this decade, despite the expansion of the base levels of consumption. The typical American model of industrialization based on standardized mass production was established particularly with the car, the radio, the phonograph, the telephone, the cinema, electricity, chemicals and the refrigerator. These new products required massive investments in infrastructure, largely financed by the state, which accelerated urbanization, while

---

25. See Tone, *The Business of Benevolence*, which clarifies that this welfare capitalism was practiced by just a few companies, and it was not very consistent.

the agricultural sector lost heavily. In 1929 5.5 million cars were produced,[26] and 20 million were already in circulation (60 per cent of American families had at least one). Again in 1929, 40 per cent of families had a telephone, 45 per cent had a radio and 70 per cent had electricity.

On the social level, granting the vote to women in 1920, eliminating some discriminatory laws, and the high demand for labour by corporations changed the role of women; they became more independent, their presence grew in the working world, and even fashion shifted towards more comfortable and less constrained clothing.[27] These were also the years of Prohibition, the ban on producing, importing, selling, and in the final years, even consuming alcohol. Introduced in 1919 with the Volstead Act (which was repealed in 1933), a side effect was the emergence of Al Capone-style organized crime to circumvent the ban on alcohol consumption. Jazz became popular, and sports expanded. All this was defined as the "American way of life", consisting of the consumption of durable goods, free enterprise and breaking traditions; which the Europeans could not allow due to their small, protected markets, which prevented the introduction of mass production. Hence Herbert Hoover's 1928 presidential campaign slogan: "A chicken in every pot and a car in every garage."

---

26. A record that was equalled only 20 years later.
27. Brown, *Setting a Course*.

The Soviet Union, 1917–39

10.1 *The October Revolution*

The First World War caught Russia in an inchoate period of its capitalist transformation; land privatization under the Stolypin reforms was in its early stages, and the industrial take-off was localized in only a few cities and areas of this immense territory (see Chapter 4). Despite this, and the fact that per capita income was one-third that of Britain, Russia was driven to participate in the Great War by the Allies under pressure from France, as well as to assert its role as a great power – a *leitmotif* that will remain typical of the country. But the Russian economy and society were not able to meet the enormous resource expenditures for a war that by then was fought on the basis of a country's industrial strength, nor were they logistically prepared to face up to the reorganization and regulation of the markets forced upon them by war. It became particularly difficult to ensure adequate food supply for the soldiers and the industrial cities that produced the arms for the war, leading to general discontent, especially among the populace that was not motivated to fight. This led to the deposition of the Czar in January 1917 in a "bourgeois revolution" which brought in a new government run by Alexander Kerensky.[1]

Perhaps the most serious error of the new government was to declare that the war would continue, without any well-grounded hopes of being able to improve the organization of the country. In the growing chaos it was relatively easy for the socialist propaganda of Lenin and the Bolshevik Party to find a receptive audience among the people; in October 1917 the Bolsheviks launched an attack on the bourgeois government, taking the Winter Palace in St Petersburg. Four years of civil war followed, during which time the

---

1. Gregory, *Before Command.*

economy operated under Lenin's War Communism.[2] This entailed a return to barter: money had been eliminated, private trade abolished, workers were militarized and paid in-kind (with vouchers) at a subsistence level, agricultural produce was requisitioned (everything that was not hidden!), industry was nationalized, and essential services (mail, housing, gas, electricity, public transport) were freely provided at a basic level. It is no surprise that the impact on production levels was catastrophic (see Table 10.1). Industrial production fell to one-fifth of what it had been in 1913, agricultural production to two-thirds, and exports and imports vanished.

Table 10.1 The Russian economic situation in 1920 (1913 = 100).

Date	Agriculture	Industry	Transport	Exports	Imports
1913	100	100	100	100	100
1920	64	20	22	0.1	2.1

Source: Gregory & Stuart, *Soviet Economic Structure and Performance*, table 8.

Some scholars maintain that this was an inevitable result of civil war; others instead hold that it was by design and a stage in implementing a complete communist revolution. Either way the Communist Party and its supporters succeeded in taking over the entire country by winning the civil war and at that point urgent decisions were necessary on the direction of the economy of the new Soviet state.

10.2 *The New Economic Policy*

In 1921 Lenin launched the New Economic Policy (NEP), which ended rationing and requisitions in an attempt to combine the market with elements of socialism. Money was reintroduced, and restrictions on trade and industry were lifted for small companies under twenty employees, but above all the hallmark of the NEP was the surprising liberalization of agriculture. Lenin hoped to induce farmers to produce more, and sell more on the market, with typically capitalist price incentives; he imposed a proportional tax of the type in force under the Czars. Of the large nationalized industrial compa-

---

2. Despite the fact that Russia exited the First World War in March 1918, after negotiating a separate peace with the Treaty of Brest-Litovsk.

nies, only those held to be strategic (the military industries, transportation, finance and foreign trade) were placed under centralized control; the others were left some autonomy, even to form trusts. These groups were allowed to independently sign contracts and follow the principles of efficiency and resource optimization, and they paid taxes to the state based on income and capital. Their general strategy alone was determined by the Supreme Council of the National Economy (the VSNKh), which was already operating during the war communism period.[3]

We can characterize the NEP as the first experiment in a mixed economy, in which the state played a general planning role and managed a series of nationalized companies, while leaving the rest to the operation of the market within a monetized economy; in this sense it anticipated the Nazi experiment during the 1930s and that of the French during the 1950s and 1960s. In terms of production it achieved positive results that allowed the economy to recover (see Table 10.2); it even attained some level of recovery in foreign trade, in spite of discriminatory attitudes by many Western powers.[4] However, the NEP had some inherent flaws and maintained aspects of the capitalist system that were unacceptable to some members of the Bolshevik Party.

The NEP's flaws have been clearly documented in an article by Johnson and Temin.[5] First, since the trusts held the prices of manufactured goods high and imposing agricultural price hikes was repugnant to a Bolshevik mentality, a "Scissors Crisis" developed which saw a widening gap (price scissors) between industrial and agricultural prices. Second, the importance of macroeconomic controls was not understood, which led to inflation and unemployment, which were further abhorrent aspects of a market economy. Furthermore, there was a longstanding disaffection by part of the party with the "favours" granted to growers and merchants – the "enemies" of the people – and the speculative component inherent in the market mechanism. Finally, the "slowness" of the market system in attaining the goals the Bolshevik Party had set for the economy, particularly that of a forced rearmament, had widened the gap between the Soviet economy and those in the West.[6]

---

3. See Graziosi, "Building the First System of State Industry in History"; Graziosi, *L'Unione Sovietica, 1914–1991*.
4. Note that this attitude had been engendered, among other things, by the USSR's refusal to recognize the foreign debt of the Czars.
5. Johnson & Temin, "The Macroeconomics of NEP".
6. For more details on the economy of the NEP and the later planned economy, see Davies, Harrison & Wheatcroft, *The Economic Transformation of the Soviet Union, 1913–1945*.

Table 10.2   Soviet economy indicators in 1928 (1913 = 100).

Date	Per capita income			Other indicators in 1928	1913 index = 100
	in 1990 $	1950 index = 100	Annual growth rates		
1913	1,488	52	–	Grain production	87
1928	1,370	48	–0.5	Cast iron	79
1937	2,156	76	5.1	Steel	102
1940	2,144	75	0	Coal	122
1947	2,126	75	0	Cotton textiles	104
1950	2,841	100	9.5	Transportation	104
1973	6,059	213	3.3	Electricity	203
1989	7,112	250	1.0	Exports	38

Source: Gregory & Stuart, *Soviet Economic Structure and Performance*, table 9; Maddison database.

All these contradictions and discontents erupted after Lenin's death, which resulted in three alternative economic strategies emerging.[7]

1 The vision of the left wing of the party, led by Preobrazhensky, recommended an industrial "great leap", especially in heavy industry. He advocated an unbalanced industrial growth to the detriment of agriculture, which he held should be left in private hands.
2 The vision of the extreme right of the party, advocated by Shanin, which argued for a return to Russian agrarian traditions, on the basis that higher agricultural productivity would increase savings and keep the cost of food low, allowing industry to grow without inflation.
3 The vision of the right wing of the party, supported by Bukharin, advocated balanced growth to continue along the lines of the NEP.

While the debate unfolded, Stalin, as General Secretary of the Communist Party, did not offer an independent contribution, but rather aligned himself instead with Bukharin's position; he emphasized the positive results of the NEP and ridiculed the left's proposal of super-industrialization. However,

7. See Gregory & Stuart, *Soviet Economic Structure* and also Sherer, *Industry, State and Society in Stalin's Russia 1926–34.*

the USSR's foreign relations worsened in 1927, while the internal problems of grain availability in urban markets multiplied. To increase availability Stalin ended up adopting increasingly coercive measures, personally directing the grain harvests in Siberia. He became increasingly convinced there was no way to achieve the industrial growth projects pressing on the party other than by crushing the farmers once and for all.[8] From this his unexpected and increasingly drastic version of the left's vision of forced super-industrialization at the expense of agriculture emerged. Distinguished mathematicians assured him that a means existed for planning the economy without using money, by using input-output models and identifying goals in physical terms, which reinforced his intention to abolish the market and transition to a command economy.[9]

10.3 *Soviet planning*

In October 1928, Stalin – by then party leader after the purges had removed, among others, Trotsky – launched the first Five Year plan in the midst of another grain harvest crisis. Stalin's response was not slow in coming, and in the autumn of 1929 he declared the collectivization of land. Protests were widespread, not only in the countryside but even in some cities that had seen vast immigration by peasants, and this only strengthened Stalin's tendency to govern with violence. Thus, in 1929, the era of Soviet planning began. How did it operate? The central coordinating body was the Gosplan (State Planning Committee); it had existed in the 1920s but had been marginalized by the VSNKh, and the latter was now superseded. Gosplan set the annual goals – and only those goals – that the economy should achieve, and the party's Politburo directly controlled the main ones. The operational plans for each industrial sector and for each company were worked out from the Gosplan goals, which constituted an integral, top-down *dirigiste* system. Raw materials were distributed to plants with volume based input-output matrices and prices were set by Gosplan according to criteria that were consistent with the plan's goals, using price discrimination and multiple prices.

It was precisely this last characteristic of fully administered prices that caused

---

8. Historians do not agree that this decision by Stalin was inevitable. See, for example, Allen, "Agricultural Marketing and the Possibilities for Industrialization in the Soviet Union in the 1930s" who concludes that "Stalin was wrong – there was no need to force Soviet peasants to sell food. They would have done it anyway – voluntarily" (407).

9. See Allen, *Farm to Factory*.

prices in the USSR to lose their connection with production costs and the scarcity or abundance of goods with respect to their relative demand, resulting in the phenomena of excess supply or demand. Excess demand was dealt with by rationing and queues rather than by price hikes. These same administered prices explain the enormous difficulties encountered by Western observers in valuing the USSR's national income; the figures presented by Soviet sources were not comparable with that of other countries and presented serious recalculation problems, since it was not clear which prices to use in the operation.[10]

But the flaws in Soviet central planning go well beyond the problems of administered prices. The rigidity of the Five Year Plan was one of the central weaknesses: as it was impossible to perfectly predict the future, it became necessary to modify the plan, which typically happened after a long delay and with negative repercussions on the affected supply chain.[11] Paradoxically it was precisely to obviate these problems that the market, which had been driven out the door, had its revenge; factory managers were forced to turn to informal markets to get rid of excess product and acquire what they lacked in order to meet the objectives of the plan.[12] Frequently, however, the plan's objectives were completely unattainable.

Another serious problem, perhaps the most serious of all, was technology. During the NEP more than 2000 German engineers had helped the Soviets to catch up technologically, while many Soviet engineers were sent abroad to learn. According to Sutton, between 1917 and 1930 home-grown Soviet technology was non-existent; rather, the country limited itself to introducing Western models.[13] At the beginning of Stalinist planning the American models of products, but especially of production processes were preferred, not least because they were better adapted to the enormous size of the Soviet factories. During the years from 1930–33[14] the Americans provided massive technology injections, such that in a second volume covering the period, 1930–45 Sutton

---

10. There were also deliberate alterations in the data, particularly the demographic data, to conceal certain realities; see Davies, Harrison & Wheatcroft, *Economic Transformation*, 29.

11. Zaleski, *Stalinist Planning for Economic Growth, 1933–1952*. See also Carr, *History of Soviet Russia, Vol. IV*.

12. Temin, "Soviet and Nazi Economic Planning in the 1930s", writes that in 1930 there were 2,500 "barter agents" in Moscow alone (575).

13. Sutton, *Western Technology and Soviet Economic Development 1917 to 1930*. An attempt to produce a Soviet tractor is perhaps the only example of an attempt at originality, but it was soon abandoned in favour of introducing American models such as Fordson, Caterpillar and Harvester. Even attempts to improve Western models were abandoned because they slowed down the production process.

14. The majority of foreign engineers left the USSR in 1932.

maintained that under Stalin also there was no possibility of the Soviet Union producing a native technology, with the partial exception of synthetic rubber.[15] The real problem in a planned system is the difficulty of producing technology endogenously, given that the timing and characteristics of new technologies are not plannable in advance. It is also well known that research requires spaces for intellectual freedom that are unthinkable in a police state such as Stalin's.[16]

Table 10.3   Results achieved by Soviet planning, 1928–40.

	1928	1937	1940
Structure of GNP per productive sector (%)			
Agriculture	49	31	29
Industry	28	45	45
Services	23	24	26
Transformation of the industrial sector			
% heavy industry	31	63	–
% light industry	69	34	–
Structure of GNP per end use (%)			
Personal consumption	82	55	49
Public services	5	11	11
Public administration and defence	3	11	21
Investment	10	23	19

Source: Gregory & Stuart, *Soviet Economic Structure and Performance*, tables 10, 16.

Even the introduction of foreign technology presented problems, often attributed to acts of sabotage, resulting in even more vicious purges,[17] but in reality they were due to the technical unpreparedness of both Soviet engineers

---

15. Sutton, *Western Technology and Soviet Economic Development 1930 to 1945*.
16. Sutton produced a third volume that covered the years up to 1965 (*Western Technology and Soviet Economic Development 1945 to 1965*, in which he maintained that the USSR was not innovative even after the war, receiving technical assistance from the West in many cases or remaining undeveloped in many others. The one exception was the military complex, where many foreigners worked, in which there were no limits on resources and people enjoyed some limited freedom. His conclusion was that the lack of liberty and the planning system made technological creativity impossible.
17. It has been calculated that at least 2 million people were killed in Stalin's purges.

and workers – many of which were taken directly from the fields – in addition to the inevitable errors in the plans. The fact remains that, according to Western estimates, both the first (1928–32) and the second (1933–37) Five Year Plans reached 70 per cent of their objectives.[18] Despite all these difficulties, a number of important results desired by the planners did succeed (as can be seen in Tables 10.2 and 10.3). Industry's "great leap" meant that national income grew at a sustained rate; although income growth was not dramatic, it was achieved at a time of great crisis in Western capitalist economies (see Chapter 11). Agriculture instead saw some dramatic turns of events. Indeed, forced collectivization created a crisis in which the farmers themselves primarily bore the consequences. Its worst year was 1932, with a famine that killed between six and eight million people.[19] Agriculture did then recover, but with output fluctuating around levels barely above those of 1913. Within the industrial sector, heavy industry in particular was privileged, with a strong shift in the composition of GDP from consumption to investments and defence. Over all we can conclude that Stalinist planning produced a forced industrialization that benefited defence industries and the country's infrastructure, which was accompanied by a small increase in per capita personal consumption, driven by an increase in the consumption of manufactured products.[20]

10.4 *Victory in the Second World War and its aftermath*

We can easily understand why the country found itself in better shape to face the Second World War than it had the first. Wartime mobilization was much more efficient in improving infrastructure and increasing military production capacity and the central control of agriculture avoided disorganization in the food supply. However, we should not forget two other significant factors that explain how the USSR defeated the much more advanced Germans. The first, known already to Napoleon, was the vastness of the territory and the sheer size of its population, which together wore down the enemy. Consider that during the Second World War Russia lost 9 million soldiers, in addition to over

---

18. Gregory & Stuart, *Soviet Economic Structure*, table 11.
19. The estimates are imprecise because they are indirect, given that the regime hid the true extent of the disaster.
20. Allen, *Farm to Factory*, ch. 7, proposes a more favourable revision of the results of the early Soviet plans, based on the standard of living of the population.

16 million civilians.[21] The second factor is one of the ironies of history. After the battle of Stalingrad, in which the Russians showed themselves to be at the limits of their ability to hold out, the Americans launched a vast operation in support (estimated at around $10 billion of the time) providing fighter planes, tanks, jeeps, trucks and canned food; communications equipment, which the Russians did not have, was particularly important in coordinating operations in such a vast territory as Russia.

According to Harrison, the American aid, calculated in Soviet prices, amounted to about 10 per cent of Soviet GDP during 1943–4; this was a sum that did not have to be subtracted from its already tight consumption, and it also included goods that could not be produced in the Soviet system.[22] This highlights the vital role American aid played in allowing the Russians to win the war alongside the Allies – an outcome that later turned against the Allies. This is why we spoke of an irony of history: America contributed towards a decisive victory by the Russians, who then were the only nation to oppose America's great power status until the mid-1980s!

21. In the First World War, 2 million soldiers were killed, and another million during the civil war; 11 million civilians disappeared, most of them due to the civil war. See Harrison, *The Economics of World War II*.
22. Harrison, *Accounting for War*. For a long-term view, see Werth, *Storia dell'Unione Sovietica*.

11

The first major international crisis

11.1 *The theories*

At the end of the 1920s a crisis developed in the Western capitalist countries on a scale never seen before. While it is true that economists and economic historians have always observed that the capitalist system is cyclical, there is much disagreement over the interpretation of these cycles.[1] There are essentially four schools of thought on the matter:

- The *instability* school, which holds that the capitalist system is intrinsically unstable; Malthus, Marx and Keynes were among its adherents. Marx wrote of the internal contradictions of the system due to the anarchy of the market and chronic underconsumption (the latter an aspect Malthus had already described), contradictions that would lead capitalism to self-destruct. Right after the Great Depression, Keynes formulated a theory of stabilizing interventions by the state in order to counter a drop in effective demand; this is a theme we will consider at the end of this chapter.
- The *stability* school, which holds that the market is capable of absorbing the shocks of various sorts to which it is subject, and of restoring equilibrium to the system. This school includes most neoclassical economists, and it has never had an interest in proposing specific measures of economic policy.[2]

---

1. Kindleberger has worked extensively on the cycles, particularly the financial ones, identifying a long list in his *Manias, Panics and Crashes*.
2. In *The Great Crash*, J. K. Galbraith sketched a vivid picture of reassuring statements by economists of the time, who insisted on not considering the crisis as a serious one, even after the entire world had suffered.

- The *cyclical* school places the cycle at the centre of its theorizing. The best known exponent is Schumpeter, with his long run development cycle inspired by the Russian economist Kondratieff, whom we discussed at the beginning of Chapter 7.[3] We should also mention Kuznets's theory of the infrastructure cycle of 15–20 years, which accompanies and reinforces the long cycle created by technological change.[4] Market saturation is a key feature of development cycles. This saturation can be the effect of a thorough dissemination of an existing technology, which leads to demand only for worn-out replacement goods, and gives rise to long-term stagnation if no innovations are produced. There can also be a "spurious" saturation due to the growth of inequality: if the rich become ever richer and the poor do not increase their income, there will be a high availability of capitals for investments, but the effective demand will not increase.[5] This generates overproduction and a tendency for capital to seek financial investments, which creates financial bubbles and widespread crises. During the 1920s in the United States there was precisely this increase in inequality, which produced a "spurious" stagnation of effective demand (see Figure 11.1, which also reports the analogous increase in inequality recorded prior to the 2007 crisis).
- There is also a *financial* cycle theory, which seeks to explain how financial bubbles are created, from euphoria to panic. Hyman Minsky is credited with developing this financial cycle theory[6] which is essentially a stage theory, with the length of the final stage, when the crisis reaches a floor, dependent on whether an effective and comprehensive intervention plan takes shape.

The cycle theories are especially useful for explaining what happened between the late 1920s and the early 1930s, but before doing so a brief overview of the particular historical global circumstances will be useful.

---

3. See van Duijn, *The Long Wave in Economic Life*; Zarnowitz, *Business Cycles* and Thygesen, Velupillai & Zambelli, *Business Cycles*.
4. Each new technological paradigm requires investments in infrastructure: consider the locomotive with its railways, cars and their roads, electricity with its dams and long-distance transmission, the aeroplane with airports, and so forth.
5. There were enormous dividends to shareholders during those years.
6. Minsky, *The Financial Instability Hypothesis* and *J. M. Keynes*.

Figure 11.1 Income percentage of the top 1% of US population, 1913–2011

Notes: ■ including capital gains □ excluding capital gains

Source: Piketty & Saez, "Income Inequality in the USA 1913–1998", *Quarterly Journal of Economics*, 2003, (updated to 2011).

11.2 *Facts and interpretations*

The traditional starting-point for the Great Depression was the collapse in share prices on the New York Stock Exchange over a series of "black" days, beginning 24 October 1929. There had been signs of a downturn earlier, and we should restate that the German economy – which became the second centre of the crisis – had already entered severe difficulties a year earlier at the end of 1928.[7] The economies of many countries then crashed without seeing a recovery until 1932–3;[8] the industrial sectors in particular contracted, (Table 11.1), and international trade collapsed to one-third of its value (due to the fall in prices) and 40 per cent of its volume.[9] Germany (as well as Austria) and the United

---

7. Weder, *Some Observations on the Great Depression in Germany.*
8. As in Austria, Canada, the United States, Czechoslovakia and Poland. In Spain, which was relatively untouched by the crisis, there was great economic disruption when civil war broke out in 1936.
9. Findlay & O'Rourke, *Power and Plenty*, 450.

States were the two hardest hit countries. Since the German crisis began first we can say that this was a bipolar crisis, with a locus both in Europe and in the United States, although the latter has been studied much more. The duration and severity of the crisis were greater than any previous crisis in the industrial capitalist system.[10] Even those European countries that seemed to weather the storm in terms of income were to suffer more negative consequences at other times (as we will see in Chapter 12). Japan was largely spared.

Table 11.1   The fall in income and industrial production between 1929 and 1932.

Country	GDP in 1932 (1929 = 100)	Industrial production in 1932 (1929 = 100)
Austria	79	62
France	84	74
Germany	83	61
Britain	94	89
Italy	94*	84*
The Netherlands	89	86
Spain	93	84
Japan	97	–
United States	71	62

Note: *a recent revision places the level of Italian industrial production at 74 and GDP at 84.

Sources: Maddison database; Maddison, *Monitoring*; Feinstein, Temin & Toniolo, *The European Economy Between the Wars*.

There is a vast literature on the reasons for such a large-scale crisis, which we cannot review here, but a certain amount of consensus exists around the following causes.[11]

---

10. The crises of the pre-industrial era were less cyclical and were related to wars, famines and epidemics, which could be so devastating as to wipe out entire populations or decimate generations, setting the economy back decades or even centuries.

11. Eichengreen's works have summarized and clarified the conclusions reached by the literature; see his *Essays in the History of International Finance 1919–39* and *Golden Fetters* as well as "The Origins and Nature of the Great Slump Revisited". See also Rowland, *Balance of Power or Hegemony?* and Temin, *Lessons from the Great Depression*.

- The structural changes in the economy that had taken place during the 1920s had made both the products market (by increasing the degree of monopoly) and the factors market (particularly the labour factor) much less flexible than before, which made it more difficult to automatically re-establish equilibrium after a shock.
- The international monetary system had reintroduced the gold standard during the 1920s, but under highly imbalanced conditions (as described in Chapter 9). Furthermore, the United States had changed its role from that of a net debtor to that of a net creditor, but without following the rules of the game for the proper functioning of the gold standard and without allowing net transfers from Europe (see Chapter 9). This made the system unstable and barely functional.[12]
- The role of the New York Stock Exchange crash has been over-emphasized both as a trigger and as its main cause; production, income, investments and prices had begun to decline at least three months earlier in the United States and a year before in Germany. There have been stock market crashes, both before and after the one in 1929, that have been larger but without such serious consequences.[13]
- What immediately made the crisis so severe were tight monetary policies[14] in both the United States and Germany, which, in the absence of a lender of last resort, produced financial panic, chains of failures and deflation.[15] (We shall see later that in some countries there was a more or less timely and effective intervention plan that acted at the national level.)
- The propagation of the crisis from those countries that generated it to other economies was helped by the mechanisms of the gold standard, the lack of coordination between economies, falling prices accompanied by a poorly interpreted fiscal orthodoxy (there was still a belief in balanced budgets, even when revenue reductions drove governments to cut spending and increase taxes right in the middle of the crisis), and growing protectionism (in 1931 all countries, including the United States, which

---

12. See Boyce, *The Great Interwar Crisis*, who writes: "Leading international bankers privately acknowledged as early as July 1927 that the international payment system was severely dislocated" (243).

13. The measurement of the Dow Jones index between October 1928 and September 1929 has been called into question, due to the inclusion of many new companies that gave an exaggerated positive impulse to the index itself, while the economy was clearly losing steam.

14. There is boundless literature on this point; see, for example, Parker, *Reflections on the Great Depression* and the interesting comparative essays in White, *Crashes and Panics*.

15. The absence of an international lender of last resort is the chief explanation for the crisis offered by the well-known work by Kindleberger, *The World in Depression 1929–1939*.

did not have balance of payments problems, substantially increased their levels of protection, with so-called "beggar thy neighbour" policies).

It is reasonable to say that the economic policies that had until then been pursued with generally positive results were shown to be inadequate, because a series of near simultaneous events deprived domestic economies and the international economy of compensatory factors. Take protectionism, for example: if a country increases its protections it may import less and export more, but if all countries increase their protections simultaneously the decrease in imports by all countries will decrease the exports of all countries, given that on the whole imports and exports at the world level are of equal value. The decrease in exports will cause a decrease in income resulting in a downward spiral. This also applies to fiscal policy; while in general a balanced budget is a good rule, when faced with a grave crisis it is necessary to put counter-cyclical compensating factors into effect, as Keynes taught the world in *The General Theory of Employment, Interest, and Money* (1936) written in the wake of the dramatic events of the Great Depression.

Completing this negative set of circumstances was deflation, which, since it was not countered, continued to lower prices; this created economic difficulties even for healthy companies, as they produced at prevailing prices and wages but were forced to sell at lower prices. Furthermore, the lack of either absolute or relative income support mechanisms for the unemployed caused effective demand to collapse into a bottomless spiral.

11.3 *Repercussions on banking*

It is clear from what we have said so far that the banks did not play a leading role in the 1929 crisis; however, when the crisis worsened, they were incapable of supporting the burden of so many outstanding loans. The chain of events linked to the ensuing banking crisis was the most spectacular; it showed the level of interconnectedness attained by the global economy and the need for international economic governance, which was set in place only after the end of the Second World War.[16] We shall follow it in some detail. The banks' situation began to worsen in the spring of 1931, with the failure of Austria's largest mixed

---

16. See Wicker, *The Banking Panics of the Great Depression*. On the lessons of the financial crisis of the 1930s see Minsky, *Can "It" Happen Again?*.

bank, *Creditanstalt* in May.[17] Not unlike the story of the Italian mixed banks in the 1920s, the difficult conditions in the country drove the *Creditanstalt* – under pressure from the Austrian government – to increasingly support the companies linked to it, resulting in the acquisition of 60 per cent of the shares of Austrian public joint-stock companies. At the time of its failure, bad debts accounted for 70 per cent of its losses.[18] Furthermore, unlike the Italian banks, 50 per cent of its shares were in foreign hands (primarily due to the breakup of the Austro-Hungarian Empire), and 40 per cent of its activities were outside the country.[19] Since requests for help went unheeded (we have already mentioned that there was no mechanism for international intervention), the Austrian government intervened through the central bank, but only after a long delay. Controls on exchange rates were not introduced until October 1931, and the state decided to become the bank's major shareholder, which put the bank back on its feet without altering how it operated as a universal bank.

The inability to prevent the failure of the Viennese bank had even more serious repercussions; the contagion spread to the Hungarian banks, who were the first to go into crisis, then the German banks quickly followed. Between the end of May and mid-June the *Reichsbank* lost half of its gold reserves (recall that the gold standard was still in effect). The United States had to rush to Germany's aid, and on 20 June President Hoover agreed to a moratorium on reparations payments and war debts, overcoming France's hostility only with difficulty. Attempts were made to organize an international loan, but with little success. In July the banking crisis exploded with the failure of the *Danat*, one of the country's four largest banks. The German government decided to close the banks and stock market for a week; it prepared a package of measures, among them raising the interest rate to 10 per cent and injecting liquidity into the mixed banks. The *Danat* was merged with the *DresdnerBank*, and as with the *CommerzBank*, its majority ownership became public (public participation in the *DeutscheBank* was only one-third). In these instances as well the banks' operations were not changed, and they became private again at the end of the 1930s[20] (see Table 11.2).

---

17. On the behaviour of the European banks during the interwar period, see the excellent collection, Feinstein, *Banking, Currency and Finance in Europe Between the Wars*.
18. All this information is derived from Schubert, *The Credit-Anstalt Crisis of 1931*.
19. This made the subsequent bailout even more difficult, necessitating separating out the foreign activities of the bank, which was then merged with other banks, making it even more the national banking "champion". See Stiefel, "The Reconstruction of the Credit-Anstalt".
20. Temin is of the view that it was not bad management of the German banks that led to these difficulties, but the repercussions of a restrictive monetary policy; see Temin, "The German Crisis of 1931".

Table 11.2 Bailouts of large German universal banks by the Central Bank and by the German state.

Property as % of capital after the bailout	Deutsche Bank	Dresdner Bank*	Commerz Bank
Private	69	9	30
Central Bank	31	23	56
State	–	68	14

Note: *incorporating the Danat.

The effects of the German banking crisis spread throughout Europe, with a run on gold that ended up putting pressure on the Bank of England, which had only modest reserves due to the difficulties in the British economy in the 1920s (see Chapter 9).[21] There were widely diverging opinions on how best to address the banking crisis, to the point of provoking a crisis of government. The new National government that formed on 28 August 1931 increased taxes and reduced expenditures in a desperate attempt to balance the budget. However, on 16 September a strike by Royal Navy sailors stationed at Invergordon protesting at a reduction in pay was overblown by the press as a mutiny, which provoked further serious losses of gold by the Bank of England. The decision to abandon the gold standard loomed as inevitable, and on 19 September the Bank of England informed the Federal Reserve and the *Banque de France* of the decision. On 21 September Britain exited the gold standard, with particularly negative repercussions on the many countries that remained.

The crisis spread to Italy, where in September 1931 the directors of the three largest mixed banks had to ask Mussolini for help. Mussolini instructed his trusted man Alberto Beneduce (who became known as the economic dictator in the 1930s) to see to it.[22] Beneduce organized a two-phase bailout. In November 1931 he founded a new long-term public industrial credit institution, the *Istituto Mobiliare Italiano* (IMI), which assumed the role of financier in place of the mixed banks; he then relieved the mixed banks of their shareholdings through another public institution, the *Istituto per la Ricostruzione Industriale* (IRI), which was to manage the shares as a large holding. Finally, in 1936 a new banking law was enacted that abolished mixed banking practices in Italy, reducing the former-mixed banks to commercial banks owned

---

21. Williams, "London and the 1931 Financial Crisis".
22. Zamagni, *Economic History of Italy.*

by the IRI. The effects of the 1929 banking crisis in Italy were structural and enduring, as we will shall see in Chapter 12.

France was the only European country spared from financial crisis, due to its ample gold reserve (equal to 24 per cent of the global stock). Its most serious problem seems to have been unloading its reserves of devalued sterling without losing too much. However, this relative tranquillity did not prevent its economy from worsening; it did not recover, while the others slowly did (as we shall see in Chapter 12).

The 1931 banking crisis impacted the United States as well, with a serious increase in bank failures (see Table 11.3). On 7 October 1931 President Hoover, seeing that the Federal Reserve was not able to address the crisis, pushed the bankers to create the National Credit Corporation (NCC) for the purpose of stopping bank failures by direct interventions, but with little success. A year later he restructured the NCC as the Reconstruction Finance Corporation with public financing, but the organization was still unable to resolve the banking crisis, which dragged on until early 1933, when the entire American banking system was at risk. The new President Franklin Delano Roosevelt,

Table 11.3 American bank trends, 1921–33.

Date	Total number of banks	Total failed banks
1921	29,788	505
1922	29,458	366
1923	28,877	646
1924	28,185	775
1925	27,638	618
1926	26,751	976
1927	25,800	669
1928	24,968	498
1929	24,026	659
1930	22,172	1,350
1931	19,735	2,293
1932	17,802	1,453
1933	14,440	4,000

Source: Wicker, *The Banking Panics of the Great Depression*, 52.

shortly after taking office in early March, had to close the banks for a week. On 9 March an Emergency Act was issued, later incorporated in June into the Glass–Steagall Act, which maintained the small sizes of the American banks but divided their activities: deposit banks could not make long term investments, and investment banks could only place their own capital at risk, because they could not attract deposits. Deposit insurance was also introduced, paying interest on demand deposits was prohibited, the intervention powers of the Federal Reserve were broadened, and setting up a bank required authorization. An agency was also set up to monitor the stock market, the Securities and Exchange Commission, or SEC. These banking system regulations remained in force until the 1980s.

11.4 The lack of international cooperation and the emergence of an alternative way of thinking

While a few hesitant attempts were made at the international level to direct some flow of aid towards the growing hot spots in the crisis, the aid was completely inadequate, intermittent and negotiated bilaterally. As we've seen the only noteworthy initiative the international community was able to take was to oversee the reparations payments, which prompted the foundation of the Bank of International Settlements (or BIS) in Zurich on 20 January 1930. This institution lost its remit with Hoover's moratorium, and when Hitler decreed the end of payments it became a meeting place where central bankers could arrange international loans. The BIS was also a privileged place for training economists with international expertise, who were then hired by postwar international organizations, as well as a place for showcasing ideas and plans for reorganizing the international economic system. In the postwar years it functioned as a place for informally coordinating interventions by European central banks, anticipating European Central Bank (ECB) functions.

The June 1933 London Economic Conference is also worth mentioning; the decision to hold it was made at the end of 1932 and its aim was to explore measures to tackle the crisis. However, in April 1933, shortly before the meeting, the United States also left the gold standard. France and Italy remained, as part of the "gold bloc", as did Germany who could not leave according to the dictates of the Treaty of Versailles. There was now little hope of reaching a common opinion on how to fight the crisis, not least because all countries placed their own internal recoveries as their highest priority. They were not able to discuss reducing protectionism, stabilizing their currencies or even launching a common public expense program. The Conference ended with a few marginal agreements for show, such as those on grain sales and the price of silver.[23] It was not until 1936 that the Tripartite Accord was negotiated between the United States, Britain and France, which offered reciprocal support to each other's currencies in order to stabilize exchange rates. Additionally, if necessary, the United States agreed to provide gold or dollars to the other two countries at a price agreed in advance. It was a limited agreement and is generally remembered only because it was the first. As we shall see in Chapter 13, the international agreements signed after the end of the Second World War were much more substantial and enduring.

In conclusion, we can say that on the one hand the absence of international cooperation[24] made the gold standard a straitjacket that obstructed implementing a lender of last resort, while on the other the internal policies that aimed to balance the budget only worsened the situation. The automated mechanisms and customary economic orthodoxies no longer had a grip on a tightly interrelated global economy that was much more complex than the first industrial revolution. Without proper governance, the global economy became disjointed and discriminatory, with the emergence of economic blocs, all the while sliding towards a new worldwide conflict, a topic that we will develop in Chapter 12.

The Great Depression taught the industrialized world an important lesson, even though what was learnt was not put into practice in the 1930s. It is fair to say that Keynes, who was already active in the 1920s, drew inspiration from the events of the crisis to propose a general theoretical system for economic policies that was to become an alternative to the prevailing orthodoxy.[25] Starting from the demonstration that an economy can be caught by a low level equilibrium trap, with persistent unemployment and an unsatisfactory use of productive capacity, Keynes recommended counter-cyclic economic policies, with expansive monetary and fiscal policies when faced with falling demand, and restrictive policies when faced with excess demand. Keynes's thought had a profound influence on the postwar industrialized economies, and particularly that of the United States, although even today it has many critics.

---

23. See Clavin, *The Failure of Economic Diplomacy*.
24. Many economic historians have spoken of the "costs of non-cooperation", based on game theory. Among these, see Redmond, "The Gold Standard between the Wars".
25. Keynes, *The General Theory of Employment, Interest and Money*.

12

The 1930s and the Second World War

During the 1930s, the global economy suffered its only downturn since the Napoleonic Wars; see Table 8.1, which shows that since 1820 the interwar years were the only ones in which international trade was falling.[1] The domestic events within the principal European countries followed different paths, because they responded differently to the financial crisis and had different strategies of rearmament.[2] The drama of the events that plunged Europe into a new period of barbarism and violence, which was overcome thanks only to the resolute intervention of the United States, merits detailed analysis. In this chapter we will evaluate the crucial steps that led Germany to Hitler's dictatorship, Italy's imperialistic adventures and subsequent alliance with Hitler, and France's total unpreparedness for war. While the British economy was the only one that had a nearly normal recovery, it turned out to be insufficient to prepare it to withstand the German onslaught without America's decisive help.

12.1 *Britain and the gold standard*

We saw in Chapter 11 that Britain had been forced to leave the gold standard in September 1931. Over the course of 1932 the pound devalued by about

---

1. See Roselli, *Money and Trade Wars in Interwar Europe*.
2. For a comparative overview of the reactions to the crisis, including Britain, Sweden, Germany, France, the United States and Eastern Europe, see Garside, *Capitalism in Crisis*. Some interesting reflections on the cultural and moral import of the events during the 1920s and 1930s can be found in Overy, *The Interwar Crisis 1919–39*. See also Kaiser, *Economic Diplomacy and the Origin of the Second World War*.

30 per cent against the dollar and the French franc; however the benefits to the British economy should be measured by taking into account other currencies as well, against which the pound lost little or no value. The average devaluation in 1932 was actually around 13 per cent, and the following year it was down to 9 per cent.[3] But this was not the most important benefit for the British economy of leaving the gold standard; decoupling from the gold standard finally allowed an expansionist internal monetary policy, with low interest rates to incentivize investments, particularly in the construction industry. Indeed, industrial production and construction recovered significantly, positioning Britain in a select club of countries that had a consistent recovery through the 1930s.[4]

Although unemployment decreased, it still remained at the high levels of the 1920s (see Table 9.3), which has given rise to a vast literature speculating on the causes of such high unemployment. Some scholars have held that it can be attributed to the lack of a Keynesian fiscal policy, pointing to the fact that public spending did not increase until after 1938, when Britain had to rearm itself.[5] Others lean towards structural causes: investments were largely in making companies more efficient through mergers, and these initiatives were largely concentrated on new industries, while the traditional, older British industries did not benefit, which is where unemployment was largely concentrated.[6]

Britain initiated a policy of rearmament only from 1938 onwards, when concerns about German rearmament became truly serious. It was clear to British politicians at the time that British military resources were not on a par with Germany's accumulated weapons stocks. However, Britain felt it could count on its privileged relationship with the United States. Indeed, Viscount

3. See Redmond, "An Indicator of the Effective Exchange Rate of the Pound in the 1930s". For a general overview see Hentschel, "Indicators of Real Effective Exchange Rates of Major Trading Nations from 1922 to 1937".
4. In 1937 the index of industrial production was 30 per cent higher than in 1929, exceeded only by the Scandinavian countries, which left the gold standard along with Britain and Greece.
5. All agree that a more expansive public spending policy could have helped in the circumstances, but many raise doubts on its feasibility in a setting such as the 1930s; see Middleton, *Towards the Managed Economy* and Dimsdale & Horsewood, "A Model of the UK Economy in the Interwar Period".
6. Among the many contributions see: Booth & Glynn, "Unemployment in the Interwar Period"; Peden, "Keynes, the Treasury and Unemployment in the Late Nineteen-thirties"; Hatton, "Unemployment Benefits and the Macroeconomics of the Interwar Labour Market"; Broadberry & Crafts, "The Implications of British Macroeconomic Policy in the 1930s for the Long Run Performance".

Halifax, the Foreign Secretary, stated in 1939 that "it would be reasonably safe to assume that when the war had continued for some time the attitude of the US would be sufficiently favourable to us to enable us to win the war".[7] The war was won, but the Americans were the ones who won it; in the process they anchored their hegemony throughout the world, while Britain became a weaker power.

One final aspect of the British economy during the 1930s should be mentioned, due to its important consequences after the war ended. At the end of 1931 Britain also returned to protectionism;[8] international conditions no longer existed for it to continue to be the standard-bearer for free trade, but under the Ottawa Agreement it granted preferential trading status to countries in the Commonwealth. This favoured further concentration of British foreign trade with the colonies: at the end of the 1930s half of Britain's exports and around 40 per cent of its imports were with its colonies.[9] According to Drummond, this was obtained at a high cost of concessions to the colonies, which marked the beginning of favourable conditions for decolonization.[10] In 1938 only 30 per cent of British exports were to Europe, which dropped to 20 per cent after the end of the war. The implications of this were that Britain initially had little interest in the process of European integration, and the British economy suffered a serious postwar impact due to decolonization.

12.2 *Germany's reflation and rearmament*

We said in Chapter 11 that Germany applied the deflationary policies that all countries practised, but that they applied them in the extreme. Taxes were ruthlessly increased and interest rates soared to unimaginable levels, which heralded the collapse of the German economy, (see Table 11.1).[11] All this

---

7. Parker, "Economics, Rearmament and Foreign Policy", 645.
8. The effects of the reintroduction of protectionism on Britain's international trade, as in the case of the devaluation of the pound, are difficult to assess, given the profoundly altered conditions of the time. See Capie, *Depression and Protectionism*.
9. Rowland, *Commercial Conflict and Foreign Policy*. Note that during the interwar years France and Japan also increased the concentration of their trade in the colonies (see Table 8.5).
10. Drummond, *Imperial Economic Policy 1917–39*. See also Clayton, *The British Empire as a Superpower 1919–39*.
11. See Balderston, *The Origins and Course of the German Economic Crisis, 1923–1932* and James, *The German Slump*.

provoked progressive dissatisfaction with the Weimar Republic among its citizens.[12] Several studies have shown that as unemployment gradually increased there was growing consensus towards extremist political parties, in particular Hitler's National Socialists.[13] It's of no surprise that historians have wondered if things could have gone differently and whether less restrictive economic policies would have been workable. To understand the difficulties the German rulers had to face, and particularly Chancellor Brüning, we must consider the following factors:

- There had been no influx of foreign capital since 1928, so in order to pay the reparations[14] it was necessary to provide funds through a balance of payment surplus; for that to happen German economic policies had to be much more restrictive than other countries, for whom achieving a balance was sufficient.
- The collapse of the German economy could lead to the cancellation or suspension of reparations (which in effect happened).
- The mark could not be devalued under the terms imposed on Germany by the Versailles treaty (however, exchange rate controls were introduced in July 1931 that effectively isolated the mark from the worst effects of its appreciation against currencies that gradually lost value).
- Devaluation of the mark would have increased the real debt burden.
- Wages were inflexible (due to the power of the unions), and this inflexibility would have prevented much of the effectiveness of fiscal policies.
- There were no significant contemporary proposals in Germany for alternative economic policies.[15]

Given these considerations Borchardt has argued that Brüning had no viable alternatives to the extremely tight policy he followed.[16] As noted already,

---

12. Von Krüdener, *Economic Crisis and Political Collapse*.
13. Stögbauer, "The Radicalisation of the German Electorate".
14. On this point see Houwink ten Cate, "Reichsbank President Hjalmar Schacht and the Reparation Payments (1924–1930)".
15. Actually, there was a small group of German intellectuals in contact with Keynes who were pushing reflationary ideas, but their influence on public opinion and the government was quite marginal. See Garvy, "Keynes and the Economic Activists of pre-Hitler Germany".
16. Borchardt, *Perspectives on Modern German Economic History and Policy* and Borchardt & Ritschl, "Could Brüning Have Done It?". Using a Keynesian model provides additional support for Borchardt's argument, although from a different point of view; see Ritschl, "Reparation Transfers, the Borchardt Hypothesis and the Great Depression in Germany, 1929–32".

the policy discredited the Weimar Republic, which had not recovered even when von Papen, who replaced Brüning in mid-1932, attempted to revitalize the economy. A recent work has argued that if these attempts to revitalize the economy had been successful, they would have been effective in opposing Nazism.[17] Instead, the Nazi party had considerable success in the elections at the end of 1932, which brought Hitler to power in January 1933.[18] Many historians have highlighted the perverse role of the disgraceful German reparations policy, linking it initially to hyperinflation and destabilization of the German economy, and then to economic crisis; and finally to Germany's rejection of democracy and its embrace of revenge and violence.

Once in power Hitler did not immediately devote himself to rearming, as an older historiography has maintained. Rather, he worked to revitalise investments in construction and transport (the Nazis founded Volkswagen), as Overy's works have now clearly shown, restoring full employment before beginning large-scale rearmament.[19] This economic growth strengthened and stabilized the regime, as it had done in Italy during the economic boom of the early 1920s with Mussolini's rise to power.[20] This result was obtained by a significant increase in public spending, which went from 15 per cent of national income in 1928, to 23 per cent in 1934, and 33 per cent in 1938; this increase was made possible by an ingenious expansion of credit by Schacht, the president of the *Reichsbank*. Rather than simply increase the money supply – which was not feasible given that Germany could not officially leave the gold standard – he issued credit certificates that could be used as payment only by banks and also for the purpose of paying taxes. This is how he avoided the new money being used for consumption, which only recovered to 1929 levels.

Large scale rearmament began in 1936 with a Four Year Plan, and was strengthened with the construction of the "Westwall" (also known as the Siegfried Line) in 1938. In economic terms it presents an interesting case-study of a new type of mixed economy: some resources were under direct state control through "priority markets" and others were left to the market.[21]

---

17. Stögbauer & Komlos, "Averting the Nazi Seizure of Power".
18. See Kershaw, *Weimar: Why Did German Democracy Fail?* Regarding the question of what support large industries gave Nazism, we seem to be able to say that there was no collective action, as in the case of Mussolini's rise to power, but there were individual industrialists who supported Hitler. See Turner, *German Big Business and the Rise of Hitler*.
19. See his survey work, Overy, *The Nazi Economic Recovery 1932–1938*.
20. As noted by van Riel & Schram, "Weimar Economic Decline, Nazi Economic Recovery and the Stabilization of Political Dictatorship".
21. See the excellent article by Schweitzer, "Plans and Markets".

Hitler's goal was to create a stockpile of armaments that would allow an irresistible *Blitzkrieg* ("lightning war"), given that he did not consider it politically appropriate to extract too many resources out of the civil economy. However, due to the ineffectiveness of Göring's management and to Hitler's decision to go to war earlier than anticipated, that goal was slow to be achieved, and the rearmament was not fully effective.[22] In any case the stock of available weapons at the beginning of the war was sufficiently impressive for the Allied powers to systematically overestimate Germany's productive capacity, as Klein unequivocally shows.[23]

In addition to planning, the Nazis employed two other means for mobilizing the resources for rearmament, those of autarky and exploiting the countries of south-central Europe, both of which had results well below expectations. In the case of autarky, the chemical industry had some success[24] in producing substitute materials, but in 1939 Germany remained heavily dependent on countries outside its influence for oil, iron and many other metals, particularly those used in alloys for producing aeroplanes. With the policy of *Lebensraum* ("living space") that sought domination over many countries in south-central Europe and that saw the annexation of Austria in 1938 and Czechoslovakia in 1939, there is no doubt that German trade turned in their favour, but the impact remained modest. If we take the group of countries made up of Bulgaria, Greece, Romania, Turkey, Yugoslavia, Italy and Spain, German imports from these countries went from 9.8 per cent in 1929 to 18.7 per cent in 1938, and exports went from 11.2 to 20.8 per cent, yet these could not slake the German economy's thirst for raw materials. However, through "clearing" mechanisms favourable to Germany, many of these economies ended up financing Germany's war effort,[25] while German industry established itself on a grand scale in Austria and Czechoslovakia.

In conclusion we can say that Nazism used its economy as a weapon for

---

22. For these and other arguments see Overy, *War and Economy in the Third Reich.*
23. Klein, *Germany's Economic Preparation for War.*
24. I. G. Farben, the giant chemical monopoly, was dismantled by the Americans after the war, who accused it of having supported Nazism. The facts seem far more nuanced; see Hayes, *Industry and Ideology.*
25. *Clearing* was a bilateral system created to avoid having to make disbursements for international trade. The agreement provided that if one country had an excess of exports that it could not compensate with imports, it could not claim monetary payment to settle the account; the assumption was that the following year the balance could be reduced by higher imports. If this did not happen, a credit was issued to the country with excess imports. This was precisely the case of Germany with nearly all the above mentioned countries that, for one reason or another, continued to import less from Germany than they exported.

military purposes; it achieved neither perfect efficiency nor perfect synchrony between production cycles and military operations, but it nonetheless launched a powerful and technologically advanced war machine.

12.3 *Italy: ragamuffin imperialism*

Through Beneduce's bank rescue operations, which saw the creation of IMI in 1931[26] and IRI in 1933 (as noted in Chapter 11), the Italian state found itself owning 21.5 per cent of all the capital of Italian joint-stock companies but it controlled fully 42 per cent of the capital of those companies, particularly in certain sectors. IRI controlled all arms production, 80 to 90 per cent of ship-building, shipping lines, airlines, telephones, 40 per cent of the steel industry, 30 per cent of electricity, 25 per cent of the engineering industry and 15 per cent of the chemical industry (the largest company, Montecatini, remained private). It owned the former mixed banks, Comit, Credit, and the *Banco di Roma*, and together with other public banks, around 80 per cent of the banking sector was in state hands. IRI also owned a string of other companies in various sectors that it attempted to sell to private owners.

IRI's management worked to streamline managing all this by creating subholding companies, such as STET for telephones in 1933, Finmare for shipping companies in 1936 and Finsider for steel in 1937. In 1937 the IRI, which had been designed as a temporary agency, was made permanent. In 1936 banking reform began, which made the *Banca d'Italia* public and abolished the mixed bank; the gold standard was abandoned, and the lira was tied to the dollar. The banking sector was organized around short-term banks and long-term investment institutions, the latter all in public hands.[27] It remained that way until the 1993 legislation adopted the European banking sector liberalization directives, which not only privatized banks and opened markets to foreign banks, but also returned to the universal bank.

Although a series of bankruptcies were avoided in Italy by the timely action of the *Banca d'Italia* and Alberto Beneduce, and its recession was not among the most serious, the country's economic situation did not substan-

---

26. Lombardo, *L'Istituto Mobiliare Italiano*.
27. After becoming public in 1946, the three former mixed banks created one of these institutes, the *Mediobanca*, so they would not become wholly separated from their traditional activity of financial engineering; run by Beneduce's son-in-law Enrico Cuccia, it became the most active and famous. See Petri, *Storia economica d'Italia*.

tially improve. Due to its commitment to a strong lira in 1926, the fascist regime did not consider devaluing the lira until 1936; this inevitably made for a restrictive monetary policy, although it was mitigated by exchange controls and "clearing" agreements. Actually, two interventions were formulated, which the regime hoped would create popular support and economic benefits, but both turned out to be quite modest in scope.

The first was the integral land reclamation policy already discussed in Chapter 9, which continued at full speed during the crisis years, although it was carried out where reclamation had been understood and appreciated, since private involvement was necessary to implement the projects. In south and central Italy there was little progress because there was little or no collaboration by private parties; with the looming necessity of shifting to expropriations, which the regime did not want to do, in 1934 it instead removed Arrigo Serpieri, the capable reclamation administrator and reclamation subsequently lost its impact and economic sense, dragging on in a weary routine.

The second intervention was to introduce the *corporazioni*; announced in 1928, they were planned at length and then eventually formed in 1934. The *corporazioni*, similar to guilds, were to be a means of overcoming conflicts between capital and labour, and the *Camera delle Corporazioni* (the Chamber of Fasci and Corporations) was where their common interests were represented. This was the strategic body for implementing the "Third Way" between liberalism and planning, which fascism accredited as its "advanced" politico-ideological characteristic.[28] The reality was that the Chamber of Fasci and Corporations was not very effective, limiting itself to overseeing the cartels (the "*consorzi*"), investment decisions, prices and labour contracts. For example, IRI was administered separately, and its president, Beneduce, reported directly to Mussolini; even the decisions listed above were frequently made outside the *corporazioni* and simply ratified by them. The effectiveness of the ability of the *corporazioni* to function may also have been affected by the new political and military context in Italy after 1935, which imposed a more government-driven *dirigisme* on the country.

Indeed, by 1934 the Italian economy still showed no consistent signs of recovery; at which point something snapped in Mussolini and his entourage, and it was then that the regime took a sinister, warmongering turn. If we look at the impact of the regime's arms expenditures on total public spending before 1933, we find that it was less than during pre-war liberal governments. In 1934, perhaps following the wave of Nazi propaganda, or

---

28. Note that Nazism's "New Economic Order" imitated the fascist approach, although it is difficult to say just how much Hitler believed it.

internal economic difficulties, Mussolini began speaking of expanding the Italian people into Africa and planning a military intervention there. This actually began in Ethiopia on 3 October 1935, leading to its conquest in 1936 and the proclamation of the empire. All this went against international agreement that there would be no more colonial campaigns in Africa, and the League of Nations levied economic sanctions against Italy.[29] The Ethiopian campaign initiated a rearmament race, which continued with Italian support of General Franco in the Spanish civil war and then with the progressive rapprochement with Hitler; it culminated with the Pact of Steel in 1938, which was a forerunner to the adoption of the racial laws against the Jews and of entering the Second World War in June 1940.

Mussolini sought to imitate Hitler's autarky, with even less satisfactory results; in 1939 only 21 per cent of raw materials necessary for the Italian economy were produced in the country. There was also a significant shift in its foreign trade towards Germany; imports from Germany increased to 27 per cent in 1938 and 40 per cent in 1940. The efforts to produce alternative materials in Italy as well launched research and new plants that did not immediately produce important results, but turned out to be significant and useful for the postwar recovery.[30]

In conclusion, in contrast to Germany, whose recovery was triggered by investments in the civil sector, Italy's recovery was predominately based on rearmament – although the results were wholly inadequate for the characteristics and conditions of the Second World War.

12.4 *France: from crisis to defeat*

Because of its large gold stock and low level of unemployment due to its relative vitality during the 1920s, France's economy was not initially hard hit by the depression; however, after the devaluation of the pound it began to suffer a significant fall in exports and tourist revenue.[31] The attachment to the

---

29. These sanctions were only partially effective, given that they were not applied by all countries, but they did cause imports and exports to fall significantly, which created difficulties in covering the balance of payments. See the interesting work by Ristuccia, "1935 Sanctions Against Italy".
30. In particular, see Petri, "Innovazioni tecnologiche tra uso bellico e mercato civile".
31. For a detailed examination of the French economy between the wars, see Sauvy, *Histoire économique de la France entre les deux guerres*. For a more general picture and a more recent bibliography, see Broder, *Histoire économique de la France au XXe, 1914–1997*.

"Franc Poincaré" precluded a devaluation; this meant the continuation of a restrictive monetary policy and a deflationary spiral of wage and price cuts until late 1936, when France decided to devalue. It is strange that France, which during the 1920s had drawn so many advantages from a weak franc while Britain suffered from the pound being artificially maintained too high, did not learn its lesson and align itself with the devaluation of the pound. The fact is that it became stuck in a downward spiral that prevented any recovery.

When the country became aware of the inability of those in power to alleviate their suffering, it sought change by electing a leftist government, led by Léon Blum and supported by the socialists and communists (the *Front populaire*). The new government's first decision was not to devalue the franc; rather, with the Matignon Agreements it increased wages and reduced working hours. The incongruity of these measures with the state of the French economy was immediately grasped by business owners;[32] fearing the worst they began exporting capital, which made the devaluation of the franc inevitable and certainly did not help restart investments and productive activity. The franc was devalued, but the situation remained tense. In June 1937 Blum asked parliament for extraordinary powers to address the crisis, but his request was rejected.[33] The political process was paralyzed from June 1937 to April 1938, with very short duration governments; among them was a new Blum government that lasted only one month. Finally in May 1938 a person of real resolve, Edouard Daladier, took charge; he appointed Paul Reynaud to govern the economy.[34] The forty-hour working week was moth-balled, investment incentives were enacted, research and statistics compilation were promoted, and a massive rearmament program was begun. Although industrial production rose, it was too late to counter the German attack in 1940; France found itself absolutely unprepared to face it, and it was crushed over a massive 40 day campaign.

There was much debate in France over the reasons for this debacle. The experiment of Blum's leftist government was certainly a failure, not because Blum was a particularly mediocre politician, but because his advisers were not up to the task and poorly informed. An entire elite was involved, who were incapable of conceiving the necessary policies to breathe life back into

---

32. The wage increase caused prices to rise before broadening the internal market, while the shortened working week made it difficult to organize labour in a country in which unemployment was modest, even despite the crisis.
33. For more on the event, see Minot, "La chûte du premier gouvernement Blum et l'action des commissions des finances 1936–37".
34. Reynaud was the only man in France, since 1934, to recommend devaluing the franc.

the economy, which made the final defeat inevitable.[35] There was no lack of dissenting voices, which at the time went unheard, particularly among a group of technocrats inspired by the ideas of Saint-Simon and who became active in various governments, particularly after the war.[36] Among them we should mention André Tardieu, the prime minister at the end of the 1920s who had prepared a plan to modernize industrial plants that was never approved. In the early 1930s a group of graduates from the École Polytechnique in Paris formed a club called "X-Crise", or "Crisis X", to study ways out of the crisis.[37] Among its participants were figures who later became promoters of postwar planning, such as Jacques Rueff, Alfred Sauvy, Jean Ullmo and Paul Reynaud (the hapless minister of the economy at the end of the 1930s). The experience of the Pétain government is also worth mentioning. Condemned by everyone because of its collaboration with the German occupation, it is nonetheless of some interest from an economic viewpoint. The government in fact set itself to improve production methods in French industry, increasing productivity on the basis of a ten-year plan of factory modernization and a better and more efficient collection of statistical data. Jean Bichelonne led the Ministry of Industrial Production, which was organized in committees by sector (*Comités d'organization*) that involved business-owners as well; a model that was taken up again after the war.

12.5 *The United States and the New Deal*

The New Deal is justly famous because it profoundly altered the US economy and society. It significantly changed the nation's macroeconomic practices, achieved through increased spending by the federal government. While spending by the states and municipalities remained more or less unchanged, federal spending quadrupled over the course of the 1930s,[38] bringing the impact of public spending from 11 per cent in 1929 to 17 per cent in 1939. The importance of federal spending (excluding defence spending and interest payments

---

35. Kemp, *The French Economy 1913–1939* discusses a social structure crisis. Sauvy discusses the prevalence of a "Malthusian" mindset.
36. See Kuisel, *Capitalism and the State in Modern France*. Jean Bichelonne, Ernst Mercier, Pierre Ricard, Pierre Mendes France, François Bloch-Lainé, Michel Debré and Jean Monnet were among the key players.
37. "X" denoted an unknown, indicating the incomprehensibility of the crisis and the necessity of finding a solution.
38. See Dowd, *The Twisted Dream*.

on the debt, which were already a feature) on total spending doubled by the end of the 1930s, and it subsequently increased to over half of all public spending by the end of the twentieth century.

In addition to the Glass–Steagall Act, (discussed in Chapter 11), what were the main provisions that characterized the New Deal? Initially, in the early phase, it was primarily for emergency interventions. The FERA (Federal Emergency Relief Administration) created jobs in public works and infrastructure; during the winter of 1933–4 two million workers benefited from it. The AAA (Agricultural Adjustment Administration) pursued the goal of raising the prices of agricultural products, which had fallen to intolerable levels; the NRA (National Recovery Administration) introduced similar measures for industry. The success of Roosevelt's policies was such that the Democrats took control of Congress as well. The second phase of the New Deal began in the winter of 1935, in which the emergency provisions of the first hundred days became permanent components of US macroeconomic policies.

In agriculture the AAA was reproposed as a permanent system of agricultural price support; this included controlling the quantity produced, which was provided by a mechanism administered by the Soil Conservation and Domestic Allotment Act of 1936. The legislation introduced for the industrial sector was far more complex and innovative. The NRA was abolished, but was replaced by three different types of interventions. The Wagner Act of 1935 created the National Labor Relations Board (NLRB), which ensured official recognition of the labour unions and enabled them to represent workers in labour disputes. Furthermore, the Fair Labor Standards Act was passed in 1938, which established a minimum wage, a limit on hours worked and overtime compensation. The second intervention was in the area of social security, which had not been generally adopted in the United States. The Social Security Act passed in 1935[39] restructured the pension system, unemployment insurance and support systems for the disabled and orphans. Finally, the third intervention was in the area of public works, through employees of the Public Works Administration (PWA) and the various specialized agencies set up from time to time to implement various projects, such as the well-known TVA (Tennessee Valley Authority) whose reclamation and flood control provided electrical generation across several states.

The beneficial effects of this new legislation were slow in coming, partly because it was not easy to recover from a crisis of such proportions, but also because European politics was descending towards a new war. This redirected

---

39. Note that the United States was the first to use the term "social security"; see Silei, "Dalle assicurazioni sociali alla *Social Security*".

investments into the arms industry, for a war that proved to be more destructive than any previous conflict.

12.6 *The Second World War*

As we've seen, the recovery in Europe during the 1930s varied from one country to another because it was driven substantially by internal mechanisms, at least until the general rearmament that set in at the end of the decade. Japan too had high growth in heavy industry during the 1930s. In 1934 two-thirds of Japanese industrial employment was in textiles (silk and cotton), but by 1942 that was down to 20 per cent, and 60 per cent had shifted to heavy industry. These developments were due to the policies of a military elite, which began with a war of aggression against China and Japan's invasion of Manchuria in 1931 and ended with Japan attacking the United States at Pearl Harbour in 1941.

In conclusion we can compile a table summarizing the performance of the six major countries, along with the macroeconomic policies they followed, to draw a few final observations. If we look at Table 12.1 we can clearly see that Japan and Germany were the countries with the best growth results; the crisis had been contained in Japan, while Germany's recovery was remarkable. Britain was at an intermediate level, particularly because its crisis was modest; Italy had a weak recovery, which might explain Mussolini's decision to give imperialism a try. France and the United States suffered the worst performances; France because its recovery was very weak, and the United States because it suffered a very serious crisis and an insufficient recovery.

Note that the best performing economies enjoyed expansionist monetary policies, while the German economy took advantage of effective economic policies from all approaches. The US economy was instead ruined by wholly inadequate policies at the beginning of the crisis and saw its productive capacity not recover fully until the war, which it long sought to avoid.

In the heat of battle the Second World War consumed a staggering quantity of resources (Table 12.2), even more than was expended during the First World War.[40] Looking at the table we see that Italy had the most modest mobilization, probably because the fascist regime did not believe in the war

---

40. For general aspects of the war, see Overy, *The Origins of the Second World War*. During the First World War Britain employed about one-third of its national income for war purposes, and Germany employed about 40 per cent.

Table 12.1 Performance and policies in the 1930s.

Country	GNP growth rate 1932–38	GNP level in 1938 (1929 = 100)	Monetary policies	Fiscal policies	Intervention plan
France	2.0	95	Restrictive	Orthodox	No
Germany	6.6	123	Expansionist	Expansionist	Yes
Britain	3.3	114	Expansionist	Orthodox	No
Italy	1.3	102	Restrictive	Expansionist	Yes
United States	3.7	89	Restrictive	Orthodox	No
Japan	3.7	121	Expansionist	Orthodox	No

Source: Maddison database.

Table 12.2 Military spending during the Second World War as a percentage of
national income (at current prices)

Date	United States	Britain	Soviet Union*	Germany	Italy	Japan
1939	1	15	–	23	8	22
1940	2	44	17	40	12	22
1941	11	53	28	52	23	27
1942	31	52	61	64	22	33
1943	42	55	61	70	21	43
1944	42	53	53	–	–	76

Note: *at 1937 prices.

Source: Harrison, *The Economics of World War II.*

all that much, and it did not think it possible to expect heavy sacrifices from citizens who believed in it even less; moreover, it lacked the raw materials to be able to produce any more.[41]

The escalations by Germany and the Soviet Union in 1942 and by the United States in 1943 are very evident. The very high levels attained by Germany and particularly the Soviet Union, which was still a very poor country, are partly explainable by the fact that both countries, as well as Britain, could count on additional resources from foreign sources; the United States assisted Britain and the Soviet Union, while Germany drew from its occupied countries. An estimate of the contribution by the United States to the Allies and the flow of resources to Britain and Germany can be found in Table 12.3. As noted in Chapter 10, the US contribution to the USSR was substantial, of the order of 10 per cent of Russian GDP.

During the long years that war ravaged Europe, both Germany and Britain were drawing up their proposals for reorganizing the world after the war. In Germany the basic idea was of a New Order; its contents were not uniformly interpreted within Nazi circles, but in any case it included the following elements: a fascist, corporatist state; planning, although within a mixed economy with a strong state presence rather than in a Soviet-style central-ized system; autocracy; and "living space" (*Lebensraum*), or a sort of German hegemony over the European economy.[42]

41. See V. Zamagni, "Un'analisi macroeconomica degli effetti della guerra".
42. Barkai, *Nazi Economics.*

Table 12.3   Outbound (–) and inbound (+) resource flows as a percentage of national income.

Date	United States	Britain	Germany
1938	–2	5	–1
1939	–1	8	1
1940	–2	17	7
1941	–2	14	12
1942	–4	11	17
1943	–6	10	16

Source: Harrison, "Resource Mobilization for World War II".

The "living space" was interpreted coercively, through annexation and occupation of those countries that would be required to contribute to the German economy. The collaborationist Pétain government in France gave the most important support to the German war effort, although it was mostly required to produce goods for the civilian market, which freed up German productive capacity for armaments. Norway was important for obtaining strategic raw materials, and Belgium and the Netherlands for their production capacity. During the occupation of the northern part of Italy since late 1943 Italy was made to pay heavy war compensation. Milward maintains that Eastern Europe, in which Germany had placed much hope, was not very useful because the nations there were so underdeveloped.[43]

Germany tried to implement integrated production plans, with the major German companies opening new factories. However, precisely because the entire system rested on coercion and violence, the Germans had to face the serious problem of organizing a frequently unruly labour force. Among the Nazi hierarchy, Sauckel preferred forced internment in Germany where it could be better controlled, even when the labour force was free, but that raised formidable logistical problems; Speer favoured letting the work remain in-country, which left greater room for sabotage. The fact is that, due to the constraints of each choice, there was no optimal solution.

In Britain the primary problem was finding resources to cope with a war that, with France's defeat, became increasingly long and costly. The aid coming from the Commonwealth quickly proved inadequate, and as had been predicted it had to turn to the United States, which was not yet at war.

---

43. Milward, *War, Economy and Society, 1939–45*.

In the summer of 1940 the United States suggested that the British liquidate their foreign investments, but that provided only temporary relief. In March 1941 the US Congress approved a law – the Neutrality Act – that stated that any aid to the countries at war would be provided without requiring compensation; the purpose was to avoid repeating the perverse effects of inter-Allied war debts after the First World War, the effects of which were understood only later.

In May 1941 Britain sent a delegation to the United States, headed by Keynes, to negotiate an aid plan. Keynes had expected to remain in America for just a week; instead he remained for three months due to the differences that arose between the US and British governments. The Americans wanted precise commitments by the British on liberalizing their economy after the war and the reintroduction of the gold standard; Keynes was reluctant to sign to these terms, because he thought that Britain would need many controls to put its economy back in order during reconstruction. A compromise was eventually reached, and the Atlantic Charter entered in force in August 1941.[44] It explicitly stated the principle of multilateralism and called for a cooperative global system to expand production, employment and trade, eliminating discriminatory practices and reducing barriers to free trade. Following that agreement the Mutual Aid Agreement was approved in February 1942 with the Lend–Lease aid plan; it provided $30 billion worth of weapons, of which $10 billion was distributed to Russia, as previously noted, and lesser aid to other countries. One of the most interesting aspects of this event is that Keynes was still under the illusion (and many after him) of being able to negotiate with the United States as an equal, while in reality no European country could compete with the United States by then.[45]

The turning point in the war was the direct participation of the United States in 1942,[46] which immediately restored some balance to the fortunes of war, with the ultimate victory of the Allies. Actually, with the United States, in 1942–3 the Allies could count on a stock of resources that was more

---

44. Discussions on the subject were later resumed.
45. There was no lack of Europeans who were aware of this, but without the ability to effect a change in policy. For example, in September 1915, when asked his opinion regarding a customs union between Germany and the Hapsburg Empire, the German politician, Clemens von Delbrück responded: "We are no longer fighting for the mastery in the internal [European] market, but for mastery in the world market, and it is only a Europe which forms a single customs unit that can meet with sufficient power the over-mighty productive resources of the transatlantic world" (quoted in Milward, *The New Order and the French Economy*, 147–8).
46. The Japanese attack on Pearl Harbour happened on 7 December 1941.

than double that of the Axis powers, and that gap increased to three and five times respectively in 1944 and 1945.[47] With their decisive contribution the United States gained a predominant role in defeating Germany and Japan, and this made them the keystone of the subsequent peace. The war ended with 55 million dead (just under half of whom were Russian), vast destruction throughout Europe, especially to infrastructure, and a second collapse of Germany.[48]

---

47. After Mussolini's arrest on 25 July 1943, Italy decided not to continue the war, resulting in the armistice of 8 September 1943. It subsequently declared war on Germany, which divided the country into two parts, with a German-occupied North where the Republic of Salò was established.

48. See Ferguson, "The Second World War as an Economic Disaster".

13

Postwar reconstruction and decolonization

13.1 *The United States and postwar Europe*

The American involvement in the Second World War was so intense that it was immediately clear that it was impossible for it to return to its old isolationism. To the contrary, beginning in 1943 America found itself needing to launch an aid plan for the civilian population, which it did so through UNRRA (United Nations Relief and Rehabilitation Administration); it provided around $4 billion in food aid to Europe until 1947.[1] In addition there was the problem of administering the occupied German zones (see Figure 13.1), where the economy was no longer working and the monetary system had once again been destroyed.[2] The biggest problem, however, was designing a European reconstruction that ensured a more lasting continuity than the reconstruction conceived by the Treaty of Versailles.[3] The reality was that European countries, with France at the head, again began to press for reparations, while proceeding to dismantle many German factories and

---

1. After 1947 the UNRRA funds gave rise to various agencies of the United Nations: Food and Agriculture Organization (FAO), International Refugee Organization (IRO), World Health Organization (WHO), United Nations Children's Fund (UNICEF) and United Nations Educational, Scientific and Cultural Organization (UNESCO).
2. Germany was divided into four zones; one was under British control, one was under French control, a third was under the control of the United States, and a fourth was under the control of the Soviet Union; in Berlin they had a joint presence. The British, French and US zones were coordinated and administered with the US Government Administration of Relief in Occupied Areas (GARIOA) funds.
3. For a comparison of the two postwar periods, see Meier, "The Two Postwar Eras and the Conditions for Stability in Twentieth-Century Europe".

procrastinate over every proposal to rebuild the German economy.[4] Another looming problem was Soviet expansionism, which was leveraging the existing communist parties in various European countries, seeking to draw as many countries as possible into its sphere of influence.

Confronting this situation was the need to rebuild. Not that the European countries were not already hard at work, but since they were all poor in raw materials, and having lost their foreign exchange reserves to finance imports, they very quickly found themselves trapped in a vicious circle: only by exporting could they import raw materials, but without raw materials they could not produce anything to export.[5] Over the course of 1947 the United States became aware of the choice it now faced: it could either let Europe's spiral downward continue, which would obstruct a successful reconstruction, or it could intervene with a new aid plan. In the first case the United States would find itself without a trading partner, with the risk of another large scale crisis, and without a solid bulwark to oppose Soviet expansionism. In the second case, it was clear that it would have to include Germany among the beneficiary countries of a new aid plan, which suggested making it broadly multilateral.

On 5 June 1947, during a speech at Harvard University the American Secretary of State George Marshall announced that the United States had decided to finance a multi-year reconstruction plan for all European countries that wished to join it. The plan was called the European Recovery Program, but is better known as the Marshall Plan. Its aim was to fill European countries' balance of payment deficits with American aid in order to allow them to restart their production process without inflationary trends or engendering political instability. The Americans proposed their own growth model to the Europeans based on increasing productivity and introducing scientific management, which would enable them to increase their national income and limit their serious income distribution conflicts.[6]

But the Americans did not limit themselves to offering funds; they also designed a system for distributing them – which remains unique among its kind – based on two principles:

---

4. Note that the German problem was particularly acute for the Americans, who found themselves having to literally support the German population because of the disarray of the German economy; see Gimbel, *The Origins of the Marshall Plan* and also Turner, *Reconstruction in Post-war Germany*.
5. This vicious circle has been termed the "dollar gap", referring to the shortage of dollars for financing imports.
6. See Meier, "The Politics of Productivity". See also Hutton, *We Too Can Prosper*.

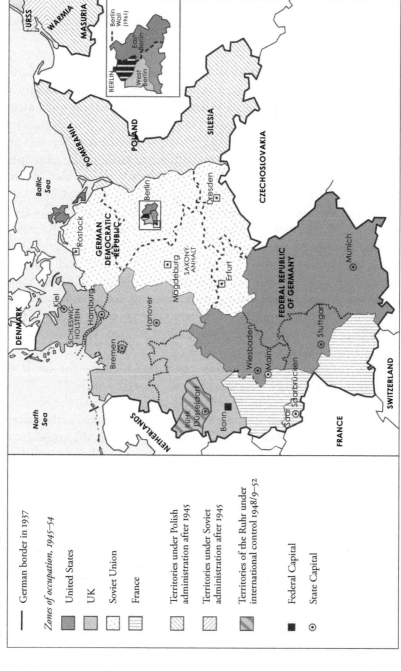

Figure 13.1 The occupation of German territories after the Second World War

Source: Duby, *Atlante storico* (Turin: Sei, 1995)

- requested goods were transferred directly; and
- all decisions required US agreement, since it had ultimate responsibility of the whole system.[7]

Although the plan was multilateral (i.e. it was offered to multiple countries at the same time), offices were subsequently opened in each country that adhered to it. The list of goods negotiated for each country was based on a four year growth plan and annual operational plans. The United States sourced and directly purchased the goods, either in their own markets or on global markets, and they were delivered without payment to the participating countries.[8] Each national government organized their sale on their domestic markets using local currency, and the proceeds were retained in a "counterpart fund", the use of which had to be agreed to by the US. The type of goods sent to Europe clearly reveals the predominance of goods necessary to restart the production process: 33 per cent raw materials, 29 per cent food products and fertilizers, 16 per cent energy products (coal and oil), 17 per cent machinery and vehicles, and 5 per cent other goods. The ERP resulted in goods worth $12.5 billion flowing to Europe and, formally, lasted for four years, from mid-1948 to mid-1952.[9] In 1952, due to concerns raised by the Korean War, it became a much more limited military aid plan, the MSA (Mutual Security Agency).

Table 13.1 shows the participating countries and how the funds were divided. Note in particular that there are two countries in the list – Portugal and Turkey – that, given their peripheral role in the war, we would not expect to find there. Included by the US for geopolitical reasons, they received only limited resources. Britain and France were among the countries that most benefited, receiving just under half the aid, followed equally by Germany and Italy and then by the Netherlands, which had been severely

---

7. The Marshall Plan sent goods instead of dollars to Europe in order to avoid financial speculation and uncontrolled use of the funds. With the mechanism that was put in place, the Americans could easily control the process and avoid the market seizing up and prevent hoarding. That of course implied a high level of American interference in the development projects of all participating countries, which is precisely why the Russians refused to take part.

8. The geographical sources of the goods distributed under the Marshall Plan were as follows: United States 69 per cent, Canada 12 per cent, Latin America 8 per cent, participating countries 5 per cent, other countries 6 per cent. See Hogan, *The Marshall Plan* and also Wexler, *The Marshall Plan Revisited*.

9. This flow of resources was equal to over 2 per cent of the United States' GDP during these years.

Table 13.1 ERP funds distribution by participating country, April 1948 to December 1951.

Region	US$ millions April 1948–January 1951	% of total
Austria	634	5.1
Belgium and Luxembourg	546	4.4
Denmark	267	2.2
France	2,576	20.8
Federal Republic of Germany	1,317	10.6
Greece	614	5.0
Ireland	146	1.2
Italy	1,347	10.9
The Netherlands	1,000	8.1
Norway	241	1.9
Portugal	50	0.4
Sweden	118	1.0
Turkey	176	1.4
UK	2,866	23.2
Total*	12,384	100

Note: *the total does not include administrative costs and costs allocated to multilateral institutions such as the European Payments Union and other small countries.

Source: Brown & Opie, *American Foreign Assistance*, 222.

Table 13.2 Aid sent to Europe, 1942–52 (US dollar billions).

	Period	Current US$	Purchasing power per US$ in 1948	% from the United States
Lend–lease	1942–45	44.6	62	98
UNRRA	1943–47	4.0	5	72
Interim Aid – GARIOA	1945–48	16.3	20	100
ERP	1948–52	12.5	12	100
Total			99	

destroyed. Greece also received a significant amount of aid relative to its small economy, which was used partially to end its ongoing civil war by defeating the communists.[10] We shall examine the role the ERP and counterpart funds played in the reconstruction history of the four largest European countries in §13.5.[11]

Finally, it is interesting to set the ERP in the context of overall aid sent to Europe, (see Table 13.2). The flows relative to the various aid plans have been carefully, if approximately, deflated in order to make a correct comparison. The total amount of aid comes to around $100 billion (1948) dollars, which corresponds to roughly $850 billion (2015) dollars, of which at least two-thirds were weapons. These were the resources provided to Europe, largely from the United States, to win the war against Germany and to restart the European economy, but the organizational contribution the US made was at least as important. Only a country like the United States that was accustomed to running and administering companies of colossal size could so effectively address such a large scale wartime mobilization and a vast and coordinated presence in Europe to support reconstruction, along with creating new international bodies to provide the governance of international economic relations that had previously been lacking.

13.2 The Marshall Plan and the beginnings of the process of European integration

In addition to the role it played in the material reconstruction of the European economy, strategically the Marshall Plan acted as midwife to the birth of a new collaboration among European nations.[12] After the United States announced the Marshall Plan, Britain and France sought to dominate the Plan's administration from the European side by becoming allies and setting themselves at the head of the group of participating nations. On 12 June 1947 the Committee for European Economic Co-operation was established in Paris, with representatives from each country. The Committee's task was to carry out technical studies of the European economies to facilitate each country formulating its own four year plan and to make each country's goals

---

10. Greece continued receiving US aid long after the Marshall Plan ended: see McNeill, *Greece: American Aid in Action 1947–1956*.
11. For a general discussion, see Ellwood, *Rebuilding Europe*.
12. See Milward, *The Reconstruction of Western Europe 1945–51*.

compatible at the aggregate level. On 16 April 1948 the group was reorganized as the Organisation for European Economic Co-operation (OEEC) in order to give it a higher profile and official status.[13]

The Americans saw the OEEC as a welcome federalist structuring of Europe and entrusted it with important tasks, such as dividing the Marshall Plan funds among the European countries. However, the OEEC was quick to demonstrate its lack of decision-making power in the face of European countries clinging jealously to their national identity and not wishing to delegate to supranational bodies. The organization's political dimension soon became entirely secondary, although it continued to function well at a technical and consulting level until 1961 when it was reorganized as the OECD (Organisation for Economic Co-operation and Development), with the inclusion of other developed countries such as Canada, Australia and Japan.

The organization was not the winning move on the way to European integration. In reality the US had underestimated the strong resistance within Europe to a political solution to European conflicts through a federalist structure similar to that of the United States. Fortunately, history did not end there because Europeans had strong incentives to find cooperative solutions, partly due to the Americans' insistence and to the presence of the Marshall Plan, which alleviated their most urgent needs. It was however the emergence of another serious problem that proved much more fruitful for creative solutions. With the operation of the Marshall Plan it had become clear that reconstructing the German state and economy could be put off no longer, though a state partly weakened by the subtraction of the Soviet controlled zone (which was established as an independent state within the Soviet Bloc). The French feared the re-establishment of German heavy industry and pressed for the creation of an overseeing authority to monitor the Ruhr, although the problem was that it was not clear who should lead such an authority. The French did not want it to be led by the Americans while they were aware that Britain, with whom they had originally thought to share leadership in Europe, increasingly did not consider itself an economically integral part of continental Europe (for the reasons we have seen in Chapter 12).

Robert Schuman, the French Foreign Minister, had the courage to propose a wholly innovative solution,[14] which he did not inform the British of ahead of

---

13. Regarding the OEEC, see Griffith, *Explorations in OEEC History*.

14. The plan, however, was prepared by Jean Monnet, a passionate proponent of the idea of a united Europe and the first President of the ECSC. Monnet subsequently worked to prepare the European Common Market, which we will discuss in Chapter 14. See Preda, "The Schuman Plan".

time, knowing full well, as Milward has noted, that it would mean the end of Anglo-French cooperation.[15] Schuman's solution was a direct agreement with Germany to establish a joint supranational body with full decision-making powers, open to participation by other countries, to control the coal and steel sectors.[16] In Schuman's own words, the implications for France and Europe:

> The pooling of coal and steel production should immediately provide for the setting up of common foundations for economic development as a first step in the federation of Europe, and will change the destinies of those regions which have long been devoted to the manufacture of munitions of war, of which they have been the most constant victims.[17]

This agreement, known as the European Coal and Steel Community (ECSC), was signed on 18 April 1951 between France, Germany, Belgium, Holland, Luxembourg and Italy.[18] In subsequent years the ECSC – initially with ERP funds – created a common market for coal and steel. It removed tariffs, quotas and other restrictions, and it harmonized technology and wages, demonstrating that a supranational institution could work for the interests of all its members.[19] Precisely due to this demonstration of successful collaboration and to the Franco-German alliance on which the ECSC was founded, the institution proved to be strategic in opening the long but effective and cumulative road towards European economic integration. Britain did not wish to participate, increasingly isolating itself from Europe until the turn of events at the end of the 1960s (as we shall see in Chapter 15).

Together with the ECSC, another institution, the European Payments Union (EPU), was brought into operation on 19 September 1950. At a time

---

15. Milward, *Reconstruction*, 396: "He had the courage to act quickly. Britain had not even been consulted and the proposals were made in the full knowledge that they might mean the end of the Franco-British cooperation in Western Europe on which French policy towards Germany had been based since the end of the war". See also Dell, *The Schuman Plan and the British Abdication of Leadership in Europe*.
16. See Gillingham, *Coal, Steel and the Rebirth of Europe 1945–1955*.
17. Translation of Schuman's words by the then US Secretary of State Dean Acheson in his work *Present at the Creation*, 384.
18. Ranieri's work documents important economic and diplomatic aspects of Italy's participation in the ECSC; see Ranieri, "Il Piano Marshall e la ricostruzione della siderurgia a ciclo integrale", and its bibliography.
19. Milward has argued that European supranational institutions does not mean that the nation has been superseded, but that they operate to protect national interests in a global economy that does not allow small nations, such as the European countries, to maximize their interests in isolation; see Milward, *The European Rescue of the Nation State*.

when the European central banks were short of reserves, the EPU was to finance temporary deficits in the balances of payments so as not to impede the flows of imports and exports (due to the lack of means of payment).[20] The EPU, conceived and aided by the United States who financed it with the ERP, was the first experiment in monetary cooperation.[21] It improved its methods of intervention in financial markets, but above all it accustomed nations to negotiations that could achieve benefits for everyone, which showed the Europeans the superior effectiveness of cooperative actions. Due to the EPU, many barriers to trade that were in force were eliminated, but trade and money were soon operating in a renewed global context, which we will recount in the next section.

In conclusion, we can say that the Marshall Plan reintroduced multilateral agreements after the negative experiences of bilateralism during the inter-war years. It gave a strategic impetus to the process of European integration, launched an era of great global economic expansion (which we will consider in Chapter 14), extended the areas of international negotiations, and spread the US model of economic organization within Europe. That a victor country would help rebuild both its allies and the defeated nations had never been seen before in history, solidifying the United States dominance that it had earned on the field.

13.3 *The creation of international institutions: GATT, IMF and the World Bank*

In 1946 a preparatory committee was formed within the United Nations[22] to draw up a convention for establishing a body responsible for overseeing international trade. In 1947 the organizational charter of the International Trade Organization (ITO) was issued; it was never ratified by the United States because it was considered too binding. The GATT, or General Agreements on Tariffs and Trade, replaced it in 1948 as a forum for trade negotiations, and was

---

20. The EPU was only a temporary institution; ending in 1958, with a return to fully convertible currencies.
21. See Kaplan & Schleiminger, *The European Payments Union* and also Eichengreen, *Reconstructing Europe's Trade and Payments*.
22. Although established in 1945, the origins of the United Nations date back to an agreement signed on 1 January 1942 by 26 nations, in which they committed to fight the Axis powers until victory was won.

quite successful. Three criteria were established for conducting negotiations: firstly, non-discrimination, although this included the general application of the "Most Favoured Nation" (MFN) status (see Chapter 7). Some exceptions were envisaged, including anti-dumping clauses and customs unions, and pre-existing preferential agreements (such as the British Commonwealth) were allowed. Secondly, the elimination of quantitative restrictions, or quotas; and thirdly, reciprocity, granting the same trading terms and conditions to all partners, although, here too exceptions were made for the most undeveloped countries.[23]

The negotiating rounds began in 1947 in Geneva with 123 agreements reached by twenty-three countries. They agreed to continue the negotiations, creating the GATT the following January. There was another round in Annécy in 1953, followed by four more rounds of negotiations during the 1950s that eliminated nearly all quantitative restrictions and lowered tariffs. In the 1960s, the "Kennedy round", named after the American president under whom it began, succeeded in reducing tariffs on industrial products by one-third. The last round, the "Uruguay round", ended in 1994 with important results, such as extending international trade negotiations to the agricultural and service sectors, which were formerly excluded. It also created the stronger body that had originally been rejected in 1947, the World Trade Organization (WTO), which began operating in 1995, and has sanctioning powers that were denied to the GATT.[24]

On the monetary front, after the joint declaration by the US and Britain of the Atlantic Charter in 1941,[25] US Treasury official, Harry Dexter White continued to study a plan on behalf of the United States to reintroduce the gold standard; it was made public in 1943 and suggested the creation of a fund with intervention powers in support of fixed exchange rates. In the meantime, Keynes prepared a counter-proposal that had significant elements of difference (see Table 13.3). Keynes's project was much broader and would have led to a truly global governance of financial flows; through centralized

---

23. Beginning in the 1970s, these exceptions became systematic with the adoption of the Generalized System of Preferences (GSP) by developed countries; these provided a whole series of concessions to developing countries that were explicitly not reciprocal.

24. On the current problems of the WTO, see Jones, *Reconstructing the World Trade Organization for the 21st Century*.

25. The Atlantic Charter was a statement issued by the UK and the US on 14 August 1941, that defined the Allied goals for the postwar world, which included, no territorial changes against the wishes of the people; self-determination; restoration of self-government to those deprived of it; reduction of trade restrictions; global cooperation to secure better economic and social conditions for all. This statement became the basis for the United Nations.

monitoring it would have attempted to eradicate imbalances in balances of payments by introducing disincentives for countries, both those in deficit and those in surplus, to remain in their unbalanced states. There was to be a clearing union at the head of this integrated governance of financial flows, with its own money to be used only in transactions between central banks. The US government did not wish to accept the creation of such a *super partes* body and supported its own project, creating an intervention fund that was controlled by the country who had contributed the most resources to it (the United States). It did adopt a few amendments inspired by Keynes's ideas, one of which was the creation of a world bank, although with very different characteristics than those Keynes had wanted.

Table 13.3   Main features of the two alternative proposals put forward at Bretton Woods.

Clearing union – Bancor (Keynes)	Stabilization fund – Unitas (White)
1. Initial quotas provided by creation of international credit	1. Initial quotas levied by way of a general subscription of capital
2. Quotas represent a claim to overdraw on international account	2. Quotas represent a right to purchase the deposits of other members
3. Requirement that exchange transactions be centralized with the Clearing Bank through national controls	3. Presumption that individuals remain free to deal in exchange with one another for "current account" purposes.
4. Control over capital movements implying prior scrutiny of all transactions and preventive action	4. Control over capital movements in principle, but in practice by *ex post facto* use of correctives
5. Correctives deliberately applied (at least equally) to the stronger party	5. Sanctions provided against the weaker party
6. General intention to be "expansionist"	6. General intention to share existing foreign resources, but to stop short of expansion
7. Special attention paid to smaller and poorer countries	7. Countries ruined by war receive nothing but the mobilization of blocked balances

Source: Van Dormael, *Bretton Woods*, 69–70 (from Keynes's own notes).

In June 1944 a meeting was convened by the member countries of the United Nations in the small American city of Bretton Woods, New Hampshire. The project was discussed and ratified by 45 countries in 1945, giving rise to the creation of the International Monetary Fund (IMF) and the World Bank (called at the time the International Bank for Reconstruction and Development); both began operations in 1947.[26] Note that, despite its name, Article XIV of the Statute of the World Bank prevents it from taking part in European reconstruction, for which the Americans had launched the Marshall Plan. In reality the World Bank quickly became a development bank for underdeveloped countries, with no connection to the clearing union that Keynes had conceived as the world's central bank.[27] The IMF had two main tasks: oversight of the new system of fixed exchange rates, and financial support interventions for countries in temporary difficulty. The IMF's oversight of the "gold exchange standard",[28] reintroduced in 1947, was impeccable. However, it could not prevent the gold reserves of the United States, which made up over two-thirds of the gold in the world at the start of the Bretton Woods system (as the fixed exchange rate system was commonly called), from diminishing to 20 per cent in the late 1960s, which along with other factors, created the conditions for abandoning the gold standard in 1973, with the declaration of the inconvertibility of the dollar. From then on a global system of fluctuating exchange rates was in force, which no longer necessitated an intervention fund.

The IMF's second role was limited by a shortage of the resources the fund had available to it. Accordingly, an intervention model was developed that assigned the fund the role of guarantor and first responder. The IMF was charged with inspecting the country requesting a loan, agreeing on a plan of political economy measures and granting a small loan; this was then complemented with other funds on trust that the debtor nation would align with the IMF's requirements. This is still the IMF's current role; many today would like to change that, partly because its resources have become wholly inadequate with respect to the financialization of the global economy, a topic we will discuss in Chapter 16.[29]

In conclusion, we can say that after the Second World War there was a high level of international institutional activism at the economic, political

26. Horie, *The International Monetary Fund*. On the operation of the Bretton Woods system, see Bordo & Eichengreen, *A Retrospective on the Bretton Woods System*. On Keynes, see also Skidelsky, *John Maynard Keynes 1883–1946*, Piffaretti, *Reshaping the International Monetary Architecture* and Cesarano, *Gli accordi di Bretton Woods*.
27. Baum, *Investing in Development* and Ayres, *Banking on the Poor*.
28. Only the dollar was convertible into gold. All other currencies could be converted to gold at a fixed exchange rate with the dollar.
29. Keynes, who died in 1946, did not live long enough to see – and perhaps criticize – the operation of the Bretton Woods system.

(the United Nations) and military (NATO, the North Atlantic Treaty Organization, was created in 1949) levels. The experiences of two world wars and the Great Depression had brought home the need to monitor and prepare for the shocks the world would inevitably suffer from natural causes, and conflict in order to mitigate their effects. Furthermore, the creation of international bodies contributed to multilateralizing negotiations; this produced more efficient and equitable outcomes from decisions made, since all interested parties were present at the negotiating table. If the world had enjoyed over a half-century of relative peace and prosperity it is certainly due to these "lighthouses" that guarantee safe harbours for ships sailing through tempestuous seas, and that establish places for negotiations to peacefully resolve conflicts. There is ample space today for improving the institutions that emerged after the Second World War, but the direction for building international institutions devoted to deal with specific issues has been irreversibly mapped out.

13.4 The reconstruction of France, Germany, Italy and the UK

Here we offer a few observations and comments on some basic aspects of reconstruction of the four largest European countries, the detailed events of which we have already charted.[30] First, we can note that the latest research has clarified that the productive capacity of various countries was destroyed much less than their infrastructure. Italy lost no more than 10 per cent of its industrial productive capacity, and the postwar productive capacity in the engineering industry was greater by one-third than pre-war levels.[31] Abelshauser has shown that at the end of the war Germany's fixed capital in the industrial sector was 11 per cent greater than in 1936, and much of it had been only recently built.[32] France had no significant loss, but the industrial apparatus suffered from the lack of recovery after the Great Depression. Britain came out of the war nearly intact, but with an ageing fixed capital because of a lack of investment in civil infrastructures and all its previous problems connected with industrial decline.

Productive industrial capacity was not what was lacking. As we've previously noted, what was missing was a favourable international context for

---

30. For a comparative overview see Dornbusch, Nölling & Layard, *Postwar Economic Reconstruction and Lessons for the East Today* and Di Nolfo & Vigezzi, *Power in Europe II: 1945–50*.
31. Zamagni, *Come perdere la guerra*, 37.
32. Abelshauser, "Germany: Guns, Butter and Economic Miracles".

productive recovery. This is precisely what the various international organizations provided,[33] which started the recovery, and the results can be appreciated in Table 13.4.[34] The most impressive results were obtained by Germany – although they started from a very low level in 1948 – followed by Austria, Italy and France, while all other countries showed increases of between 10 and 17 per cent. It is interesting to briefly consider how the counterpart funds were used (see Table 13.5). Indeed, the countries with the best results were those that used more of the counterpart funds for productive purposes, which indicates particular attention to strengthening industrial capacity and competitiveness, supply-side economic policies. In particular the slowness of the British economy during these years, which was a prelude to later years of slow growth, is linked to the scant attention the British gave to increasing investments and updating their technologies,[35] and probably to their lack of participation in the ECSC. However, this should be set alongside the enactment of the National Insurance Act inspired by the 1942 Beveridge Report,[36] which introduced a national health service, family allowances and old-age pensions, and the extensive nationalizations in coal, steel, electricity, gas, air and rail transport, rubber, and telephones made by Labour governments. This is not so much a distinctive trait in itself (there were many other public and nationalized companies in other European countries); however in Britain the nationalizations were made on mostly ideological grounds, while in other countries either they were inherited from the past (as in Italy and Germany) or were made to achieve precise political economy goals, as in France. Differently from France, the presence of an extensive nationalized sector in Britain was not combined with a strong industrial policy; this prevented an expansive utilization of public companies, which were generally managed as state monopolies.

---

33. Note Abelshauser's interesting interpretation of the role of the Marshall Plan in Germany: he held it to be quantitatively of little effect but significant strategically because, in a very different setting than the one prior, it allowed Germany to rebuild largely with its own resources and without political or military impediments. See Abelshauser, "American Aid and West German Economic Recovery".

34. Note that the levels attained in 1952 were higher than pre-war levels, which had already been recovered by nearly all countries, except Germany, between 1948 and 1949.

35. See Tomlinson, *Democratic Socialism and Economic Policy*.

36. William Beveridge, a noted progressive and social reformer, championed a complete system of social security to provide universal protection from the negative consequences of unemployment, disease, accidents and old age. His proposal was essentially a universalization of the social security system that Bismarck had already introduced, based on the Northern European model.

Table 13.4 National income increase between 1948 and 1952 (1948 = 100).

Country	Index
Austria	144
Belgium	113
Denmark	113
France	127
Federal Republic of Germany	161
Greece	114
Ireland	113
Italy	131
The Netherlands	111
Norway	113
Portugal	106
Sweden	114
UK	105
United States	114

Source: Maddison database.

So three of the four principal European countries stand out for their particularly spectacular performance, which was linked not only to the Marshall Plan but to a series of political economy measures. In Germany, three measures should be highlighted:

- the 1948 monetary reform, which made the market economy functional again and restored German industry to full operation;
- the adoption of a *social market economy*, that is, a mixed economy that respected the market but was careful to correct its more unacceptable distributional effects;[37]
- cooperation between capital and labour that allowed for co-management (*Mitbestimmung*, introduced in 1951), or the presence of trade union representatives on companies' boards of directors.

---

37. See Zamagni, "L'economia sociale di mercato nella storia".

Table 13.5 Counterpart fund use (%).

Region	Redemption of public or unused debt	Productive purposes
Austria	46	54
Denmark	83	17
France	8	92
Federal Republic of Germany	9	91
Greece	45	55
Italy	14	86
Norway	100	0
The Netherlands	62	38
UK	100	0
All participating countries	46	54

Source: Brown & Opie, *American Foreign Assistance,* 244.

The policies and international conditions discussed above worked together to allow Germany a very rapid recovery and then its "economic miracle", which we will consider in the next chapter.

In France there were no easy solutions to the problems of controlling the macroeconomy, with recurrent balance of payments and inflation crises, but the productive system was restarted by De Gaulle's decision in January 1946 to rely on a planned system. A small *Commissariat du plan* (planning commission) was established at the Presidency of the Council of Ministers with Jean Monnet at its head. He was quite skilled at obtaining national and international consensus around several basic production goals, initially for coal, steel, electricity, cement, farm machinery and railways, formulated in his first five year plan (the *Plan de modernisation et d'équipement*). Even the method was innovative: realistic and mutually compatible goals were set, a coordination system was set up for those involved in implementing the plan, and finally appropriate incentives were created. The results of the first plan initiated in 1947 were so positive that planning became a permanent part of France's political economy until the end of the 1970s; and it inaugurated the strong involvement of the French government in the economic development of the country, which remained a feature even after planning had been abandoned.[38]

---

38. See Estrin & Holmes, *French Planning in Theory and Practice.*

Italy had to work hard to restore a democracy that had been lost for over twenty years; a strong communist party, in alliance with the socialists, threatened to win the elections and push the country back into dictatorship, although in the opposite direction.[39] On 18 April 1948 the Christian Democrats, a centrist party, won the elections. It administered the Marshall Plan with pro-productive and pro-European choices and brought Italy into NATO, thereby tightly linking Italy's fate to the advanced Western democracies.[40] Italian entrepreneurs, once placed in contact with the American model, were able to restructure their largest enterprises, while also demonstrating the ability to creatively reorganize the vast scope of artisanal work and small companies; this launched the country into its own "economic miracle" comparable to that of the Germans in terms of the strength of its results.[41]

13.5 Decolonization

While the building of a new architecture for Europe was the greatest global turn of events after the Second World War, another was that countries formerly under colonial dominion gained independence, the long-term effects of which are still ongoing. This process had actually already begun in the eighteenth and nineteenth centuries in the Americas and Oceania, but between 1945 and 1975 over seventy new independent states were created, primarily in Africa and Asia. The Atlantic Charter enshrined the principles of people's self-determination that Woodrow Wilson had already advanced at the end of the First World War. However, fully realizing those principles met with serious difficulties, in part due to the Cold War between the American and Soviet blocs.[42] The bloodiest events were those in Korea and Vietnam. Between 1949 and 1952 over two million people were killed in the Korean War, which ended with the division of the country between North and South Korea. The North, supported by China, became a brutal military dictatorship; the South, with American support, proved to be one of the most notable economic

39. See especially Fauri, *Il piano Marshall e l'Italia*.
40. Lombardo, *L'Istituto Mobiliare Italiano II*.
41. In addition to Chapter 11 of my work *An Economic History of Italy*, in which I discuss the industrial policy options made during reconstruction, see the first 1996 issue of *Studi Storici*, devoted to "Italia, Europa, America. L'integrazione internazionale dell'economia italiana (1945–1963)".
42. For a general overview, see Droz, *Histoire de la décolonisation au XX siècle*.

success stories in Asia (see Chapter 16). The Vietnam War dragged on much longer and with much more devastating consequences. Indochina had a long history of domination by the French, before being invaded by Japan during the Second World War. When liberated by forces led by Ho Chi Minh, the French attempted to regain control, which in 1954 resulted in the creation of four countries: Laos, Cambodia, North Vietnam and South Vietnam. We cannot follow here the complicated events in those countries, but we cannot ignore that the United States' heavy involvement in defending the governments of South Vietnam from the North's attacks had profound global political and economic resonances; it ended in 1975 with the fall of South Vietnam and the unification of the country under the leadership of Ho Chi Minh. At that point, the governments of Laos and Cambodia were replaced by brutal communist dictatorships, one such the Khmer Rouge. Only the fall of the Soviet Union and China's evolution towards a market economy (see Chapter 16) permitted the political and economic evolution of these countries.

India was among the less traumatic cases of decolonization, which was negotiated with the British government and fulfilled in 1947.[43] The original unitary project was partially set aside by the creation of Pakistan that same year and the creation of Bangladesh later in 1971. Political and economic life has not proven easy for any of these countries, although over the long term India has shown itself capable of much more substantial progress (see Chapter 16). Regarding the complex turns of events in Africa, here we can only remark a few points. The first is that the decolonization of the Mediterranean areas of Africa was complicated by France's unwillingness to cede sovereignty, which led to several wars.[44] The creation of Israel in 1948, further introduced a permanent destabilizing factor in the region. If we add to that the presence of oil reserves, which had previously been developed by Anglo-American multinationals and were now becoming gradually nationalized by the newly independent states, and the question of poorly drawn state boundaries, there is good reason to understand why serious conflicts, civil wars, genocides, and population flights have arisen.

The acculturation of sub-Saharan Africa[45] had just begun when new states were created. Some were poorly drawn, others were without adequate leadership, all struggled to put tribal allegiances behind those of country; resulting

---

43. Darwin, *Britain and Decolonization* and Low, *Eclipse of Empire*.
44. See Pervillé, *De l'Empire à la décolonisation*.
45. Gifford & Louis, *Decolonization and African Independence* and Hargreaves, *Decolonization in Africa*.

in endemic civil wars, military dictatorships and enormous economic difficulties, and still with no end in sight. In South Africa the white minority's power survived independence and it maintained the racial segregation policies of apartheid, to which Western countries responded with embargoes to economically isolate the country; these were lifted with Nelson Mandela's release and his ascent to the presidency of the country in 1994. But there was no lack of problems for South Africa's new course.

While the process of decolonization redrew the political map of the world, it did not mean an upturn in the economic conditions for all the new states. The legacy left by the former colonial power (see Chapter 7), as well as local cultural traditions, were what made the difference. The third industrial revolution (discussed in Chapter 7) was significant for opening new economic opportunities for countries that had been cut off from global developments, but even then their ability to take advantage of these opportunities were constrained by their history.

14

The age of European growth and the return of instability

In this chapter we will limit ourselves to discussing the salient aspects of events in Europe during the second half of the twentieth century, drawing on the work of many others.[1] Although Europe had never before experienced such growing prosperity of the sort that existed during the era of the "economic miracles" between reconstruction and the mid-1970s, this dynamic process of growth was interrupted by events that greatly slowed down its growth rate and triggered a series of effects that would eventually produce another great crisis (which we will consider in Chapter 17). In this chapter we will explore the reasons for such a sustained period of growth and then the factors responsible for subsequent difficulties.

14.1 *Economic miracles: facts and interpretations*

The first fact to restate is that when we speak of Europe until the fall of the Soviet Union, we are referring to Western Europe. Eastern Europe had its own very different political and economic turns of events, closed off as it was by the Iron Curtain that sought to isolate it from being "contaminated" by Western capitalism. The Soviet model of the elimination of private property and the pursuit of central planning had been imposed on it, which was enforced more or less rigidly. Their economic relations with the Soviet Union were predominately confined within an exchange organization known as COMECON; it was to be analogous to the European Community (which we will discuss in the next chapter), but in reality it was much less successful, operated as it was for the exclusive interests of the Soviet Union and

---

1. One of the most recent is Eichengreen, *The European Economy since 1945*.

crushed by bureaucratic management. The literature on the economic events that happened in each of the countries under Soviet hegemony[2] is not large, because the little that could be accomplished was squandered[3], and in large measure even destroyed, by the failure of the Soviet model and the difficult phase of subsequent transition.[4]

Resuming our discussion of Western European countries, we shall first document the high increase in productivity, then consider its mechanisms and problems. A look at Table 14.1 shows the results attained during the years of high expansion until 1973; they subsequently increased incrementally, even though global growth rates dropped significantly, as we will see later. We can see that the Western European countries and Japan caught up with the leading country, the United States. Indeed, average European and Japanese growth rates were higher than those of the leading country, such that in 1950 the relative levels approached those of the United States, although the gap had not entirely closed. While Western Europe notably improved overall, note that the countries that grew the most were those with the lowest starting levels, although the negative correlation is not perfect[5] (see Figure 14.1). Britain is a paradigm case: in 1950 it was among the best situated countries in Europe with a level of 72 with respect to the United States, and it remained in that position until 1973, having been reached and in some cases exceeded by most Western European countries. No wonder then the continuing decline of Britain remains the subject of much research.[6] Ireland also had a disappointing relative performance, rising only from 36 to 46, as did Norway, rising from 52 to 67, while Italy had an absolute growth rate among the highest and equal to that of Germany. The three Mediterranean

---

2. Of course, for a more detailed discussion of this area it is necessary to follow in detail the developments of recent years: see Berend, *Central and Eastern Europe 1944–1993* and Offe, *Il tunnel.*

3. The Eastern European countries repeated what had already happened in the Soviet Union: as long as there was room to build infrastructure and military expenditure, centralized planning showed some results, with discreet income growth rates. However the system was to subsequently falter, with even the most basic factories becoming obsolete, and fail. We will further discuss this failure in Chapter 17, as well as in §15.2.

4. A comparison between Eastern and Western European countries can be found in V. Zamagni, "Institutional Innovations and Economic Growth in Europe in the Post-world War II Era".

5. For an insightful analysis of the process of convergence, see Broadberry, "Convergence: What the Historical Record Shows".

6. Among others, see Pollard, *The Wasting of the British Economy* and the comprehensive work by Crafts & Woodward, *The British Economy Since 1945.* See also Comfort, *The Slow Death of British Industry.* Note that the relative performance of Britain has improved from 1980 onwards.

Table 14.1 Per capita gross domestic product in Europe 1950–73 (international 1990 US dollars).

Country	Annual growth rates 1950–73	Levels (USA = 100)	
		1950	1973
Austria	4.9	39	67
Belgium	3.5	56	73
Denmark	3.1	70	84
Finland	4.3	43	66
France	4.0	55	79
Germany	5.0	45§	72*
Italy	5.0	36	64
The Netherlands	3.4	61	78
Norway	3.2	52	67
Sweden	3.1	70	81
Switzerland	3.1	93	109
UK	2.4	72	72
Greece	6.2	20	41
Ireland	3.1	37	46
Portugal	5.7	22	44
Spain	5.8	25	52
United States	2.4	100	100
Japan	8.0	20	69

Note: *only Federal Republic of Germany.

Source: Maddison, *The World Economy*.

countries of Greece, Portugal and Spain, which started from levels similar to those of Japan and lower than other Western European countries, experienced overall growth greater than any other European country,[7] but well

---

7. Many works offer a comparative analysis of the principal European countries; among them see Graham, *Government and Economies in the Postwar World*; Crafts & Toniolo, *Economic Growth in Europe Since 1945* and Schulze, *Western Europe: Economic and Social Change Since 1945*.

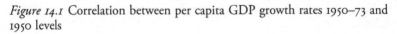

Figure 14.1 Correlation between per capita GDP growth rates 1950–73 and 1950 levels

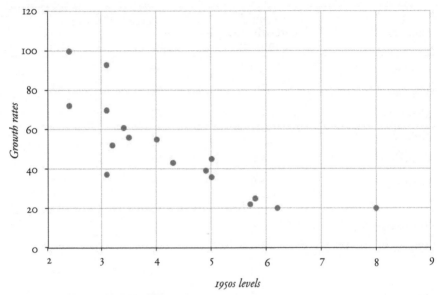

Source: Maddison, *The World Economy.*

below that of Japan;[8] in 1973 they remained distant from the rest of Western Europe.

Having summarily illustrated the quantitative data on which the expression "golden age" is based, the period of Western Europe's robust postwar expansion, we can now review some of the factors underlying it:

- The creation of new institutions that proved particularly adapted to the promotion and coordination of economic policies, as illustrated in Chapter 13. To these international institutions we should add the processes of European integration, considered in the next chapter.[9]
- The existence of a vast reserve labour force that was underemployed or unemployed, particularly in agriculture, and which was ready to pour into industry without claiming wage increases. This allowed the industrial

---

8. Regarding the transformation of the Japanese economy, see Dore, *Taking Japan Seriously* and Flath, *The Japanese Economy.*
9. A formal analysis of the impact of the institutions on postwar Europe can be found in the previously cited works by Eichengreen, as well as in Eichengreen, "Institutions and Economic Growth".

sector to expand through accumulated profits, which created a *capital widening* process that raised median productivity and hence consumption.[10]

- The "advantages of backwardness" – recalling Gershenkron's phrase, otherwise called the "technology gap" – that allowed Europe to follow the United States' lead and "Americanize" itself in various ways.[11]
- The great, progressive liberalization of international trade through the GATT, which on the one hand allowed better labour specialization, and on the other increased competition, both factors that increased efficiency in the use of the world's resources.
- Low growth of the prices of raw materials, and therefore favourable "terms of trade", a ratio of the growth of export prices to the prices of imports.
- Low levels of financial speculation, due to the Bretton Woods system of fixed exchange rates, and strong incentives for direct foreign investment through the growth of the multinationals.
- Expansive domestic economic policies, mostly through qualifying and supporting industrial policies, although there were a few (and not the most fortunate) purely Keynesian cases that supported the demand side.

These favourable conditions came together in a way that had never happened before. These were also fortunate years for the distribution of the fruits of this growing prosperity: with the introduction or expansion of the welfare state, growing inequality was contained and the idea that growth by its very nature is able to spread well-being throughout the population – an idea that unfortunately has been lost – had some credence.

14.2 *The welfare state*

Social inequalities have characterized society from its earliest days, but the principle of solidarity, inherent in European civilization through its Christian

---

10. This interpretive element derives from a 1954 article by Lewis, "Development with Unlimited Supplies of Labour", and is systematically organized in Kindleberger, *Europe's Postwar Growth*.

11. A vast literature also exists on the Americanization of Europe, which is discussed and summarized in Zeitlin & Herrigel, *Americanization and its Limits*. See also Gourvish & Tiratsoo, *Missionaries and Managers*.

roots, worked to remedy this. Consider the institutions of religious benevolence during the Middle Ages and the modern era that provided aid to the
needy, orphans and other vulnerable strata of the population. With the industrial revolution, this solidarity gradually evolved into institutional solutions
such as progressive taxation (in which the wealthy are taxed at a higher rate
than the poor) that allowed education to be publicly financed and an increasingly broad range of insurance measures against risk, paid through employers'
contributions as well as public subsidies.

After the Second World War there was a further progression of such
measures in the search for a more equitable and just society. The main
areas of intervention were public education, national health services, benefits for unemployment or verified cases of need, pensions, and assistance for
particular types of disadvantages (insurance coverage for work-related accidents was already widespread by the end of the nineteenth century). Other
related aspects should be added to these, such as access to culture – libraries,
museums, theatres and organized public events – and environmental protection, understood as a space to defend for ethical, aesthetic and health reasons
for the benefit of all citizens.

There are two models of European welfare: the German model and the
Nordic model.[12] The German welfare state model is known as the *social
market economy*. It is distinguished by being mainly financed by employers,
with a modest participation by workers and a more substantial contribution
by the state, particularly for assistance and contributions other than those
directly linked to workers. It was introduced by Bismarck during the 1880s for
the employees of large companies and was generalized after the Second World
War, together with the introduction of co-management (*Mitbestimmung*),
which assured workers a presence on the boards of directors of large companies.

The Nordic model of the *universal welfare state* resembles the German
model in its architecture, in the sense that there is broad and solid public
commitment to protecting citizens, but it is built on different foundations.
Where in Germany the social state came about from industrial development,
in Sweden the opposite happened, in that the social rights of all citizens were
leveraged to trigger economic growth. Furthermore, social aid is provided as
a right of citizenship rather than as a work-related benefit, and it is financed
entirely by taxation. In 1946 the new social democratic government enacted
a reform program that entailed a high level of state debt to support building
the social state. The impact on the productive system was extremely positive.

---

12. Esping-Andersen, *Politics Against Market*.

A new generation of workers were better educated and prepared, and the country's companies were able to leap forward in productivity. The standard of living of the population was more stable and increasing, and which in turn created an important internal market. The higher taxes obtained from the increased income went to offset and reduce the initial public debt.

The United States has long criticized the European welfare models, having always maintained that it is a matter of individual responsibility to obtain sufficient levels of well-being through one's own work, with help for the less fortunate provided by philanthropic individuals, foundations, religious groups and associations.[13] Only after the 1929 crisis with the enactment of the Social Security Act did Roosevelt's New Deal introduce assistance for people in difficulty (see Chapter 11). Even so, this was still a system that aimed to minimize the state's commitment; social risk was left to individuals, with the exception of those in poverty. Only during Barack Obama's presidency was there an attempt, which was highly opposed, to help citizens who were not poor enough to benefit from public assistance but who were not well off enough to afford adequate insurance policies and acceptable pensions.

In spite of allegations to the contrary, the European welfare state in and of itself was not a reason for inefficiency in the economic system – at least as long as its finances were compatible with economic growth rates, and it was not implemented at a time of high state budget deficits. In Table 14.2 we can evaluate the impact the welfare state has had on public spending, which reports the data from 1980 to 2013 (previous years are omitted due to inconsistency in the sources). We see that its impact increased over that period, sometimes greatly (note Portugal and Greece) and the exceptionalism of the United States emerges clearly with its public social spending lower than any other country. The two "Anglo-Saxon" European countries, Ireland and Britain, show a lower impact than other European countries, but higher than the United States. France tops the list of those countries with the highest impact, followed by Belgium, Finland and Denmark. Interestingly, Sweden, which was traditionally the country with the highest impact, contained it after 2005. Only Germany lowered its impact between 2005 and 2013 due to a highly contested but very effective reform, which also improved its competitiveness.[14]

---

13. Brandes, *American Welfare Capitalism, 1880–1940*.
14. Regarding the effects of cuts to the welfare state made particularly after the 2008 economic crisis, see Atkinson, *The Economic Consequences of Rolling Back the Welfare State*.

Table 14.2 Impact of social spending on gross domestic product.

Country	1980	1990	2005	2013
Austria	22.1	23.4	26.8	28.3
Belgium	23.5	24.9	25.6	30.9
Denmark	24.4	25.0	27.3	30.2
Finland	18.0	23.8	25.0	30.6
France	20.6	24.9	29.6	32.0
Germany	21.8	21.4	27.0	25.6
Italy	18.0	21.4	24.9	28.7
The Netherlands	24.8	25.6	21.8	24.6
Sweden	26.0	28.5	28.7	28.2
UK	16.3	16.3	20.2	22.5
Greece	10.3	16.5	21.1	24.3
Ireland	16.0	17.2	15.8	21.9
Portugal	9.6	12.4	22.8	25.8
Spain	15.4	19.7	20.9	27.3
United States	12.8	13.1	15.5	18.6
Japan	10.3	11.1	18.4	23.1

Note: the figure for Japan in the last column is for 2011.

Source: OECD database.

14.3 *Regime changes during the 1970s*

Many of the conditions that sustained the economic miracles could not last indefinitely. Wages soon became quite dynamic, with union protests during the late 1960s and early 1970s. May 1968 in France, the labour riots in late 1969 in Italy and many other protest movements marked a discontinuity in growth, which by then was linked more to growth patterns, that needed to be linked more to productivity increases (to pay for higher wages) than to investments aimed at expanding production capacity.

The fixed exchange rate system of the gold exchange standard (the Bretton Woods system) was abandoned in 1973 with the declaration of the inconvertibility of the dollar. That opened the way for flexible exchange rates and the return of speculation on the many futures markets that proliferated in anticipation of change in many economic variables.

On top of this, the prices of some raw materials rose sharply (particularly oil, which quadrupled between 1973 and 1974), resulting in terms of trade that tended to be unfavourable, but were in any case highly volatile. Ultimately a third industrial revolution was underway (the implications of which we shall discuss in some depth in the next section), which ended the period of high European growth and paved the way to the return to a more unstable global economy. This created local crises throughout the 1980s, but it did not trigger a global crisis until 2007, which we will discuss in Chapter 17. Europe sought to face this changed global context by continuing the process of European integration (see Chapter 15), while rapid growth and development was initiated by countries outside of Europe, as we will see in Chapter 16. Table 14.3 gives an account of the impact of these global changes on European income growth rates. From 1973–1995, although European growth rates were more than halved, in general they remained higher than American rates; the process of convergence continued, albeit at much slower rates. Between 1995 and 2007, however, the landscape changed with many European countries growing less than the United States. Consequently, the rankings of European per capita incomes compared to the United States show limited changes, with fluctuations from country to country.

What forcefully emerges from these data is that the process of convergence seems to have been arrested before its ultimate end was attained, that European and Japanese incomes equal American incomes. However, this needs further comment. We must keep in mind that GDP is the result of different variables; it includes production, certainly, but also employment rates and annual hours worked. There are notable differences between these variables from country to country, but particularly between Europe and the United States, which lead us to conclude that the convergence in productivity between the United States and the main European countries (certainly not all, in particular the new EU members are still behind – see Chapter 15) was completed prior to the end of the twentieth century. However, this does not clearly emerge from the per capita GDP data because Europe generally works fewer hours than the United States and employment rates are frequently lower, as a result also of the more widespread part-time employment.[15] We cannot here consider the reasons why the European per capita level of income shows as lower than the US level, but the implication of highly convergent

---

15. See the development of these observations in Van Ark, O'Mahoney & Timmer, "The Productivity Gap Between Europe and the United States".

levels of productivity per hour worked is that the process of imitating US technology has been substantially concluded. Europe must equip itself for innovation, something that until now it has been slow to do, apart from in some small areas of the continent.

The worsening of the European position after the 1990s is bound up with the financialization of the global economy (see §14.5) and the recent global crisis, which we will discuss in Chapter 17.

Table 14.3 Per capita gross domestic product trends 1973–2013 (purchasing power parity).

Country	Average annual growth rates of per capita income			Levels of per capita income (US = 100)			
	1973–95	1995–2006	2007–13	1973	1995	2007	2013
Austria	2.2	2.1	1.1	67	84	81	85
Belgium	1.8	2.0	1.1	73	80	76	79
Denmark	1.7	1.9	0.8	84	82	81	83
Finland	1.6	3.5	-0.2	66	69	78	75
France	1.7	1.6	0.5	79	76	71	71
Germany	1.7	1.3	1.4	72	79	77	81
Italy	2.2	1.2	-0.6	64	77	70	66
The Netherlands	1.6	2.1	-0.2	78	79	90	87
Sweden	1.4	2.8	0.3	81	78	85	85
UK	1.7	2.5	-1.0	72	72	78	73
Greece	1.4	3.8	-1.4	41	47	60	49
Ireland	3.4	6.0	-2.8	46	65	97	87
Portugal	2.2	1.8	0.3	44	52	52	53
Spain	2.4	3.6	-1.1	52	58	68	63
United States	1.8	2.1	0.5	100	100	100	100
Japan	2.5	1.0	0.2	69	80	70	69

Note: the EU sources do not entirely match the Maddison database (which ends in 2006) due to slightly different criteria in calculating purchasing power parities. I have used the Maddison series until 2006 for growth rates and for 1973 levels; other data are from official EU sources.

Sources: growth rates, 1973–2006, Maddison database; 2007–1013, official EU sources; levels: 1973, Maddison database; 1995, 2007, 2013, official EU sources.

14.4 *The third industrial revolution and globalization*

As explained in Chapter 7, the third industrial revolution, which began to spread contemporaneously with the re-emergence of global instability in the 1970s, led to significant changes in production systems where fixed assembly lines were increasingly abandoned and so-called "flexible manufacturing" was introduced. Flexibility within the factory saw the introduction of robots and automated systems that allowed the manufacture of models with countless variations and the use of machines for heavy and hazardous work. There was also flexibility in that factories themselves could be dispersed in many different places, with each one specializing in a particular production phase. Global trade became primarily trade in intermediate products that were then assembled elsewhere. This is the globalization of production: the world itself is the locus of the various phases of production, such that for more complex products it no longer makes sense to talk of where they are made, because they are made *in the world*. The product is designed by a parent company that then parcels out the various parts of production to subsidiaries or independent suppliers, choosing the most specialized or the one able to make it at the lowest cost, depending on the opportunity.

Companies that once had the capacity to make everything in house are now compelled to outsource in order to achieve advantages unavailable to them in their original location. During the second industrial revolution companies were well placed in the most advantageous locations, from which they had no incentive to move. However, with the possibility of control at a distance provided by electronics and the greater ease of transport, companies have fragmented and have included in their production chain even highly specialized small and medium companies, or companies with low labour costs in developing countries. Third industrial revolution companies are organized in networks, with links that go beyond the market, involving various contractual relationships. This process has spawned on the one side a race in developed countries to get into high value added sectors and processes to be able to pay their high salaries, in addition to not having to compete with new entrants, and on the other side a tendency to outsource lower value added production to countries with low labour costs.

Another feature of the third industrial revolution is that office work has been made more efficient by the development of dedicated software, useable by even the least specialized employee. The impact on the labour market is significant: during the second industrial revolution it broadly had the shape of a pyramid, with generic labour forming a broad base, white collar work forming a substantial middle level, and management occupying the narrow top. Now it has the shape of an hourglass: generic labour is still necessary, and management has greatly expanded, but the middle layer has contracted. The process of imitation has become much more rapid – giving rise to the dramatic growth of the BRIC economies (see Chapter 16) – and has created a veritable race to produce innovations in response to the driver of technological obsolescence, never before so acutely experienced. Thus companies that want to compete in advanced market sectors necessarily must have research laboratories, participate in international research networks and "go international" by being present in various global markets.

It goes without saying that the implications of the third industrial revolution have made productive activity much more complex and competitive for entrepreneurs in advanced countries, while going international requires at least a medium size company.

14.5 *Deregulation and the financialization of the economy*

Even during the gold standard a gap had opened up in the controls on international financial flows with the emergence of the eurodollar market in 1963, the year when for the first time the Soviet Union deposited dollars in Western banks with no intention of exchanging them into local currencies. After that Western European banks found themselves holding dollar deposits, which they began to employ *as dollars*, there being no law prohibiting such use. This credit circuit was not subject to any regulation, since the central banks had authority only over their own currencies, and the US Federal Reserve could not extend control beyond its own borders. During the 1970s, with the growth of oil revenues in the Gulf countries, the eurodollar market soared. In 1973 it amounted to $315 billion, and ten years later it had reached $2,278 billion. The eurodollar market made many banks appreciate the lack of regulation that permitted higher returns, although with higher levels of risk. Thus a series of financial crises began in the early 1980s due to excessive credit extended in the eurodollar markets to countries with little chance of repayment.

The problems of failed repayments is precisely what prompted a series of "financial innovations" designed to make loans more liquid. First, loans were *securitized* so they could be sold at discounts on the amounts receivable, which recovered liquidity for use for other purposes. From there a plethora of complex financial instruments emerged – derivatives, hedge funds, Asset Backed Securities (ABS), Credit Default Swaps (CDS) and Collateralized Debt Obligations (CDO) – that were intended to allow higher returns to both banks and savers while seeking to balance the risks these high returns implied. Banks changed from being service providers of credit for production and consumption into profit producers through financial engineering. The high returns offered by these securities created a stampede to invest in them – the less regulated the market the more rapid the investments – until international capital markets were liberalized in 1990.

This spike in global financial activity was energised by a large change that occurred in the United States. Since the Glass–Steagall Act of 1933 (discussed in Chapter 7) nothing much had changed in US finance until the early 1980s, when it became clear that the United States was increasingly cut off from new developments happening in the financial world. The process to liberalize the financial sector, known as *deregulation*[16] was begun by President Reagan in 1980 and proceeded unabated, eliminating size restrictions, favouring mergers and the creation of branches, until the Glass–Steagall Act was finally abolished in 1999, which allowed banks to use customer deposits for their own activities. It has been said that this made the US banks "universal" banks, in the sense of the European model (which was discussed in Chapter 8 and also in Chapter 5 with reference to Germany) however there is a great difference between the two. In fact the German model of universal bank was able to use deposits for industrial investments, and it offered various services to its entrepreneurial clients. These were therefore long-term investments of a productive nature. US banks, which had become universal without a firm tradition of industrial investments, caught the favourable wind of investing in securities purely for buying and selling to generate short-term profits. Accordingly, their investments were for the very short term, for speculative purposes rather than in support of productive activities or private savings. Deregulation continued even after 1999, which exempted large swathes of financial activity from control by the authorities and which created significant opacity in the system – a large part of the difficulty in assessing the size of the speculative bubble in 2007–8, to be discussed in Chapter 17.

---

16. A sketch is available in Sherman, *Short History of Financial Deregulation in the United States.*

15

The process of European integration

15.1 *The Treaty of Rome and the customs union*

Immediately after the ECSC (see Chapter 13), Europe tried to build the European Defence Community (EDC); it was a resounding failure, which reinforced the belief that the economy was the ground for the process of European integration. Gathering the suggestions that came from previous attempts to form customs unions (only one of which had succeeded, the Benelux countries), the foreign ministers of the six countries participating in the ECSC met in Messina, Sicily; from that meeting the proposal emerged to create a customs union and share other economic policies in transport and energy. The UK was again invited to participate in the negotiations, and again it rejected the idea of sacrificing part of its national sovereignty to supranational institutions. Two treaties of extraordinary importance were signed in Rome on 25 March 1957. One established the European Economic Community (EEC), known at that time as the European Common Market (ECM), and the other created the European Atomic Energy Community (Euratom). Euratom was not very successful, even though it contributed to maintaining Europe's competitiveness in the field of nuclear energy.[1] The ECM, however, was crucially important; not only did it abolish the customs barriers within the six countries, expanding the intra-European market for the first time, it made the ECM a single player in international trade negotiations.

After the ECM came into force in 1958, the elimination of internal customs barriers was staggered over ten years, achieving the elimination of all tariffs in July 1968. During this period trade in the six countries boomed, with the

---

1. Europeans established other cooperative agencies in nuclear physics, among them CERN (European Organization for Nuclear Research) which is particularly important.

progressive redirection of flows within the customs union. Exchange within the ECM went from just under one-third to over half the foreign trade of the member countries, which clearly had the effect of creating new trade, at least in industrial products. In response to the evident success of the ECM those Western European countries not part of it created the European Free Trade Association, or EFTA, which eliminated internal tariffs but left the member countries free to negotiate their foreign tariffs, which perpetuated the problems for smaller countries. However, as noted above, and after some initial hesitation, the ECM became a single player in international trade negotiations, initially within the GATT.[2] It then initiated its own Generalized System of Preferences (1971) trade policy with developing countries, and agreements with some former colonies – renamed the ACP (African, Caribbean and Pacific) countries – were initiated in Yaoundé in 1963 and continued in Lomé from 1975 onwards.

Little by little, partly due to other European countries successively joining (discussed further in §15.2), the European Union (EU)[3] became the most important player in international trade, surpassing even the United States. It also contributed to liberalizing international trade, although maintaining high protections for its agriculture (see §15.4) and a series of protections or subsidies for sectors in crisis (steel, cars), mature sectors (textiles, clothing), or those considered strategic (aeroplanes, electronics). Many of these protectionist measures were heavily criticized, particularly by the United States, which did not take lightly to losing global leadership in trade, even asserting the idea that the EU was as closed as a fortress. That was unfair as the EU was certainly not the only advanced area to practice protectionism (Japan had for far longer, and the United States was not exempt either) and its opening up of the economy to international trade, even excluding intra-European trade, was greater than that of the United States and Japan.[4] Another important trait of European foreign trade was that imports and exports were fairly well balanced, compared to both the United States' high deficit and Japan's and now particularly China's surpluses.

---

2. The first GATT round in which the ECM took part as a single entity was the Kennedy round in the early 1960s, which dragged on at some length, partly because the ECM countries, and France in particular, were not always consistent in entrusting their representatives with a single mandate.

3. From here on I will always use the expression "European Union" to denote European member states as a whole, even though that designation was not officially introduced until the Maastricht Treaty in 1992 (see §15.7); previously the expression "European Economic Community" (EEC) was used.

4. Hanson, *Limits to Free Trade*.

Nonetheless it remained true to say that abolishing internal tariffs did not immediately entail the creation of a truly free European market, due to the persistence of numerous non-customs barriers to the free circulation of goods, barriers which were in large measure dismantled only after the Single European Act of 1986. Regarding movements of capital, extensive controls remained in place until their liberalization in 1990. In the field of finance, the Treaty of Rome established the European Investment Bank (EIB) as a development financing agency, but nothing was done to harmonize the banking or monetary systems. Under pressure from Italy, the free movement of workers within the EU was introduced, with equal treatment and the right to accumulate social benefits accrued in different countries, although without any effort to formulate pan-European social policies (see §15.4). The European Social Fund (ESF) was created to facilitate emigrants adjusting to their new destination countries, although with very little impact.

While the Treaty of Rome marked a fundamental step in the process of European integration, because it addressed a crucially important environment for the general economic development of the countries involved, it retained the ECSC's approach of partially resolving problems without coordinating macroeconomic policies

15.2 Subsequent accessions

In the early 1960s the success of the six ECM countries and the recession in the UK economy prompted the UK to change its policy of indifference to European integration; together with its economic satellites, Ireland and Denmark it applied to join in August 1961. However, with De Gaulle in power, the UK's perennially uncooperative attitude led France to veto the request. The attempt was repeated in 1967, with a similar denial, this time due to difficulties in the UK economy, which led to the devaluation of the pound. It became clear that negotiations with the UK could be resumed only after the De Gaulle era.

That occurred in June 1970, with Norway applying alongside the UK, Ireland and Denmark. This time the outcome was positive, and the treaty of accession for the new countries was signed in January 1972; however, it was not ratified by Norway, where a popular vote rejected it, and so the EU expanded to nine countries on 1 January 1973. Coinciding with the turmoil of cancelling the Bretton Woods system of fixed exchange rates and with the outbreak of the oil crises and a time of international instability, the UK's joining wasn't easy. In particular, the UK found the Common Agricultural Policy (see §15.3), a particular problem, requiring as it did large expenses but no advantages (only to be corrected, at Margaret Thatcher's insistence, when an agreement was reached that reduced Britain's contribution to EU revenue). In any event, it took time for UK trade to shift towards the EU and for it to again become a "European country", which it did while maintaining its distinctive attitude of not fully cooperating right up to its decision in 2016, made by referendum, to leave the European Union.[5] For Denmark and Ireland, the other two countries, economic integration into the EU was quicker and easier. For Ireland in particular, entry into the EU marked the beginning of a phenomenal development process that redeemed the country from centuries of poverty and dependence on Britain, and it soared in European rankings for per capita income.

The second expansion of the EU was with Greece, the first country to obtain an association agreement with the Community, which included various privileges, among them the unilateral elimination of EU tariffs for Greek imports of manufactured goods. This agreement was frozen after the 1967 military coup in Greece, but with the return to democracy in 1975, the request for membership was made. Despite Greece's income being much lower than the EU average, the negotiations were successful and the treaty of accession was signed on 28 May 1979 and went into effect on 1 January 1981. The effects of joining the EU on the Greek economy are somewhat contradictory; the country failed both to develop substantial export flows to the EU and to correct the outdated defects in its economy, but it did manage to remain connected to the rest of Europe, although always bringing up the rear.

Soon after Greece's request for accession, Spain and Portugal, having been freed from their dictatorships, presented requests for accession in 1977. This time the decision took longer because the EU itself was at an impasse, fearing that adding the burden of Spain could alter the balances that had been so painstakingly achieved. Only at the beginning of Felipe Gonzales's time as prime minister of Spain in 1982 were negotiations relaunched and the two Iberian countries were finally accepted, with the treaty signed on 12 June 1985 coming into effect on 1 January 1986. Both countries quickly adapted to the EU's rules and fully participated in its economic processes, undergoing a successful positive trend of growth when the two countries joined.

---

5. At the time of writing (early 2017) the exit process had not taken shape, so the tables still refer to "Europe 28".

At this point the EU included twelve countries, with others knocking at the door. By then the EFTA was moribund, and the remaining countries that were part of it resolved to apply for accession to the EU between the late 1980s and early 1990s. They obtained a prompt response from the EU, which was to sign a treaty to create the European Economic Area (EEA) on 2 May 1992 to take effect on 1 January 1993; then in 1994 the EU accepted all the former EFTA countries into the EU itself, which took effect on 1 January 1995. However, only Austria, Finland and Sweden actually joined; Norway (for the second time) and Switzerland did not ratify the treaty of accession and remained in the EEA.[6] At this point all of Western Europe, with the exception of a few fringe areas, was part of the EU.

While this historical process was being fulfilled, the Soviet hegemony over Eastern Europe collapsed. This resulted in the unification of Germany in 1990, and the new governments of the other Eastern Bloc countries immediately turned to the EU for aid, association agreements and ultimately to request actual accession. In May 1990 the EU created the European Bank for Reconstruction and Development (EBRD) alongside the European Investment Bank (EIB). The EU then initiated the accession procedure for many of the Eastern European countries, as well as others that had applied in the meantime. This required a significant commitment. It was not a new Marshall Plan, but something more: in addition to material aid, the EU engaged in a process of institution-building to help the transition of those countries' institutions towards a market economy. In 2005 ten countries (including Cyprus and Malta, which are not part of Eastern Europe) were welcomed into the EU; Romania and Bulgaria were accepted in 2007, bringing the total to twenty-seven European countries in the EU. Meanwhile the other Balkan countries, having overcome serious conflict and ethnic problems, began the process of becoming candidates for entry; as of 2016 only one, Croatia, had entered the EU (2013) which made it the twenty-eighth member. Turkey is another candidate that has been in process for some time, and as of 2016 it is still in standby. Its difficulties are not mainly economic but political in nature, since one of the requirements for becoming a member of the EU is having a solid democracy.

A comparative framework of the positioning of the various countries in the European Union can be seen in Table 15.1. Note that the new entrants, with the exception of Slovenia and Cyprus, improved their relative positions between 2002 and 2013, converging towards the EU average for per capita GDP, and Estonia, Latvia, Poland, Slovakia and Romania improved quite

---

6. To be precise, Iceland is also part of it.

substantially. Conversely, the relative situation of some historical members worsened, particularly Italy, Greece and the UK, as well as France, Belgium, Spain and Holland; only Germany and Luxembourg improved. In general, we note a marked process of convergence towards the average, with a few outlying cases.[7]

Table 15.1 Index of per capita gross domestic product, 2002–13 (purchasing power parity).

Region	2002	2013	Region	2002	2013
EU (28 countries)	100	100	EU (28 countries)	100	100
Eurozone (18 countries)	111	107	Eurozone (18 countries)	111	107
Belgium	125	119	*Lithuania*	43	73
Bulgaria	31	45	*Luxembourg*	241	258
Czech Republic	74	82	*Hungary*	60	66
Denmark	128	124	*Malta*	82	86
Germany	115	122	Holland	137	131
Estonia	48	73	Austria	127	128
Ireland	139	130	*Poland*	47	67
Greece	91	73	Portugal	78	79
Spain	100	94	*Romania*	29	55
France	116	107	Slovenia	82	82
Croatia	53	61	*Slovakia*	53	75
Italy	113	99	Finland	115	113
Cyprus	93	89	Sweden	125	127
Latvia	41	64	Britain	122	109
			United States	155	150
			Japan	111	103

Note: countries that improved are in italics.

Source: Eurostat (http://ec.europa.eu/eurostat).

---

7. See Baldwin & Wyplosz, *The Economics of European Integration*.

15.3 *The Common Agricultural Policy*

There were already provisions in the Treaty of Rome to make all active protectionist measures uniform among all countries within the ECM. Agriculture then counted much more than today in terms of people employed and value added. The goal of agricultural protection, about which France was particularly insistent, was to avoid the fate of the British agricultural sector, which had vanished after protectionism was abolished with the repeal of the Corn Laws in 1846; agriculture was deemed strategic for food security for the European population. To accomplish this it was necessary to support farmers' incomes, either through direct income integration schemes or through price supports at levels considered sufficiently profitable for agricultural companies.

At the beginning of the 1960s the ECM began to outline a Common Agricultural Policy (CAP),[8] and agreement was reached on protectionism based on price supports for some strategic products (grains, meat and dairy products) and on customs duties that were to be compensatory with reference to the variability of world prices, rather than fixed *ad valorem*. Each spring intervention prices were set for individual products, which remained fixed for the following year; these were translated into the individual national currencies at the fixed exchange rates then in force. The surpluses over the quantity sold at the set price that resulted on various markets were neutralized by buying them at the intervention price and storing them in common warehouses. This system began operation on 1 January 1962; it was administered by the European Agricultural Guarantee Fund (EAGF), which also had a small section dedicated to restructuring European agriculture. The scheme quickly proved to be costly, absorbing much of the modest budget of the EU,[9] because it maintained the prices of protected agricultural products well above world prices, although in varying degrees. In subsequent years it was extended to other products, particularly to the Mediterranean products such as olive oil, wine, citrus fruits and tobacco, demanded by newer members of the EU. The cost of this policy fell primarily on the mass of consumers who paid prices above global levels for protected food products, and more marginally on the taxpayers who financed the operating costs of the EAGF.

However, an unexpected result of this system was that it transformed the EU from a traditional food products importer into an exporter; this crowded out most of the trade flows originating from developing countries, which

---

8. Patel, *Fertile Ground for Europe?*
9. That budget item is held around 1 per cent of the Community GDP, or 2 per cent of total public expenditures of the Community countries.

came to see European markets as increasingly impervious to their exports, but it also cut into the United States' position as the pre-eminent exporter on world markets. In fact, since storing products that could not be sold in the EU threatened to irreparably overrun the warehouses, the EAGF decided to subsidize exports by covering the difference between internal Community prices and world prices; this allowed it to get rid of stocks that would have otherwise rotted. Table 15.2 gives the overall effect of the European agricultural policies on production, exports and imports.

Note that these policies succeeded first in increasing production until the mid-1980s, and then in maintaining total EU production, similarly to what happened in the United States and Japan. However, with exports the EU distinguished itself by an incomparably more dynamic export performance than the US or Japan and by a corresponding containment of its imports. This could not but provoke negative reactions by developing countries and the United States, which repeatedly threatened, and occasionally implemented, retaliatory measures.

Table 15.2 Comparative agricultural indicators for the three most developed world areas 1965–94 (volume index 1979–81 = 100).

Date		EU 15	USA	Japan
Production	*1965*	73	69	78
	1985	107	108	108
	1994	105	116	102
Exports	*1965*	37	37	38
	1985	129	76	39
	1994	169	84	46
Imports	*1965*	63	72	45
	1985	106	130	110
	1994	122	204	130

Source: Food and Agricultural Organization (various years).

The system faced its first crisis when fixed exchange rates were abolished (see §15.5) and difficulties emerged during the mid-1970s in administering the common prices. To do this, so-called "green" currencies were introduced; these values were also fixed annually, and the reference price was translated into them. However, because real currencies fluctuated, the difference between the green currencies and the market-determined value of the various currencies gave rise to monetary compensation payments, piling distortion on distortion that caused increasing discontent with the operation of the EAGF. The second crisis occurred in the mid-1980s, when the EU became aware of the excessive predominance of agrarian interests on its budget, in contrast with the inevitable decline of European agriculture, while many other urgent problems required greater attention. Moreover, in the previous round of GATT negotiations (called the Uruguay round), the Americans had applied considerable pressure to weaken European agricultural protection, and more generally to include agricultural products in GATT negotiations, which had hitherto been excluded. The EU decided to initiate a wholesale reform of the CAP, which began in 1992 as the MacSharry reform. It provided for a progressive reduction in intervention prices, a transition to direct income compensation schemes for farmers, the imposition of production quotas for products that had the highest surpluses, compensation for reforesting arable land, incentives for growing products that were not in surplus, and improvement in the quality of and greater respect for the environment.

With the approval of the Uruguay round of trade negotiations in December 1994 and the entry into force of the World Trade Organization (WTO) in 1995, agreement was reached to shift the various forms of agricultural protection to duties in order to simplify negotiations, progressively eliminate export subsidies, introduce minimum import quotas, and introduce preferential treatment for developing countries (along the lines of the previously agreed generalized preferences on manufactured goods). With the opening of the 2001 negotiations in Doha, which had the general goal of lowering agricultural protection, the EU understood that the 1992 reform was not sufficient, and it launched the Fischler reform in 2003. This was an even more radical reform, in that it altogether abandoned the market price support approach in favour of direct income support for farmers. During the transition phase that support took into account the historical payments made under the previous system, which perpetuated a series of imbalances between countries and between products, but at least it brought about a progressive alignment of internal EU prices with international prices.[10]

The entry of the new members in 2005 necessitated lowering direct interventions by the old member countries in favour of the new countries, and so beginning in 2014 a series of indicators linked to environmental management,

---

10. Cunha *et al.*, *An Inside View of the CAP Reform Process*. On the results of this reform, see also Shucksmith, Thomson & Roberts, *The CAP and the Regions*.

biodiversity, technology improvements and landscape preservation were set as the basis for payments throughout the EU (which in 2015 counted around 12 million farmers). Concurrently, in negotiations under the aegis of the WTO the EU continues to offer substantial reductions in duties, but as of 2016 negotiations could be concluded only for limited general agreements, and not for an overall cut in duties.[11]

With these major changes CAP has experienced a turn around. After decades in which agricultural protection allowed the EU to ensure a good agricultural base – without however obstructing a significant exodus of the work force from the countryside – it can now think about decreasing the cost of such protection, abandon an obsessive interest in quantity to aim more at the quality of products and the environment, and reopen the EU agricultural markets to developing countries. Even the cost impact of the CAP has been brought under control, shifting from around 75 per cent of the budget to 40 per cent, while remaining one of the pillars of the EU.

15.4 *Regional and social policies*

In the midst of the first oil crisis in 1974, when all countries had already had to deal with the inflationary pressures of abandoning the Bretton Woods system, the rise in oil prices, and finding themselves with serious deficits in their balance of payments and public accounts, the European Regional Development Fund (ERDF) was created to prevent international difficulties from worsening conditions in the less developed European regions. At first it was a small fund distributed, on the basis of national quotas, as contributions that financed up to 30 per cent of the cost of projects and it was used mainly by Italy and Ireland. When Greece, Spain and Portugal became part of the EU, interest sharply increased in how territorial rebalancing could be achieved with the ERDF. In the early 1980s the ERDF began experimenting with smaller and more comprehensive interventions through the integrated Mediterranean programmes (IMPs). This was implemented with a first reform of the fund in 1985, which replaced fixed quotas – frequently not fully used – with quantitative indicators that established maximum and minimum allocations for each country; it also more clearly identified criteria for accepting projects that gave clear preference to integrated intervention packages.

---

11. Swinnen, *The Political Economy of the 2014–2020 CAP*.

A true reform was achieved in 1988, and all structural funds were reorganized (including the social fund and the structural part of the EAGF) with a unified plan that set various objectives beyond developing backwards areas and combating unemployment; among these were supporting areas in decline and promoting sparsely populated regions. The most important aspect of the reform was that funds were no longer allocated at the national but at the regional level, with an automatic provision that allowed regions with a per capita income lower than 75 per cent of the European average to submit projects for consideration. The procedure for selecting projects also changed, giving greater importance to local municipal and regional governments and introducing a comprehensive system of evaluating project implementation phases and their results.

In the social field, in addition to funding professional training and retraining courses, various social action programmes were initiated that were designed to improve working conditions, achieve parity among workers, incentivize dialogue among the various social bodies and mutually recognize diplomas. Finally in 1989 the Community Charter of the Fundamental Social Rights of Workers was adopted, which was seen as a means for harmonizing European social legislation – a goal that remains far off, however.[12]

The Maastricht Treaty (see §15.7) gave much more prominence to the commitment to improving the development levels of the most disadvantaged regions of the Community. It significantly increased the endowment of the structural funds, and in 1993 it initiated a cohesion fund destined for the countries with a national per capita income below 90 per cent of the European average. At this point many European countries set aside their national intervention plans for troubled areas to work on co-sponsored EU projects.[13] With the entry of the new members the structural funds became increasingly important, to the point that they made up 40 per cent of the EU budget. This was partly because cross-border projects were funded, with the goal of unifying the EU from an infrastructure standpoint (particularly with high speed railways) and modernizing it by promoting new energy sources and expanding the telecommunication networks.

Given the increasing attention paid to the structural funds, and the well-

---

12. The UK was the only country not to sign the Charter and that opposed Maastricht, chiefly because the Charter was to become the social chapter of the new treaty. In 1997 the Blair government withdrew this opposition, and the Charter was incorporated into the Treaty of Amsterdam on 2 October 1997 as Article 118A.

13. Recall that Community projects are always co-financed and that the Union has a general rule of "partnership" with national, regional and communal levels of government.

known existence of pronounced income gaps within the European Union, it is very important to ask if a process of convergence has happened. There has been much pessimism on this point, which is supported by the lack of regional data that can actually be compared. Some have argued that the European economy exhibited opposite behaviour to that of the United States – where the high mobility of people favoured relatively contained regional gaps – by privileging the central regions to the detriment of those on the periphery. With the publication of regional data by the EU (from the REGIO database maintained by Eurostat, the official EU statistical bureau) longitudinal analyses have been made from 1970 onwards. What emerged from these analyses is that the process of convergence has been continuous and sustained, with a common tendency by many initially more advanced areas to regress in relative terms, and even more initially backward areas to advance in both absolute and relative terms. The gap between the average per capita income of the first ten and the last ten regions (out of seventy-four regions in the EU-9) between 1950 and 1970 went from 3.7 to 2.8.[14] The same gap, recalculated with purchasing power parity, among the EU-9 regions during the period 1970–1995, went from 2.4 to 1.8. Performing the same calculation for the three countries that entered during the 1980s, we see that between 1981 and 1995, of the thirty-six regions that comprise them, only four worsened their initial position relative to the European average, and one remained stationary. Even with subsequent EU expansions, the process of convergence continued, as we saw in §15.2. It is still true that while there is a marked process of convergence between countries, that is less true between regions, particularly during the post-2008 crisis years. The central regions in each country have proven to be very dynamic, while some of the more peripheral regions, among them some regions in Southern Italy, have shown persistent weaknesses.[15]

Determining how much of this convergence was the result of new opportunities that opened up to the more backwards European regions as European economic integration progressed and how much to attribute to the effects of policies specifically designed for convergence and cohesion is beyond the scope of this chapter. There is no doubt however that by now there have been too many infrastructure projects and investments made with the support of

---

14. Recall also that the EU in the timeframe considered was still at six members, but the other three were included in the calculation in order to have a basis of comparison for the successive timeframe. In fact, Italy was the only country that demonstrated strong convergence in the EU-6 period. See Leonardi, *Convergence, Cohesion and Integration in the EU* and *Cohesion Policy in the EU*.

15. Wozniak Boyle, *Conditional Leadership*.

regional policies to deny that their contributions have been decisive.[16] We should also add that in recent years part of the structural funds have been used to partially finance large-scale connective infrastructure projects between European countries, such as the high-speed trains.

15.5 *The European Monetary System*

When the first crisis hit the exchange markets in 1971 due to the US's unilateral suspension of the direct international convertibility of the dollar to gold (which was to cease to be convertible completely in 1973, leading to the abolition of the fixed exchange rate system inaugurated in 1947), the EU countries immediately acted to maintain tightly linked exchange rates. In March 1972 the "currency snake" was launched, which provided for fluctuations of ±2.25 per cent among the EU currencies, with a link to the dollar set within fluctuations of ±4.25 per cent. The snake did not last long, because the British and Irish pound had to leave it, followed by the Italian lira a year later; France tried in vain to hold out, leaving and re-entering it several times until it finally abandoned it in 1976. At that point the French–German alliance, one of the pillars of the EU, was under threat of collapse, together with the administration of the CAP. The hope that a moderate inflation and the flexibility of exchange rates could be used to redress balance of payments disequilibria without major drawbacks died out, in face of the instability generated and the large increase in speculation.

It was not long before consultations began to create a more mature and flexible version of the currency snake, and in the spring of 1978 the German Chancellor Helmut Schmidt proposed the European Monetary System (EMS). This was premised on the European Exchange Rate Mechanism (ERM) which fixed the parity of each currency in the system to a reference currency, the European Currency Unit (ECU); its value with respect to currencies outside the Community was determined by the weighted average of the value of the Community currencies that made up the ECU.[17] When a currency diverged

---

16. Bradley, Petrakos & Traistaru, *Integration, Growth and Cohesion in an Enlarged European Union.*

17. This weighting was made on the basis of the GDP and foreign trade of each member of the Community, and it was periodically updated. In 1990 it was as follows: Belgium/Luxembourg 8.1; Denmark 2.5; France 19.3; Germany 30.2; Greece 0.7; Ireland 1.1; Italy 9.8; the Netherlands 9.4; Portugal 0.8; Spain 5.3; Britain 12.8.

from parity by more than ±2.25 per cent, that currency's government was required to intervene; if that proved too burdensome, there was the possibility of receiving some temporary aid from a fund designated for that purpose.[18] If even this proved insufficient then the exchange rates could be realigned; this was done in an agreed manner to avoid competitive devaluations and unexpected effects on other currencies.

The ECU became operational in March 1979, delayed due to differences of opinion between France and Germany on how best to structure the agricultural compensation funds. Of the countries that then comprised the Community, the UK chose not to join the EMS, and Ireland and Italy negotiated a larger fluctuation range of ±6 per cent. Spain subsequently entered in 1990, as did the UK when Italy and Ireland also abandoned the extended fluctuation range. Portugal entered in 1992, Austria and Finland entered in 1995 and Greece alone remained outside it.

The EMS went through numerous realignments (see Table 15.3), but on the whole it was successful in cutting inflation in many European countries and in increasing Europe's monetary stability. When monetary union (see §15.7) was decided on, there was a storm of currency speculation between the summer of 1992 and the summer of 1993, which forced first the Italian lira[19] and then the British pound out of the EMS, and ultimately forcing the fluctuation range to be expanded to ±15 per cent to avoid forcing out further currencies – particularly the French franc – but by then the EMS experiment was coming to an end. It had certainly served to make the advantages of monetary stability in Europe better appreciated, even to the point of suggesting that they become permanent. But before we explore the monetary union that was to follow, we must first introduce other aspects of the process of European integration.

15.6 Industrial policy and a single market

The slowdown in growth that began in the mid-1970s prompted the EU towards interventions in industry. Initially it was concerned with defensive measures in the core industries where overproduction threatened to bank-

---

18. Note that in this manner not only were those countries whose currencies were devaluating required to intervene, but also those with appreciating currencies; this produced greater symmetry of behaviour in the system.
19. The lira re-entered the EMS in December 1996.

Table 15.3 Realignments of the central parities in the EMS, 1979–1993.

Currency	24 Sep 1979	30 Nov 1979	22 Feb 1981	5 Oct 1981	22 Feb 1982	14 Jun 1982	21 Mar 1983	20 Jul 1985	7 Apr 1986	4 Aug 1986	12 Jan 1987	12 Jan 1990	13 Sep 1992	16 Sep 1992	2 Feb 1993	14 May 1993	2 Aug 1993
Belgian franc					-8.5		+1.5	+2	+1		+2		+3.5				**
Danish krone	-3	-4.8			-3.0		+2.5	+2	+1				+3.5				**
German mark	+2			+5.5		+4.25	+5.5	+2	+3		+3		+3.5				**
French franc				-3.0		-5.75	-2.5	+2	-3				+3.5				**
Irish pound							-3.5	+2		-8			+3.5		-10.0		**
Italian lira			-6	-3.0		-2.75	-2.5	-6				-3.75	-3.5	*	–	–	–
Dutch guilder				+5.5		+4.25	+3.5	+2	+3		+3		+3.5				**
Spanish peseta		Entry 19 June 1989										+3.5	-5.0	-6.0	-8.0	-7.0	**
British pound			Entry 8 October 1990										+3.5	*	–	–	–
Portuguese escudo		Entry 6 April 1992												-6.0	-6.5	-3.5	**

Notes: *exit from the EMS; **fluctuation band ± 15.

Source: *General Report on the Activities of the European Union*, various years.

rupt large enterprises. The first was the steel sector, which went into crisis in 1974. The EU financed both restructuring and the closing of mills, as well as subsidizing retraining or early retirement for thousands of workers. Then crisis hit synthetic fibres, prompting an agreement to divide up quotas and cut production capacity in 1978. Beginning in 1981, assistance was provided to naval shipyards to halve production capacity and move to improving the quality of production, and petrochemical companies were encouraged to reach agreements to streamline production.

However, dissatisfaction mounted with this merely defensive approach, which was coupled with analyses that suggested Europe was falling behind in certain core industries due to a lack of critical mass in areas of research caused by national fragmentation and European companies being too small. Therefore the idea emerged to launch EU-supported research projects that freely brought together partners in various European nations, and particularly companies and university research centres. In September 1980 the first of these projects was proposed, the European Strategic Programme for Research and Development in Information Technology (ESPRIT), in the rather weak European electronics sector. The programme was approved by the European Commission in December 1982, and by September 1983 it already included 200 proposals originating from 600 companies and think tanks. The success of this initiative caused a new course to be set, and research programmes began to proliferate, often with imaginative acronyms such as EUREKA, RACE, BRITE, BRIDGE, COMETT, and SPRINT. Beginning in 1987, the EU established programme frameworks for the principal goals it wished to achieve with relative financing over the next five years.[20] In that same year the ERASMUS (European Region Action Scheme for the Mobility of University Students) project was approved, which allowed selected students from European universities to study in other universities. The importance of the research led to the creation of the European Research Council in 2006 which became responsible for selecting research and funding scholarships on the basis of requests made by scholars and think tanks throughout the EU.

And so the conclusion was reached to re-establish the EU on deeper foundations, which was accelerated when Jacques Delors became president of the Commission in January 1985. The most ambitious project was the creation of the so-called "single market" by removing the many remaining non-tariff barriers that had made the ECM unification only partial. In December 1985 the European Council approved the Single European Act, which had as its

---

20. Mosconi, *The New European Industrial Policy*.

main objective the actualization of a single market (by December 1992). It also had other measures to reform the Treaty of Rome, among the most important of which were moving approximately three-fourths of the possible decisions to the majority rule,[21] as well as involving the Union in new regional, social, industrial, technological, environmental and monetary policies.[22] There were those such as Altiero Spinelli, a great promoter of a unified Europe, who thought the outcome more molehill than mountain, but as throughout the process of European integration there was much resistance to it, so much so that the Act only went into force on 1 July 1987, after several difficult ratifications. In any event, although not one of the steps towards unification proved decisive, the process had been set in motion and was not to stop or reverse, leading ultimately to epochal changes.

The work to implement the single market followed two guiding criteria. The first provided that European legislation be harmonized over a series of fundamentally important fields in which it was inappropriate for differences to persist. To that end agreement was reached in over 300 resolutions, which were then accepted by the several governments. The second criterion regarded the settings in which harmonization was not deemed necessary, but which envisaged the adoption of a principle of "mutual recognition":[23] products and services could be created according to the laws in force in one country in the EU and sold on all other markets in the Community, without discrimination. The market would determine the degree of customer satisfaction, which would eventually persuade the national authorities to adapt to the successful model.

Border checks of goods were progressively reduced and wholly eliminated on 1 January 1997; indirect taxation was brought back into comparable ranges; corporate subsidies were harmonized; bidding for public projects was opened to competitors from throughout the Union; in the banking sector control of each subsidiary was put under the responsibility of the country in which the

---

21. Various weights were assigned to each country according to their sizes: 10 votes to the 4 largest countries, 8 to Spain, 5 each to Belgium, Greece, the Netherlands and Portugal, 3 to Denmark and Ireland, and 2 votes to Luxembourg.

22. Article 102A states that monetary cooperation would take into account "the experience acquired in co-operating within the framework of the European Monetary System (EMS) and in developing the ECU".

23. This principle emerged from a judgement made by the Court of Justice on 20 February 1979 (in the *Cassis de Dijon* case); it established that a product lawfully manufactured or marketed in a member state must in principle be allowed on the markets of all member states of the Community.

bank had its headquarters, and opening subsidiaries was liberalized.[24] Later other services were liberalized (and often privatized), such as air transport and telecommunications.

The European market truly became an "internal" market for the first time; the remaining language, fiscal policy and currency barriers were not small, but they were no longer insurmountable, as subsequent developments showed. In fact, there was a time of intense growth in Europe between 1986 and 1990 that triggered a series of agreements and acquisitions between companies in the Community, so much so that a debate on effective antitrust legislation arose, which had never before been a matter of concern in Europe. Two articles, 85 and 86, in the Treaty of Rome prohibited the abuse of a dominant position, but recourse to them was rarely taken. Over the course of preparatory work for the single market it was considered vital to establish a more decisive means of protecting the common market against concentrations and acquisitions through the Merger Control Act n. 4064, which was approved on 21 December 1989 and went into force in 1990.[25]

To the surprise of many, not only were all these changes accomplished by 1992, but in the wake of the collapse of the Soviet Bloc, German reunification in 1990 and Jacques Delors's drive towards integration. Within that same timeframe capital markets were liberalized, social harmonization was accelerated, monetary unification was launched with the adoption of the Community Charter, and ultimately a new treaty was achieved that for the first time spoke of European union with explicit reference to political as well as economic components. These last developments were so important as to merit particular development.

15.7 *The Maastricht Treaty and the birth of the European Union*

Discussions on monetary union and on political and military union had already begun in 1988. Different views and mediation proposals were made over many successive meetings of the European Council until the new Treaty was presented at Maastricht on 9–10 December 1991. It included 252 new

---

24. The principle of control by the authorities of the country of origin and of mutual recognition was extended to many other services, among them transport and insurance. In banking, however, it demonstrated its limits with the great international crises that erupted in 2008 (see §15.9).

25. Amato, *Antitrust and the Bounds of Power*.

articles or modifications to the ECC, ECSC and EURATOM treaties, as well as 17 Protocols and 31 Declarations. Beyond a systematic reorganization of all previous economic legislation, the new Treaty that instituted the European Union also incorporated the arrangements to implement the monetary union (Economic and Monetary Union, or EMU), a foreign policy and common security policy (Common Foreign and Security Policy or CFSP), and those regarding police and judicial cooperation (Committee on Legal Affairs, or JURI). At the moment these three "pillars", as they have been called, are of different types; the EMU has characteristics that are clearly pre-federal, the CFSP has confederational traits and the JURI has characteristics that are merely inter-governmental. But, as the history of European integration has demonstrated, the important thing is that making a step forward leads to other steps forward.[26]

The EU treaty was signed on 7 February 1992 by the foreign and finance ministers of the member states, and it was then ratified over the course of the year by the member countries; there was some difficulty with Denmark, which required an extension to 1993 to overcome the negative result of the ratification referendum held in June 1992. At the insistence of the UK, and reluctantly accepted by most of the other member countries, an "opt out" clause was inserted that allowed for some member states not to adhere to individual aspects of the new decisions that were gradually being made, but it made clear that these should be exceptional cases.

Perhaps the most significant addition by the EU treaty was in Article 8, which stated that "Citizenship of the Union is hereby established. Every person holding the nationality of a Member State shall be a citizen of the Union". And yet it remains true, as all commentators have pointed out, that the European Parliament, which should express this European citizenship, does not have an autonomous decision making capacity. The EU treaty conferred on it a "codecisional" power together with the European Council (which includes the heads of the member states and which up to that point had held absolute pre-eminence in decisions) in explicitly stated areas, strengthening the jurisdictions it already had; in this way it made a step forward toward what was to eventually become the administrative body of European political union, according to the principle of subsidiarity as set out in Article 3B.

---

26. Indeed, the common mechanisms of foreign policy and security were already strengthened with the Treaty of Amsterdam, while some matters of cooperation in internal and legal affairs, such as immigration policy and external boundary controls, became subject to Community policies. The field in which majority decisions applied was also extended.

Finally, with regard to JURI police cooperation was strengthened, partly because the countries that had formed the so-called Schengen Group[27] had suppressed police checks at their borders and airports,[28] until in 2006 Frontex was created, an agency that controlled the external borders of the Union. However these measures proved to be insufficient to address the serious stability crises of the southern Mediterranean produced by the wars in Iraq, the so-called "Arab Springs", the Israeli-Palestinian conflict, the civil wars in Syria, Libya, Somalia and other African countries, and the growth of the so-called Islamic state ISIS. As of 2016 Europe has still not been able to devise acceptable and sustainable solutions aimed at safeguarding the external borders of the EU without at the same time effecting counterproductive, inhuman and scarcely sustainable closures (see also Chapter 17).

15.8 Monetary union and the euro

The Maastricht Treaty's most significant innovation was the creation of the EMU. It provided for three phases to implement a single currency. First, the establishment of the convergence criteria for the various economies, to be completed by 1998.[29] Second, the foundation of the European Monetary Institute (EMI) (in January 1994), the forerunner of the European Central Bank (ECB), the passage of the statute to make EMU central banks more independent of their treasuries (where this was not already the case, and the constitution of the European System of Central Banks (ESCB). Third, the establishment of an irrevocable parity between the EMU currencies (on

---

27. Beginning in 1995, nearly all the EU countries joined the Schengen Agreement. The two most notable exceptions were the UK and the Republic of Ireland. Other non-EU countries also joined, among them Norway and Switzerland (the latter regarding persons only and not goods).
28. A protocol attached to the Treaty of Amsterdam transposed this result into Community law.
29. The criterion of convergence (previously mentioned) is summarized as follows: inflation rate no higher than 1.5 per cent of the average of the three countries with the lowest inflation; interest rate on long-term state bonds no higher than 2 per cent of the average of the three countries with the lowest inflation; participation of the currency in the EMS for at least two years without realignments; total government deficit no higher than 3 per cent of GDP; gross government debt no higher than 60 per cent of GDP, or reducing towards that value. With the entry in force of the euro all monetary variables passed under the control of the ECB; at the Conference of Dublin in 1996 it was agreed to make permanent the agreements regarding the fiscal variables of the so-called Stability and Growth Pact, only subsequently was it understood just how lax the Pact was.

31 December 1998) and the creation of the European currency, the euro, to be placed into circulation in 2002, initially at parity with the dollar.[30]

Eleven of the fifteen EU countries committed to adhere to this programme, which happened within the prescribed timeframes; Greece was not able to meet the criteria for convergence, and for various reasons Sweden, Denmark and the UK decided to remain outside the EMU.[31]

The Euro's launch in 2002 was initially calm, but it immediately proved weak against the dollar. It later recovered to become a strong currency, but its performance was not noteworthy until the great international crisis erupted in 2008 (which we will consider in Chapter 17). In that crisis international speculators exploited the many existing imbalances within the eurozone, and the euro began to take a hammering. The Greek crisis broke first, and then those in Ireland, Portugal and Spain, and finally the Italian public debt crisis (a debt which had already begun to accumulate prior to the crisis). Beyond developments during the crisis, the structural problems in the eurozone were linked to too diverse fiscal policies and competitiveness among the eurozone countries, which produced divergent trends in prices, wages, public expenditure and balances of payments that were unsustainable within a single currency zone – as had been made clear, but not obligatory, with the introduction of the euro. The euro was at risk of collapse because it did not have the means to restore balance; the central bank's sole objective of monetary stability was too narrow, and its use of the typical central bank toolkit for counteracting crises was too limited and inflexible.[32]

Collapse was averted with several important reforms enacted in 2012: (a) a strengthened financial oversight system at the EU level; (b) the creation of a substantial anti-speculation intervention fund (the ESM, or European Stability Mechanism) of around €1000 billion; (c) the Fiscal Compact, an obligatory fiscal convergence mechanism;[33] (d) the Banking Union, which went into force at the end of 2014 and placed the 130 "systemic" (large banks with many branches) under the direct control of the ECB.[34] It is true that the Fiscal Compact created untimely austerity in Europe while overcoming the crisis, but with intelligent management it can launch the monetary union

---

30. For a general discussion, see De Grauwe, *The Economics of the Monetary Union*.
31. Other countries subsequently adopted the euro: Greece (2001); Slovenia (2006); Cyprus and Malta (2008); Slovakia (2009); Estonia (2010); Latvia (2014); Lithuania (2015), taking the total to nineteen members.
32. Sinn, *The Euro Trap*.
33. Cottarelli & Guerguil, *Designing a European Fiscal Union*.
34. De Haan, Oosterloo & Schoenmaker, *Financial Markets and Institutions*.

towards a long life. Since 2015 the ECB is heavily intervening in markets to counter deflation with liquidity injections, and the European Union is taking steps to incentivize a new wave of investments.

In any event, the opinion is now widespread among many economists that in order to operate efficiently the monetary union requires fiscal federalism, which is currently considered to be the best automatic stabilizer. (It is frequently compared to the role of effective "shock absorbers" played by the US and Canadian federal fiscal systems.) A fiscal unification would prevent pursuing risky fiscal policies, and thus destabilizing the common currency. However, fiscal federalism requires the centralization of national fiscal revenues and their relative spending decisions; at the moment it is not likely that the European states will cede this control, even just for a portion of revenue and spending, in the absence of political integration.

The opinions of politicians, officials and citizens motivated by federalist ideals are increasingly converging towards the necessity of political unification. However, even since the mid-1970s the Community projects that have focused on studying the prospects for political unification have all encountered the same difficulty in joining theoretical aspirations with the reality of nationalism.[35] In the future it will be necessary to rediscover this driving force in order for a sense of belonging to Europe, a European identity, to form, expand and assert itself that is as strong as the feeling of national identity that presently prevails. The long and arduous path of European economic integration needs new goals, an ambitious design around which common efforts can converge, and a federal Europe is certainly today the chief and most controversial of those new goals. In any case, compared to the centuries of war that have characterized European history, sixty years of peace are still an anomaly in an unstable equilibrium (as proven by the conflict in the Balkans) and not a consolidated result: the United States of Europe are therefore an essential step for an enduring "conquest of peace". Parodying Wyplosz, "the choice is not between a federal Europe and paradise",[36] but between the fragility of fragmentation and the certainty of peaceful growth within a strong unitary and cooperative system of government.[37]

---

35. For these projects from the Tindemans Report onwards, see Urwin, *The Community of Europe*.
36. "The choice is not between EMU and heaven. It is between EMU and freely floating exchange rates, with possibly poorly coordinated monetary policies, within an area gradually becoming as tightly integrated as the United States. Would the United States have passed the currency area tests a century ago? And had it failed, all things considered, was it a mistake for the country to adopt a single currency?" (Wyplosz, "EMU: Why and How It Might Happen", 10).
37. Jensen & Miszlivetz, *Reframing Europe's Future*.

In conclusion, the process of European integration has accomplished truly remarkable results in the sixty or so years of its presence. For those who live out the dragged-out decision making process of the European Union, every step can seem excessively slow. However, keep in mind that centuries of conflict and separation have resulted in widely diverging national communities; these can only be overcome by collaboration and persuasion, because no authoritarian method is compatible with the democracy practised by the European Union. The main thing is to ensure that each step improves the state of the Union, even if not immediately, and that no step back is ever made. We should also recall that, beyond the peace and free movement of persons, goods and capital that the Union guarantees, there is also the important fact that global competition today is populated by continental heavyweights, against which only a united Europe can make its relevant weight felt.

16

The demise of the USSR and the rise of Asia

If the period after the mid-1970s was less satisfying for the Western European economy than the period before, we should recall that it also witnessed the end of the Soviet Union and the opening of the Eastern Bloc. Even with all the subsequent difficulties of transition, particularly in the successor countries to the Soviet Union and the former Yugoslavia, these were events to be welcomed, because they defused any remaining possibility of a general war in Europe, and they liberated many Europeans from the circumstances that had long prevented them from improving their conditions, as had benefitted the countries of Western Europe. With the liberalization of trade, capital movements and the growth of tourism, the processes of decolonization and globalization of the economy have involved a growing number of countries, from the so-called "Asian tigers" (Taiwan, Singapore, Hong Kong, South Korea) to China, India and even Vietnam, countries that until now had remained marginalized. This is a highly significant phenomenon that we can only touch on in this book, but it is central to our understanding of the huge impact that the European development model has had on the world.

In this chapter we will chart both the rise of the Asian economies and the decline of the Soviet Union. Beginning with Japan, the only country with a non-Western culture to have taken off in the nineteenth century – we will then briefly review the success of the Asian tigers, of which Taiwan and Korea were Japanese colonies, and Singapore and Hong Kong were British colonies. We will give a brief account of the fall of the Soviet Union, before examining the rise of the two giants, India and China. We will see that the modernization that has taken place in all these economies has followed a path imitating that of the Western model – now more American than the original European one – however with significant modifications, or "substitutable factors", recalling Gerschenkron's term from Chapter 4. Most notably, the role played by the state, which was far more important than in the eighteenth and nineteenth centuries in Europe, North America and Australia.

We can identify three models of state intervention during the second half of the twentieth century and the Asian model has been by far the most successful (see Table 16.1). Indeed, the Soviet model of a *maximal* state that abolishes the market (see Chapter 4) has failed, not only in the Soviet Union but in China as well (where it endured for a much shorter time), setting back the development process in those areas where it was rooted. The predominantly Latin American model of "import substitution", or substituting imports through protectionism, has had only limited success chiefly because it promoted industrial sectors that were frequently uncompetitive over the long term, using resources inefficiently. The Asian model, which was inaugurated by Japan and then followed by others, instead privileged long-term investments in industrial development plans that sought to make its domestic companies competitive on foreign markets, and hence able to export. Foreign companies were kept at a distance, especially during the early phases of take-off, while local companies were incentivized to expand and earn monopolistic profits that were then dedicated to acquiring and then independently producing technology.[1]

16.1 *Japan: success to stagnation*

Japan's economic recovery, after its ill-advised war venture in which it challenged the United States, was greatly aided by the Americans (who needed a bastion against Russia in Asia) with an intervention plan comparable to the Marshall Plan in Europe.[2] The *zaibatsu* (Chapter 6) were dismantled, but the Japanese lost no time in reconstructing groups of similar enterprises, even without the former prominence of the families, called *cheiretsu*,[3] that continued inter-company coordination practices typical of the Asian world (and beyond). A bank and an insurer sat at the centre of the group of companies and were ready to financially support the development plans of the group.[4]

---

1. Romano & Traù, "Il ruolo delle istituzioni nello sviluppo manifatturiero del mondo emergente".
2. Allinson, *Japan's Postwar History*.
3. Molteni & Pecorari, "I Kinyuu Keiretsu in Giappone". See also Lincoln & Gerlach, *Japan's Network Economy*.
4. Aoki & Patrick, *The Japanese Main Bank System*.

Table 16.1 Per capita income trend (at purchasing power parity) in Russia and the principal Asian countries.

Country	Index USA = 100					Growth rates				Population in 2008 (millions)
	1951	1973	1989	2000	2010	1951–73	1973–89	1989–2000	2000–10	
Russia	28	36	31	16	25	3.5	1.0	−2.9	5.4	142
China	5	5	8	12	26	2.4	4.9	5.3	8.5	1,327
India	6	5	6	7	11	1.4	2.5	3.6	5.8	1,125
Japan	21	69	78	71	72	6.7	2.8	1.1	0.7	127
South Korea	8	17	35	52	71	5.8	6.5	4.9	3.7	49
Taiwan	9	21	41	58	76	5.9	6.4	4.6	3.4	23
Hong Kong	23	43	74	77	101	5.1	5.5	2.4	3.3	7
Singapore	22	36	58	74	95	4.4	5.1	3.8	3.1	5
USA	100	100	100	100	100	2.2	2.0	1.9	0.6	303

Source: Maddison database.

A trading company operated with the outside world, and provided integrated trade for the entire group's production. This was how Japan made heavy investments in steel, transport (cars, motorcycles, and ships, but not aeroplanes), factory machinery and particularly electronics; and were able to compete successfully with US companies.[5]

The Japanese economic system has always worked differently than the US economy. First, in Japan there is a division between large, efficient exporting companies and the rest of the economy, which is organized locally on a much smaller scale. Second, corporate organization tends to favour labour over capital, with lifetime employment, wages linked to career advancement, limited gap in remuneration between management and workers, unions within companies and strong corporate welfare. Finally, the state provides a supporting role for the industrial policies implemented by the *cheiretsu* through protectionist policies, infrastructure projects and diplomatic support. This organizational system, which could hardly be more different from the American form, has generated the capacity to support long-term investment plans and to implement important organizational innovations within the company, such as increased quality through continuous product improvement (*kaizen*) and just-in-time manufacturing, or the progressive elimination of waste in maintaining raw materials stocks and intermediate products by precisely calculating materials requirements and process times.[6] Japan's success in electronics and in transport has been the subject of many studies.[7]

However, at the end of the 1980s, just when the United States and Europe were concerned that Japan would possibly surpass them, its economy entered a period of serious difficulties, although maintaining its international competitiveness. Its currency, the yen, which previously had highly appreciated, was left to devalue with manoeuvres designed to broaden its internal market; foreign investments grew, and capital markets were liberalized under the pressure of globalization. All this dramatically increased financial speculation, particularly a housing bubble, that involved all major banks in the country. In early 1990 Japanese stock market capitalization had reached a level greater than that of the US market, and a collapse was inevitable. This not only produced unemployment but also led to the failure of several banks, which needed to be bailed out and downsized at a considerable cost to public funds. The debt-

---

5. Dore, *Taking Japan Seriously.*
6. See Imai, *Kaizen: The Key to Japan's Competitive Success* and Aoki, Jackson & Miyajima, *Corporate Governance in Japan.*
7. Among these, see Chandler, *Inventing the Electronic Century.*

to-GDP ratio[8] rose to 250 per cent. Since then the Japanese "miracle" has not been repeated.[9] Japan still remains a fully respectable economic power, but successive governments have not been able to find the right strategy to revive the economy. This is partly due to the public debt burden, but also due to the problems that all countries must face when they reach the end of their process of imitation (i.e. the limit on investments generated by the shortage of innovations; see Chapter 17 on this topic).

16.2 The Asian tigers

The four Asian territories that were to take off immediately after the end of the Second World War were strongly influenced by the UK (Hong Kong and Singapore) and by Japan (Taiwan and South Korea). Hong Kong became a British colony in the mid-nineteenth century, with successive territorial expansions, and it remained so until 1997, when China again assumed sovereignty. After the Second World War, it recorded an intense period of economic development that also greatly increased its population; with urban space so limited, it has built the most vertical city in the world. Its economy is predominately based on services, and finance is highly important, but its economic and political autonomy are undergoing severe curtailment since it became part of China. Singapore had come under the administration of the British East India Company in the first half of the nineteenth century, becoming a strong colony and an important naval base. After a brief period of Japanese rule during the Second World War it returned to the UK, which made it independent in the mid-1960s. Since then it has developed a powerful manufacturing and shipping economy, with a remarkable ability to attract tourists and foreign workers. Both city-states have highly centralized political systems, with a strong propensity towards interventionism accompanied by a high degree of economic freedom.

The story of Taiwan and South Korea is more complex. Taiwan (or Formosa, as the island has been called) was ceded to Japan in 1894, which quickly began a process of industrialization and infrastructure expansion in the country along the lines of its own model. After the Japanese were expelled at the end of the Second World War Taiwan participated in the Chinese

8. The very high level of Japanese public debt has not been a source of international speculation only because almost all of it is held internally.

9. Wakatobe, *Japan's Great Stagnation and Abenomics*.

civil war, which saw the communists defeat the Kuomintang nationalists; in December 1949 the Kuomintang took refuge on the island declaring Taipei to be the capital of the Republic of China despite losing mainland China to the communists who founded the People's Republic of China. Since international powers have progressively recognized the People's Republic of China as the legitimate government represented in the United Nations, Taiwan has remained without formal recognition, such that it remains one of the most thorny diplomatic problems. However, this has not prevented Taiwan from developing a lively economy, with a high state involvement along the lines of the Japanese model that is supportive of initiatives by private industrial groups; in Taiwan these are more "horizontal" than elsewhere, made up of small- to medium-sized companies. Its industry is highly diversified, with particular strength in electronics, machinery, petrochemicals and textiles.

South Korea is the largest and most innovative of the four tiger economies.[10] Korea became a Japanese colony in 1910, and as in Taiwan Japan began to industrialize the country, concentrating primarily on the northern areas. After the end of the Second World War the country was divided in two; the more populous and agrarian south was under US protection, and the more industrialized north was under Soviet control. On 25 June 1950 the North Korean army invaded South Korea, and the UN Security Council gave the United States a mandate to free the occupied country. The ensuing war resulted in perhaps 2 million dead and extensive destruction; an armistice was finally signed on 27 July 1953. The US did not leave South Korea, and they contributed massive aid to its reconstruction, but its economy did not take off until the 1960s with the installation of a military government led by Park Chung-hee, which adopted a five-year plan. Hopes were not high for the outcome of this plan, which was centred on promoting the light manufacturing industry, but it was successful, as was the plan that followed it.

Reassured by these results, in 1973 Park's government began to develop heavy industry, steel, petrochemicals, shipbuilding and nuclear energy. These investments were strongly supported by state-controlled banks, facilitating the rise of advanced mechanical and electronics industries. Company organization followed the Japanese model of the group, called *chaebol* in Korea, typically vertically structured and family based, with a core business but tentacles in a thousand different activities. The Korean *chaebol* were dominated by the five largest: Hyundai, Samsung, Daewoo, LG and SK Group. Hyundai started life as a small repair shop in 1940, which then entered shipbuilding and civil construction, before producing cars in 1967. Samsung has become a

10. Goldstein, *Il miracolo coreano*. See also Eichengreen *et al.*, *The Korean Economy*.

world leader in telephony and electronics; Daewoo was a conglomerate with many different industrial and manufacturing operations; the SK Group is, among other things, the main telecommunications provider in Korea; and LG produces televisions and other electrical products.

Park, who governed semi-dictatorially, was assassinated in 1979, and South Korea then embarked on a slow process of democratization. Unions, which had never operated in the country, partially organized during the 1980s; civil society began to emerge, and democratic elections were held in 1987. South Korea joined the OECD in 1996. A deep financial crisis in 1998 led to a banking collapse and highlighted the need for banking regulation and initiated multiple privatizations, while trying to limit the excessive power of the *chaebol*. What Korea lacks is a robust layer of well-managed small and medium enterprises, as well as a better organized state welfare system, but it is without doubt another example of an economic "miracle", such as Japan exhibited a century earlier.

16.3 *From the USSR to Russia*

The Russian victory in the Second World War had a significant impact on international relations; it also had unexpected internal effects, among which were: the power of the military remained intact until the 1970s; the "imperialistic" hegemony it had acquired over part of Europe and other areas sustained the inefficient Russian economic system; and Western technology continued to be acquired, at least for some time.

Victory during the Second World War, albeit with massive American aid, ended up keeping planning alive much longer than would have been possible otherwise, given the intrinsic flaws in the planning itself (see Chapter 10). Only when the power of the military ended and its imperialistic hegemony crumbled did the Soviet economy reveal its unsustainability, and it ended up being entirely swept away. The process of replacing a planned economy with a market economy inevitably proved to be slow and difficult, given the ruinous legacy of seventy years of attempts to stamp out the freedom of enterprise. Let us examine the developments in further detail.[11]

Until the mid-1970s growth remained quite positive, although in large part it was determined by the highly competitive arms race with the United

---

11. Harrison, *The Rise and Fall of the Soviet Economy*.

States.[12] When the first difficulties arose there were attempts at reform[13] but these did not improve productivity or the ability to enter sectors for mass consumption goods. After Leonid Brezhnev's death in 1982, the last winning general of the Second World War, for a few years the Soviet leadership was uncertain how to proceed, until Mikhail Gorbachev became the secretary of the Communist Party in 1985. He recognized that the system had stagnated and began to slowly abandon planning, returning to a mixed economy similar to that of Lenin (the NEP, described in Chapter 10), but the international context was not that of the 1920s. His reform policies, however, initiated changes that, thanks to *glasnost* (transparency) and *perestroika* (change), led to the end of the Cold War. In 1987 a treaty was signed to eliminate intermediate range nuclear arms in Europe and the following year marked the end of the Brezhnev Doctrine, which allowed the nations in the Soviet Bloc to return to democracy. In September Gorbachev assumed the post of head of state, and in October he was awarded the Nobel Peace Prize.

Gorbachev, however, was unable to control the internal situation and was ousted from office at the end of 1991, while the country's economy continued to unravel. Boris Yeltsin's rise to power brought about an "instant liberalization", the characteristics of which we don't have space to explore in detail,[14] but it provoked a deep systemic recession, followed by another serious crisis in 1998. Only in 1999 did the Russian economy begin to grow again, although it was heavily dependent on raw materials exports, mainly oil and gas. Its per capita income recovered 1989 levels only in 2007, only to then immediately suffer the effects of the global international crisis, while remaining at the mercy of oil prices and Putin's warmongering international policies. This explains how Russia's relative per capita income position compared to the United States in 2010 had not improved since the time of Stalin's death (see Table 16.1). Russia's life expectancy of around 66 remains notably lower than in many other countries, and its population growth is among the lowest in the world. Its road to modernization has barely begun, and is not helped by maintaining its military power, at the expense of improving civil production.

---

12. During the 1970s its spending on arms exceeded 12 per cent of GDP, which increased its impact even more.
13. Graziosi, *L'Unione Sovietica.*
14. In addition to previously cited works, see Hanson, "The Economic Development of Russia".

16.4 *The awakening of two giants: China and India*

In Chapter 1 we explored the reasons why Europe, and not China, had led the world's economic development. China was not even interested in a process of imitation. Its advanced agricultural civilization and immense geographical size meant that it had no incentives to leave its political configuration of an autocratic imperial government. Confucian philosophy supported this vertical society, in which loyalty, submission and respect for the social hierarchy were the basic principles for a harmonious life. Although education and merito-riousness were widespread (the mandarins), economic activity by merchants remained marginalized, because an alliance between the emperor and the agri-cultural class was at the heart of Chinese society. The government of the Qing dynasty (1644–1912) was particularly short-sighted, and it was precisely during this period that China stagnated, losing wars with foreign powers, none of which planned to invade the mainland, but only islands, peninsulas and ports. With the death of the last emperor in 1911 there was first a revolt of the southern provinces led by Sun Yat-sen, who in 1912 proclaimed the Republic of China, which had nationalistic traits. The Communist Party, born in 1921 and headed by Mao Tse-tung, embarked on a civil war with the nationalist forces that lasted until 1949, ending with victory by Mao and the installation of the nationalist party (Kuomintang) in Taiwan (see §7.2).

Mao's republic[15] initially thought to follow the Soviet planning model. Mao launched a first five-year plan, based mostly on building up infrastruc-ture, and a second five-year plan, known as the "great leap forward" which aimed at expanding heavy industry, together with an attempt to collectivize agriculture, which until then had been privately managed, although land remained the property of the state. That move provoked a sharp decline in agricultural production and a famine estimated to have killed between 15 and 30 million people. This failure pushed Mao to break ties with the Soviet Union at the end of the 1950s; however, he did not seem able to find a viable alternative to the Soviet model. He thought this was due to Chinese society being segmented into classes, with those at the top opposed to devel-opment. His response was to launch the "Cultural Revolution" (1966–70), which proposed to eliminate the bourgeois class by closing the universities and upper division schools and forcing everyone back into the working classes (the blue military-style garment that everyone had to wear became famous). This was an enormous, unsustainable shock for China; see Table 16.1 for just how little China grew during the 1951–73 period.

---

15. Yueh, *China's Growth* and also Krober, *China's Economy*.

During Mao's last years, and especially after his death in 1976, there was a rapprochement with the West and the Chinese economy began to change course, slowly at first and then more rapidly. A primary provision of the major reform in 1978 was the one-child policy, which brought birth rates down to rates more manageable by the economy. Agriculture was then liberalized; no longer run by the state, it was based on territorial agricultural cooperatives along the lines of the Japanese model. For the first time China recognized the need to import technologies, and Special Economic Zones (SEZs) were created in which foreign investments and trade were possible; it also became possible to set up private businesses. From then on there was a plethora of liberalizations and privatizations, but even today much of the Chinese economy remains under state control with all strategic decisions made by the Chinese Communist Party, which has made no effort towards political democratization. In 1992 China officially announced that it had become a "socialist market economy"; central planning was replaced by a mixed economy in which all companies, whether foreign, joint ventures, private or state-owned, must measure up against the market, although within strategies laid out by the Party (the five-year plans still exist, but they are strategic rather than directly operational).

It is not easy to untangle Chinese statistics, but sources suggest that around 40 per cent of Chinese companies (including the largest) are state-owned even today,[16] and local regulation remains highly invasive in non-state-owned companies. Just what a "socialist market economy"[17] is remains an open question; it is not simply a matter of the state having a more influential role, which is true of all Asian economies, but it is also characterized by a directing of the economy from above in keeping with a millennial Chinese tradition. Until now the economy has not had major problems because it is based on Western technology, but it may have trouble in the future when increasing freedom of expression and empowerment of the civil society leads to calls for greater economic freedom.

China's financial system was profoundly reformed. A single People's Bank in Mao's time transitioned to a central bank and four specialized banks in the early 1980s, however it was not until the mid-90s that they were able to get control over inflation policy. Since improving the institution of the central bank in 1994 Chinese monetary policy has been quite stable, with important and timely interventions when inflation was about to reignite. However,

---

16. Huang, *Capitalism with Chinese Characteristics*.
17. Not to be confused with the German brand of "social market economy", which is quite different; see Chapter 14.

foreign observers maintain that the debt system of the Chinese state banks is not sufficiently solid and that the state's presence in the Chinese banking system is too pervasive, despite the admission of foreign banks.

These reforms have allowed China to embark on a significant process of industrialization (in 2010 47 per cent of Chinese GDP was generated by manufacturing), pouring enormous quantities of mostly low-cost goods on to world markets, and achieving astounding growth rates in per capita GDP (see Table 16.1), given that the wage level consistent with its standard of living is still far from Western levels throughout most of the country (although not in the more urban and advanced zones).[18] One of the major factors of this success is the ease with which China (and generally all of East Asia but not South Asia, or India, as we will see) has invested in human capital.[19] China made great efforts to improve its teaching and develop its research laboratories and universities, particularly in the sciences; the number of Chinese researchers doubled between 1995 and 2007, and spending on research rose from 0.5 per cent to 1.42 per cent during that same time. Foreign investments have been used as a means for technology transfers, and many technology parks have been created.

China has many challenges still to face: capital markets, rebalancing an urban-rural divide between various areas, the regulation of its markets, population growth (the one-child policy can not continue and has already become less rigid), the need to promote internal consumption (presently kept low, with wages and exchange rates too favourable to exports), a sustainable welfare system (in particular pensions), its political structure, the role of civil society, pollution, and procuring raw materials and food. However, the world is no longer dominated by the West since China has become active.

India had a history that was quite different to that of China. Less cohesive and unified than China, its affairs have been more complex and troubled. As the economist Amartya Sen has pointed out, there was a long tradition of commercial activity, and even trade with the West, beginning with Kautilya's famous treatise in the third century BCE, which spoke of work, profit, investment and the support necessary for merchants' and farmers' activities.[20] However, the inability to construct centralized governments and armies capable of resisting invasions meant that various parts of India were conquered, the north by Central Asian peoples and the coastal areas by Muslims coming from the Middle East. Over the course of the fifteenth and sixteenth centuries India

18. China became part of the WTO in 2001.
19. Chow, *Interpreting China's Economy*.
20. Sen, *The Argumentative Indian*.

was divided into sultanates that had a prosperous trade with Arab and Italian merchants. In 1556 the sultanates unified to become the Mughal Empire, which endured until 1739; India continued on a path to commercialize the coasts and to promote manufacturing, particularly textiles, while leaving the interior undeveloped. With the death of the last emperor India returned to the sultanates, into which it was easier for the British East India Company (see Chapter 2) to penetrate commercially and impose its own fiscal excises. Indian trade therefore came to directly depend on the British, who unified the Indias (plural due to its many divisions) under the British Crown in 1858 abolishing the East India Company and absorbing all its prerogatives.

Colonization did not resolve the problems in rural areas. The density of population meant that they were always in a production deficit and they were unable to prevent the long series of famines that continued to plague the country. While between 1765 and 1858 there had been twelve famines, between 1858 and 1947, when British rule ended, there were twenty. However, British rule was not so negative in the industrial and commercial sectors; local entrepreneurs continued to accumulate wealth and know-how, such that at the time of independence around 70 per cent of all economic activity was already in their hands.[21] Note also that the British government made no attempt to abolish the caste system that dominated India; the castes were formally abolished only with the new constitution after independence, but in reality they still survive today. The independence achieved in 1947 through Gandhi's non-violent campaign of protest led to a constitutional republic, but the unification of the territory under a single government was difficult; the splits of Pakistan in 1947 and Bangladesh in 1971 had to be accepted. Economically a system of rigid top-down planning was established, with broad state intervention in managing businesses (around 70-80 per cent of jobs were in industry); this did not have positive results (see Table 16.1 for growth rates), but was maintained until 1980. Unlike the integrated planning of the Soviet model, the market system was never formally abolished in India, and governments remained tied to a democratic ethos, although with an Indian flavour (Indian leaders rarely died in their beds, beginning with Gandhi himself). With the opening of China to a process of internal reforms India too reached a time for change, but the real turning point came only after 1989.

Various liberalizations were introduced, and there was an increasing openness to foreign investment, and in the financial arena as well. This made it possible to increase growth rates, although they remained below those of

---

21. Bhagwati & Panagariya, *Why Growth Matters*.

China,[22] partly because demographic trends were not placed under the same iron control as in China, but also because industrialization had stopped well before that of China, and both the tertiary and agricultural sectors absorb a vast part of the labour force at very low productivity levels. Today about half the population still works in agriculture. Although there have been no more famines after independence, the levels of education and technology adoption in rural areas remain quite low; however, recently progress has been made in the selection of seed stocks, irrigation and the introduction of GMO varieties that are more resistant to the local climate.

There are some large companies in industry, but the vast majority of the Indian labour force is employed in small and medium sized companies that work at low cost for exports, particularly in textile products, although among the industrial sectors we should mention "Bollywood", India's very active film industry. India's service sector is distinctive in that it is able to offer low cost computer and other services to companies worldwide, attracting significant foreign investments. India still has serious problems to face:[23] the level of education remains very low, with one-third of the population illiterate; its life expectancy is sixty-four and the caste mindset persists; women are still poorly treated, despite the fact that some women have risen to high positions in national politics; there remains an extremely high percentage of absolute poverty (below subsistence levels) of around 20 per cent, in addition to deep economic inequalities.[24] The road for the country's modernization is still long, as shown in Table 16.1.

In conclusion, it is worth restating that the rise of Asian economies, the chief development of the twenty-first century, is based on a process of imitating the Western model. That these countries were more successful in doing so than elsewhere can be attributed to the historical legacy of complex and articulated cultures in which social cohesion and an active role of the state allowed them to grasp the crux of every progressive civilization: how to make itself able to participate in the global circulation of people, goods and capitals.

---

22. Rodrik & Subramanian, "From 'Hindu Growth' to Productivity Surge".
23. Jalan, *The Future of India*.
24. Banerjee & Piketty, *Top Indian Incomes, 1922–2000*.

17

The second major international
crisis and the limits of growth

17.1 *The rise of neoliberalism and the American banking crisis*

In Chapter 14 we outlined the process of deregulation of the US financial
system, which led to the rise of colossal banks, with ever more complex financial innovations. These allowed the fastest circulation of short-term capital
anywhere in the world, aided by powerful computers that are able to place,
buy and sell orders at previously unheard of speeds, with little interference
by the authorities. What controls remained were bypassed through so-called
"over the counter" operations, which are only recorded in the accounts when
they are concluded, and even then through SPV companies (special purpose
vehicles, or conduits[1]) that were not subject to regulation because formally
they were not banks. This allowed US banks, and the European banks that
imitated them, to push leverage to levels far beyond what is considered
sustainable (thirty or forty to one), or in some cases nearly infinite, in that
the real capital with which they worked was nearly zero.

How this was possible should primarily be attributed to neoliberal economic
theorizing, according to which markets are able to self-regulate and credit risks
decrease to the point of vanishing when not held in their original form, but
rather are spread out over a vast number of debtors and creditors. A robust
modelling system, which had also received the anointment of the Nobel Prize,
was established on these premises[2] and this gave a theoretical basis for the unre-
strained activities of financial operators and allowed the authorities to justify

---

1. These companies form a "shadow banking system" that in the United States in 2011 was
   estimated to be around $16 trillion.
2. S. Zamagni, "The Lesson and Warning of a Crisis Foretold".

their laxity. If we add to this the long-held idea that the goal of companies is to maximize shareholder profits, we can understand why banks rushed into unsecured loans, 100 per cent mortgages, as well as international capital transfers that sought to ruthlessly exploit and profit from countries (through public debt or the currency) or companies weaknesses. The financial market for derivatives exploded, from $80 trillion in 1998 to $600 trillion in 2007, equalling over ten times global GDP (see Table 17.1). Financial operators had substantial earnings as long as the system held together,[3] and this led both financial operators and the investors to believe that a new way had been found to become wealthy without working: the financial market. Even non-financial companies were induced to fatten their slim profits by diverting funds from productive investment to finance.

Table 17.1 Evolution of derivatives from 1998–2013 (US dollar trillions).

Date	Derivatives	Global GDP	Derivatives/GDP
1998	80	31	2.6
1999	88	32	2.8
2000	95	33	2.9
2001	111	33	3.4
2002	142	34	4.2
2003	197	38	5.2
2004	252	43	5.9
2005	298	46	6.4
2006	415	50	8.3
2007	596	56	10.6
2008	548	62	8.9
2009	604	59	10.3
2010	601	64	9.4
2011	648	71	9.1
2012	632	72	9.8
2013	710	74	9.6

Source: Bank for International Settlements.

---

3. To the point that in the United States prior to the crisis 40 per cent of one year's profits derived from the financial sector.

Before giving an account of the resounding collapse of the system between 2007 and 2008, we should recall that even in the 1990s there was first-hand experience of just how risky it was to let finance have free rein, when malfunctions, which could be temporary, provoked serious financial crises around the world. Paul Krugman has described the series of crises after financial markets were liberalized in Europe in 1990.[4] As detailed in Chapter 15, 1992 saw a speculative attack on several currencies in the European Monetary System, which were forced to leave it and launch plans to strengthen their own finances. And during those same years Japan underwent violent financial crises (mostly internal) (see Chapter 16) and between 1994 and 1995 that also happened to Mexico, Brazil and Venezuela (the "tequila" crisis, as it was called), all of which had significant financial imbalances. In 1997–8 the Asian crisis followed (Indonesia, Malaysia, the Philippines, Korea and Thailand) which was primarily generated by financial weakness more than the real economy that saw robust growth rates. The contagion spread to Russia in 1998, which was still recovering from the crisis brought about by the fall of the Communist government. Finally, the Argentine crisis of 2002 was the product of an overvalued peso, which had been pegged to the dollar.

In each of these cases ad hoc interventions were made without ever connecting the events or reflecting on their common features, which would have advised greater prudence in regulating global finance.[5] It was clear to many that the liberalization of global financial markets had shifted the burden of speculation to whatever target was identified at the time as weak and incapable of resisting, producing extensive damage that needed to be addressed by international organizations, including the United States, but any measures taken failed to eliminate the underlying causes of these recurrent events. Even the US economy slipped into a speculative bubble prior to the one that led to the collapse, providing even more supporting evidence for those who were aware that finance was becoming too speculative. We are referring to the "dot com" bubble, in which new technology companies were increasingly overvalued, that burst between 2001 and 2002. Coupled with the 11 September 2001 attack on the World Trade Center, it produced a wave of unemployment that was countered by lowering interest rates – a recipe that was to set up the next bubble.

This path lined with financial crises, which were thought to be localized, led to the general collapse that was largely unanticipated by the economics

---

4. Krugman, *The Return of Depression Economics and the Crisis of 2008*.

5. For important comparisons between the financial aspects of the 1929 crisis and the present one, see Eichengreen, *Hall of Mirrors*.

profession. We now know that the trigger was the unsustainability of so-called "subprime" mortgages, which were given to individuals with poor credit histories and so carried a higher risk of default. These mortgages, which were widely and easily available, made housing prices rise. However, when a significant number of repayments defaulted, and banks tried to recover their collateral by selling the mortgaged homes, housing prices collapsed and many financial operators – including some of the largest – became insolvent. At that point the giant house of cards built on the subprime mortgages was shaken to its foundations; many other higher-risk operations were drawn in, which produced a domino effect that was far more devastating than it first appeared. The opacity of the system was such that the size of the bubble did not become clear until the serious collateral damage became evident. The banks themselves, not knowing how many "toxic" securities (those with near-zero values) were held by their counterparts, stopped making the short-term loans that so many of their operations had relied on, and insolvencies multiplied even beyond what was necessary.

Those European countries that fully followed the US model, the UK, Iceland and Cyprus began to see similar dynamics developing. Ireland and Spain saw widespread construction speculation. Events in Portugal, Greece and Italy were different, as we shall see. But individual banks throughout Europe that had followed the US model all suffered the same consequences.

As has been said by various commentators,[6] we should emphasize that at the root of this crisis was a financial system that incentivized private individuals to take on debt beyond what was reasonable; it was in place long before serious public debt was incurred, something that happened as a result of the bailouts – a topic we will discuss in the next section.

17.2 *How national indebtedness averted a collapse similar to 1929*

Since the speculative bubble emerged in the private banking system, many would have preferred to see the banks that caused it fail. However, governments know well that a bank failure has such a devastating negative multiplier effect on the economy (see Chapter 11) that no politician today is willing to take on that responsibility. So it was that all governments decided to initiate substantial bailout operations, with the one exception of Lehman Brothers – an exception that was heavily criticized as having worsened the confluence of

---

6. Vague, *The Next Economic Disaster*.

events, and yet was avoidable because the problem for Lehman Brothers was actually liquidity rather than insolvency. Founded by the Lehman brothers in 1847, Lehman Brothers had long focused on trading in raw materials; it did not begin trading securities until 1906 in collaboration with Goldman Sachs. The last of the Lehman descendants died in 1969, and since then it grew through mergers and acquisitions, with frequent name changes to become the United States' fourth largest investment bank. Having been affected by the terrorist attack in 2001, it rebounded with very aggressive practices and ended up engaging in subprime mortgages more than was prudent. After having concealed its difficulties with accounting devices, by August 2008 the situation was no longer sustainable. There were various reasons why Lehman Brothers did not find the safe harbour offered to other financial operators, and on 15 September 2008 it was forced to declare bankruptcy with bank debts of $613 billion, bond debts of $155 billion, and business activities that were not immediately collectable, for a declared value of $639 billion. It was the largest bankruptcy in United States history.

Not even the United States administration, known for its aversion to bailouts, could accept that this failure might trigger others, and immediately afterwards on 3 October the Congress approved the TARP (Troubled Asset Relief Program) plan that permitted spending 700 billion dollars – later reduced to 475 billion by the US Treasury – for bailouts. Many more billions came from other sources (particularly the Federal Reserve) providing a total pool of $2,792 billion. $1,650 billion was used to save the two semi-public banks Fannie Mae and Freddie Mac, which were completely exposed to the subprime loans, $256 billion was used for the semi-public insurance company, AIG and the rest was used for a thousand financial institutions that included J. P. Morgan, Bank of America and Citigroup. The interventions implemented by national governments in Europe (a unified scheme was set in place only in 2014, see the next section) are given in Table 17.2. Note that UK, Irish and Icelandic banks were heavily supported, but also the extent of government bailouts in Germany, the Netherlands and Belgium was substantial.[7] In all cases, including the United States, public debt soared. Italy, Greece and Spain remained out of the crisis; their problems arose as a consequence of the euro crisis, which we will consider in the next section.

The repercussions of this financial tsunami on the real side of the economy were not long in coming. Redundancies in the financial sector, a credit crunch, or sharply lowered lending capacity by banks, falling demand in many countries, and difficulty maintaining incomes in the welfare states all drastically

---

7. The case of Cyprus, where banking assets reached 7.8 times GDP, broke out afterwards.

dropped investments and consumption, which launched the global economy into a downward spiral. The impact was certainly reduced by the bank bailouts and the counter-cyclical measures adopted by some countries, but these could not totally eliminate all the difficulties, partly because in 2010–11, when the financial bubble seemed to have been overcome, the euro crisis loomed.

Table 17.2 Government bank bailouts made in Europe prior to 2010 (euro billions).

Country	Amount	Institutions involved
Austria	28	8
Belgium	142	6
Denmark	33	59
France	85	8
Germany	417	13
UK	901	18
Greece	3	9
Ireland	105	6
Iceland	1	3
Italy	4	4
Luxembourg	7	4
The Netherlands	143	14
Portugal	6	7
Spain	11	2
Switzerland	43	1
Total	1,931	155

Source: Mediobanca, *Piani di stabilizzazione finanziaria: aggiornamento* at 31 December 2013 (www.mbres.it).

17.3 *The euro crisis*

While the banking events described above were unfolding, serious problems were taking shape in Europe that were to include those countries that had not been at the forefront of the bank failures. Before the outbreak of the banking crisis, putting the single currency, the euro into operation had created a divergence between those countries that had assumed some sort of wage discipline and had given attention to the competitiveness of their production processes and those that had not. The latter had seen growing deficits in their balances of payments and public budgets (often used in a compensatory manner) that had produced high public and private debt. In October 2009 Greece revealed a budget deficit of 12 per cent; since its debt levels were already high its interest rates went through the roof, making it impossible for Greece to finance its debt. In early 2010 the European Central Bank made its first attempts to counter speculation through the Securities Market Programme (SMP), which in practice meant purchasing government bonds, albeit in small amounts due to Germany's opposition. At the same time, both Ireland and Portugal were also experiencing a rapid rise in interest rates and were no longer able to refinance their debt. In 2010 an agreement was finally reached between the European Commission, Council and Parliament to launch a new EU financial oversight system, the European System of Financial Supervision, which went into force in 2011, however this was more about agencies necessary for prevention rather than remediation.

Throughout 2011 ad hoc bailout interventions were made for Greece and Ireland, subject to accepting restructuring programs for their economies; all this was designed and funded by the EU, the ECB and the IMF (the "Troika"). In December Mario Draghi, the governor of the ECB, launched a bank refinance programme, the Long Term Refinancing Operation (LTRO), with €1000 billion; part of this was to be used by banks to acquire public debt bonds in their countries. At the end of 2011 there were difficulties in two other countries, for different reasons: Spain was suffering the after-effects of a huge construction bubble, and Italy – which had maintained a high public debt since the 1990s to be constantly refinanced – had not, due to the impossibility of increasing its budget deficit, been able to check the fall of internal demand. These two countries were able to avoid invasive interventions by the Troika, but they contributed to endangering the survival of the euro.

At this point it became clear that an ECB unable to counter the heavy deflationary effects of European events should be put under serious question. This provided strong arguments to exit the euro for those countries in most trouble and also good reason for speculators to move their capital to bet on those exits. 2012 proved to be the crucial year for saving the euro. The creation[8] of the ESM (European Stability Mechanism, to go into effect the

---

8. Actually, the creation of the fund was already planned in 2010, but with a much smaller budget.

following October) was signed off in February of that year, as was the creation of the Fiscal Compact in March (to go into effect in January 2013). The ESM was a permanent institution tasked with finding solutions for emergency crisis cases. The Fiscal Compact focused instead on the problem of public finance; it set obligatory parameters for the deficit and debt of each country in order to rebalance public finance in the medium term, as well as the necessity for structural reforms to improve the productivity of each country. However, all this seemed insufficient to the markets. Then on 26 July 2012 at the Global Investment Conference held in London Draghi, the ECB governor, made his now famous statement in response to the governor of the Bank of England, who had strongly criticized the euro:

> The first message I would like to send, is that the euro is much, much stronger, the euro area is much, much stronger than people acknowledge today … When people talk about the fragility of the euro and the increasing fragility of the euro, and perhaps the crisis of the euro, very often non-euro area member states or leaders underestimate the amount of political capital that is being invested in the euro. And so we view this, and I do not think we are unbiased observers, we think the euro is irreversible. And it's not an empty word now, because I preceded saying exactly what actions have been made, are being made to make it irreversible. But there is another message I want to tell you. Within our mandate, the ECB is ready to do whatever it takes to preserve the euro. And believe me, it will be enough.[9]

On 2 August Draghi put the OMT (Outright Monetary Transactions) programme into operation, which provided for buying bonds of states in difficulty that had agreed to a re-entry plan. The announcement of that programme began to reverse expectations that the euro would fail. The real crux of the problem was that Germany (along with a few other EU countries) had always opposed such bond purchases just as it had always opposed issuing public EU bonds. Draghi therefore had to be patient and circumvent this, ultimately succeeding by initiating decisive actions, although obviously only monetary in nature. The final measure fielded was the Banking Union, which had long been prepared over the course of 2013 and placed in operation in November 2014. This provision conferred to the ECB the direct control of 130 "systemic" banks in the eurozone, while the other banks remained under

---

9. European Central Bank; www.ecb.europa.eu/press/key/date/2012/html/sp120726.en.html. (accessed April 2017).

national oversight and were harmonized; it also initiated a common crisis resolution system, with an annexed fund. With the launch in January 2015 of Draghi's QE (quantitative easing) liquidity injection operation to counter deflation on the model of the Federal Reserve, we have seen to full effect the growing activism of the ECB.

At this point the ECB is no longer a central bank without means of intervention, not unlike what happened to the Federal Reserve after the 1929 crisis, but Draghi has repeatedly clarified that a more active monetary policy is insufficient for Europe to pull out of the difficulties into which the global crisis threw it. Other problems remain in the real economy that must be addressed by other policies. However, bringing public finances under EU control with the Fiscal Compact was not easy, due to the necessity by governments to counter the crisis with tax reductions and spending increases. This has been the chief reason why "austerity" has been heavily criticized. A sound budget is indispensable, but trying to achieve it in a crisis situation is about the least wise course of action imaginable. Countries only became aware of this in 2014, and recommendations were then made to the EU to act with greater support for investments, but this remains an open problem in 2016.

17.4 *Underlying reasons for the crisis*

While the proximate causes of the financial crisis and its prolonged duration in Europe with the euro crisis are by now clear, it seems important, as capitalism's second great crisis, to reflect on its deeper and structural causes and what it might tell us about the state of the world in 2016.

Firstly, we should note the increase in distributional inequality. This happened also prior to the 1929 crisis but today it is more pronounced and pervasive (see Figure 11.1, which shows that in the United States in 2011 25 per cent of wealth was in the hands of 1 per cent of the population[10]) to the point that improvements in the living standards of the vast majority have come to a halt. The increase in inequality by itself is sufficient to explain many current problems, including the scant increase in the demand for consumer goods, the stagnation in investments to expand production capacity and the high availability of speculative capital for financial activities that expects high returns (and

---

10. In Europe and the rest of the advanced world the increase in inequality was a little less, but it happened nonetheless. Inequalities are generally more pronounced in developing countries. For a general discussion of the problem, see Piketty, *Capital in the Twenty-First Century*.

thus is willing to face higher risk). Two other important consequences follow. One is the lack of investment in the real economy, which defers the creative part of the Schumpeterian cycle. Some have suggested that we are entering a phase of very long term stagnation[11] brought about by the lack of sufficient innovations to sustain the growth cycle, but this can equally result from a lack of investments more than from any intrinsic difficulty in generating innovations. The other consequence is that since the elites are engaged in financial activities,[12] they oppose regulation that seeks to place limits on those activities because that would generate less profit. This sets up a vicious cycle: more risky financial activity produces greater instability and fewer real investments, but fewer real investments means more economic stagnation and a greater incentive to use income speculatively.

The second observation regards the high imbalances in balances of payments, which creates global instability and difficulty. Keynes had already considered this problem. At Bretton Woods he proposed creating a global clearing union to monitor and resolve imbalances in balances of payments; its purpose was to avoid the deleterious effects of some countries dragging out deficits over the long term and others doing nothing to eliminate their surpluses. As noted in Chapter 13, Keynes's proposal was not accepted. As long as the gold standard was in force the problem was not serious, but subsequently there was no provision for a rebalancing mechanism. This is how some countries have accumulated significant surpluses (Japan for many decades, and now China, Germany and some of the Gulf states) and others have ongoing deficits (such as the United States). The countries with surpluses use them either to finance those with deficits, which has harmful consequences, or to build "sovereign wealth funds" that acquire securities and properties all over the world, which is again destabilizing. This is a problem the IMF has not been able to address.

Finally, another structural cause of the crisis has to do with so-called "jobless growth". What happened previously in agriculture is now happening in industry: productivity is rising by replacing labour with machines, computer programs, and robots, such that even when there is investment and demand revives, employment increases only slightly and the percentage of those employed in industry declines. Advanced countries create jobs almost exclusively in services. Services, however, include many different activities that operate by very different productive processes. For example, consider on the one hand railway transport, in which there are a few large companies (when

11. Teulings & Baldwin, *Secular Stagnation*.
12. Various commentators are scathing in their criticism of the "rent-seeking" attitudes of the current elite, among them Niall Ferguson in his *The Great Degeneration*.

there is not just one state-controlled company), and on the other the multitude of coffee shops, or restaurants that are managed independently by just a few people. Services often have an important relational dimension that makes them appropriate to be managed by families or cooperatives. Expanding the ways that services can be provided is fundamental to overcome jobless growth.

More generally, there are other limits to our growth model that are perhaps more serious, such as the environment and demographics, topics we can only mention here. Regarding the environment, the worry is not just producing enough food for a rising global population but the impact of global warming and climate change, which threaten human settlements. From a demographic point of view, the contradictory trends between advanced countries that are declining demographically and developing countries that are still expanding suggest the potential for great upheaval, as well as mass exoduses from countries that do not enjoy the benefits of peace, a rising economy or acceptable governments that promote the common good. Managing these population movements, which are destined primarily to Europe, is becoming one of the most burning issues in international relations: balancing the humanitarian need of migrants with the pressure on the social and economic resources, including welfare systems, of the recipient countries has yet to be determined.[13]

---

13 There is an immense literature on this subject. Here we can only offer a few essential references, among them Parsons & Smeeding, *Immigration and the Transformation of Europe*; Collier, *Exodus: How Migration is Changing our World* and Crepaz, *Trust beyond Borders.*

Epilogue

The journey from the medieval city-states to the present-day world economy exhibited two important features: the elevation of creativity and enquiry, and the move from the local to the universal, exalting mobility over sedentariness. The transition from an agricultural society to an industrial and tertiary one showcases very well this process. The low productivity of a predominantly subsistence-based agriculture of routine and physically hard cultivation of the land by farmers tied to it enabled only a very limited section of society (10–20%) to live outside it. With industry and commerce, a much more extended layer of the population was able to escape the destiny of being peasants for work in more creative and less immobile environments, increasing productivity sufficient to allow the formation of a larger surplus that not only raised standards of living, but offered resources for infrastructure, culture, arts, science and education.

This is an irreversible process, and in itself highly positive because it favours the dignity of men, offering people who were once enslaved, or colonized, or marginalized from civilization, the chance to develop their talents productively. That many people still remain excluded from sharing in this progress; that war, terrorism, misery, lack of civil rights, bad and corrupt government still today oppress millions of people, should stave off any sense of satisfaction with the progress achieved. However there are other, more serious problems with the mechanics of economic progress that should equally concern us.

The lack of investment in research in many advanced countries threatens a future of stagnation that results when neither imitation or innovation is at work and the continuing processes of globalization and homogenization further reduce the diversity so important for innovation and creativity. The early stages of economic development were characterized by the need to overcome scarcity and to increase quantity: more was better. Today, quantity can be deadly – obesity, pollution and waste are widespread. Societies need now to turn to quality over quantity and consume less and differently. The shortage of public, relational and merit goods needs to be addressed. The success of Fordism has given the world an abundance of private goods but to prosper society needs to produce more than just private goods. Public infrastructures (physical and social), education and good health, as well as equitable relations in the workplace, home and in the wider social sphere, have always been fundamental for public well-being and for maintaining the motivation to work and to contribute to the "common good". To deal with people as factors of production in the same way as other materials and capitals is to downgrade us to the level of commodities.

The growing inequalities within developed and developing countries between those at the top, who have become richer and richer, and those at the bottom, whose lot does not improve must concern us all. Public policies that seek to mitigate this growing gap are either absent or inadequate. Arguably, the most important single factor generating such inequalities today is the excessive amount of financial assets in the world, which is both responsible for the decrease in the use of capitals for investments in the real side of the economy and in research, and the predominance of short-term investments. Stronger control of finance is necessary, even if it is hard to achieve.

The increasing and gigantic size of companies, whose market power, which can only be kept in check by antitrust legislation (there is no world antitrust authority yet), guarantees political influence, threatens us with a future where great corporations can rule the world to their advantage. With research increasingly concentrated in such companies, innovation will be achieved by corporations for the advantage of corporations. The widespread faith, which has accompanied the third industrial revolution, in the belief that technology can solve mankind's problems has discouraged thinking about the important questions of life. Philosophy has been sidelined; religion is considered irrelevant; the people who once devoted time and study to making humanity happier are now devising robots and computers to out-perform humans and increasingly out-think them. Sentiments, intimacy and human relations are intermediated, if not entirely substituted, by the relation of humans with machines.

And finally, we must resist the temptation for economics to become an end in itself. To "make money" has always been deemed useful to improve one's life, but for centuries it was considered a means to other ends. Now economics has produced an end intrinsic to it: consumption. Not a consumption to meet our needs, or to support our life missions, but a consumption that entails more consumption in a never-ending cycle. Today's economics is premised on a self-interested utilitarianism that has built an artificial man, *homo economicus*, who is a maximizer of self-utility (the acquisition of private goods) and nothing else. Most of the world's economic models embody this assumption, with the result that ethics and the other dimensions of man no longer have a place in economic thinking[1]. Instead, egoism, personal or corporate, predominates. Although this paradigm of economics is not shared by all scholars – for example there are efforts to revive other lines of thinking, like that of the civil economy and public happiness[2] – there needs to be more awareness and understanding of the disasters produced by *homo economicus* before a change in mainstream economic thinking and in economic policy can take place.

I would like to end with a quotation from John Hicks, an economist who was one of the first to receive the Nobel Prize, in 1972. In an article written in 1941, he insisted that an economist should learn not only economics, statistics and commerce (management), but also history and politics. He concluded his arguments with the following words, which I still consider are of great importance today:

> In the field of economics, over-specialization is doubly disastrous. A man who is a mathematician and nothing but a mathematician may live a stunted life, but he does not do any harm. An economist who is nothing but an economist is a danger to his neighbours. Economics is not a thing in itself; it is a study of one aspect of the life of man in society. It scarcely ever happens that the decision on what policy to adopt on any practical issue can be made (or at any rate should be made) on economic grounds alone. Other things – political questions (internal or foreign), administrative questions, educational questions in a broad sense, moral questions and so on – always come in as well. Now, it is quite hopeless for an economist to pretend that he can give advice on purely economic grounds, and that some other specialist will put in an appearance to fill the gaps ...
>
> No, if the economist is to be of any use in the world, he must be more than an economist ... The economists of the Ricardian epoch knew very well what to advise: their advice was sometimes wrong, but it was not

---

1. All the great economists have been clear on this. Keynes, for example, envisaged man's "return to some of the most sure and certain principles of religion and traditional virtue – that avarice is a vice, that the exaction of usury is a misdemeanour and the love of money is detestable, that those walk most truly in the paths of virtue and sane wisdom who tale least thought for the morrow. We shall once more value ends above means and prefer the good to the useful. We shall honour those who can teach us how to pluck the hour and the day virtuously and well ..." (*Essays in Persuasion*, 360–65).
2. For the civil economy approach, see Bruni & Zamagni, *Civil Economy*.

a narrow advice; it was not based solely upon economic reasoning, but on social philosophy as well. The economist of tomorrow ... will also know what to advise, on economic grounds; but, if through increasing specialization, his economics is divorced from any background of social philosophy, he will be in real danger of becoming a dodge-merchant, full of ingenious devices for getting out of particular difficulties, but losing contact with the plain root-virtues, even the plain economic virtues, on which a healthy society must be based. Modern economics is subject to a real danger of Machiavellism – the treatment of social problems as matters of technique, not as facets of the general search for a Good Life.[3]

---

3. Hicks, "Education in Economics", pp. 6–7.

Bibliography

Abelshauser, W. "American Aid and West German Economic Recovery. A Macroeconomic Perspective", in C. Meier (ed.), *The Marshall Plan and Germany: West Germany Economic Development Within the Framework of ERP,* pp. 367–411. Oxford: Berg, 1991.

Abelshauser, W. "Germany: Guns, Butter and Economic Miracles". In M. Harrison (ed.), *The Economics of World War II,* pp. 122–76. Cambridge: Cambridge University Press, 2000.

Abramovitz, M. "Catching up, Forging Ahead and Falling Behind". *Journal of Economic History* (1986) 46:2, pp. 385–406.

Acemoglu, D. & J. A. Robinson. *Why Nations Fail.* New York: Crown Business, 2012.

Acemoglu, D., S. Johnson & J. Robinson. "Institutions as the Fundamental Cause of Long-Run Growth". In P. Aghion & S. Durlauf (eds), *Handbook of Economic Growth,* v. 1A, pp. 385–472. Amsterdam: North-Holland, 2005.

Acemoglu, D., S. Johnson & J. Robinson. "The Colonial Origins of Comparative Development: An Empirical Investigation". *American Economic Review* (2001) 91, pp. 1369–401.

Acheson, D. *Present at the Creation: My Years in the State Department.* New York: Norton, 1969.

Albert, M. *Capitalism Against Capitalism.* Hoboken, NJ: Wiley, 1993.

Aldcroft, D. *Education, Training and Economic Performance 1944 to 1990.* London: Routledge, 1992.

Aldcroft, D. H. & S. Morewood. *Economic Change in Eastern Europe Since 1918.* Cheltenham: Elgar, 1995.

Allen, R. C. "Agricultural Marketing and the Possibilities for Industrialization in the Soviet Union in the 1930s". *Explorations in Economic History* (1997) 34:4, pp. 387–410.

Allen, R. C. *The British Industrial Revolution in Global Perspective.* Cambridge: Cambridge University Press, 2009.

Allen, R. C. *Farm to Factory: A Reinterpretation of the Soviet Industrial Revolution.* Princeton, NJ: Princeton University Press, 2003.

Allen, R. C., T. Bengtsson & M. Dribe (eds). *Living Standards in the Past.* Oxford: Oxford University Press, 2005.

Allinson, G. *Japan's Postwar History.* Ithaca, NY: Cornell University Press, 1997.

Amato, G. *Antitrust and the Bounds of Power: The Dilemma of Liberal Democracy in the History of the Market.* Oxford: Hart, 1997.

Amatori, F. & A. Colli. *Business History: Complexities and Comparisons.* London: Routledge, 2011.

Aoki, M., G. Jackson & H. Miyajima (eds). *Corporate Governance in Japan: Institutional Change and Organizational Diversity.* Oxford: Oxford University Press, 2007.

Aoki, M. & H. Patrick. *The Japanese Main Bank System.* Oxford: Clarendon Press, 1994.

Armitage, D. & S. Subrahmanyam (eds). *The Age of Revolutions in Global Context, 1760–1840.* Basingstoke: Palgrave Macmillan, 2010.

Atkinson, A. B. *The Economic Consequences of Rolling Back the Welfare State.* Cambridge, MA: MIT Press, 1999.

Ayres, R. L. *Banking on the Poor: The World Bank and World Poverty.* Cambridge, MA: Harvard University Press, 1983.

Bacci, M. Livi, *A Concise History of World Population,* sixth ed. Chichester: Wiley, 2017.

Bacci, M. Livi, *A Short History of Migrations.* Cambridge: Polity, 2012.

Bacci, M. Livi, *Population and Nutrition.* Cambridge: Cambridge University Press, 1991.

Baccini, A. & M. Vasta, "Una tecnica ritrovata: interlocking directorates nei rapporti tra banca e industria in Italia (1911–1936)". *Rivista di Storia Economica* (1995), pp. 221–51.

Bairoch, P. *Economics and World History: Myths and Paradoxes.* Chicago, IL: Chicago University Press, 1995.

Balderston, T. *The Origins and Course of the German Economic Crisis, 1923–1932.* Berlin: Haude & Spener, 1993.

Baldwin, R. & C. Wyplosz. *The Economics of European Integration.* New York: McGraw Hill, 2015.

Banerjee, A. & T. Piketty. *Top Indian Incomes, 1922–2000.* London: CEPR, 2002.

Barkai, H. *Nazi Economics: Ideology, Theory and Politics.* Oxford: Berg, 1990.

Baten, J. (ed.). *A History of the Global Economy 1500 to the Present.* Cambridge: Cambridge University Press, 2016.

Battilani, P. & H. Schröter (eds). *The Cooperative Business Movement, 1950 to the Present.* Cambridge: Cambridge University Press, 2012.

Baum, W. C. *Investing in Development: Lessons of World Bank Experience.* New York: Oxford University Press, 1985.

Baumol, W. J., R. R. Nelson & E. N. Wolf. *Convergence and Productivity.* Oxford: Oxford University Press, 1994.

Becattini, G., M. Bellandi & L. De Propis (eds). *A Handbook of Industrial Districts.* Cheltenham: Elgar, 2009.

Belussi, F. & A. Sammarra (eds). *Business Networks in Clusters and Industrial Districts: The Governance of the Global Value Chain.* London: Routledge, 2009.

Bentham, J., *An Introduction to the Principles of Morals and Legislation* [1780], Oxford: Clarendon Press, 1907.

Berend, I. T. *Central and Eastern Europe, 1944–1993.* Cambridge: Cambridge University Press, 1995.

Berend, I. T. & G. Ranki. *Economic Development in East-Central Europe in the Nineteenth and Twentieth Centuries.* New York: Columbia University Press, 1974.

Berghahn, V. (ed.). *Quest for Economic Empire: European Strategies of German Big Business in the Twentieth Century.* Providence, RI: Berghahn, 1996.

Bhagwati, J. & A. Panagariya. *Why Growth Matters: How Economic Growth in India Reduced Poverty and the Lessons for Other Development Countries.* Bangalore: Public Affairs Center, 2014.

Bhattacharyya, S. C. *Energy Economics: Concepts, Issues, Markets and Governance*. Heidelberg: Springer, 2011.

Bolt, J. & J. L. van Zanden. *The First Update to the Maddison Project: Re-estimating Growth Before 1820*. Maddison Project Working Paper 4. Groningen: Groningen Growth and Development Centre, University of Groningen.

Booth, A. E., & S. Glynn. "Unemployment in the Interwar Period: A Multiple Problem". *Journal of Contemporary History* (1975) 10:4, pp. 611–36.

Borchardt, K. & A. Ritschl. "Could Brüning Have Done It? A Keynesian Model of Interwar Germany 1925–1938". *European Economic Review* (1992) 36:2–3, pp. 695–701.

Borchardt, K. *Perspectives on Modern German Economic History and Policy*. Cambridge: Cambridge University Press, 1991.

Bordo, M. & B. Eichengreen (eds). *A Retrospective on the Bretton Woods System*. Chicago, IL: Chicago University Press, 1993.

Borzaga, C. & L. Becchetti (eds). *The Economics of Social Responsibility: The World of Social Enterprises*. London: Routledge, 2012.

Borzaga, C. & J. Defourny. *The Emergence of Social Enterprises*. London: Routledge, 2004.

Boyce, R. *The Great Interwar Crisis*. Basingstoke: Palgrave Macmillan, 2009.

Bradley, J., G. Petrakos & J. Traistaru (eds). *Integration, Growth and Cohesion in an Enlarged European Union*. Berlin: Springer, 2010.

Brandes, D. S. *American Welfare Capitalism, 1880–1940*. Chicago, IL: University of Chicago Press, 1976.

Brandt, L., D. Ma & T. G. Rawski. "From Divergence to Convergence: Re-evaluating the History Behind China's Economic Boom". *Journal of Economic Literature* (2014) 52:1, pp. 45–123.

Brandt, L. & T. Rawski. *China's Great Transformation*. Cambridge: Cambridge University Press, 2008.

Broadberry, S. N. "Convergence: What the Historical Record Shows". In B. van Ark & N. Crafts, *Quantitative Aspects of Post-War European Economic Growth*, pp. 327–46. Cambridge: Cambridge University Press, 1996.

Broadberry, S. & N. Crafts. "The Implications of British Macroeconomic Policy in the 1930s for the Long Run Performance". Centre for Economic Policy Research, Discussion Paper 386, 1990.

Broadberry, S. & M. Harrison (eds). *The Economics of World War I*. Cambridge: Cambridge University Press, 2005.

Broadberry, S. & K. H. O'Rourke (eds). *The Cambridge Economic History of Modern Europe Volume 1, 1700–1870*. Cambridge: Cambridge University Press, 2010.

Broadberry, S. & K. H. O'Rourke (eds). *The Cambridge Economic History of Modern Europe Volume 2, 1870 to the Present*. Cambridge: Cambridge University Press, 2010.

Broadberry, S. *et al.*, *British Economic Growth 1270–1870*. Cambridge: Cambridge University Press, 2015.

Broder, A. *Histoire économique de la France au XXe, 1914–1997*. Paris: Ophrys, 1998.

Brosio, G. & C. Marchese. *Il potere di spendere. Economia e storia della spesa pubblica dall'unificazione ad oggi*. Bologna: Il Mulino, 1986.

Brown, D. M. *Setting a Course: American Women in the 1920s*. New York: Twayne, 1987.

Brown W. A. & R. Opie. *American Foreign Assistance*. Washington, DC: Brookings Institution, 1953.

Bruni, L. & S. Zamagni. *Civil Economy*. Oxford: Peter Lang, 2007.

Brunschwig, H. *French Colonialism 1871–1914: Myths and Realities*. New York: Praeger, 1966.

Brynjolfsson, E. & A. McAfee. *The Second Machine Age: Work, Progress and Prosperity in a Time of Brilliant Technologies*. New York: Norton, 2014.

Calomiris, C. W. "The Costs of Rejecting Universal Banking: American Finance in the German Mirror 1870–1914". In N. R. Lamoreaux & D. M. G. Raff (eds), *Coordination and Information*, pp. 257–315. Chicago, IL: Chicago University Press, 1996.

Cameron, R. "A New View of European Industrialisation". *Economic History Review* (1985) 38:1, pp. 1–23.

Cameron, R. & L. Neal. *A Concise Economic History of the World*. Oxford: Oxford University Press, 2002.

Capie, F. *Depression and Protectionism*. London: Routledge, 1983.

Cardini, F. & M. Montesano. *Storia Medioevale*. Florence: Le Monnier, 2006.

Caron, F. *An Economic History of Modern France*. New York: Columbia University Press, 1979.

Carr, E. H. *History of Soviet Russia, Volume IV: Foundations of a Planned Economy*. London: Macmillan, 1980.

Carreras, A. "An Annual Index of Spanish Industrial Output". In N. Sanchez Albornoz (ed.), *The Economic Modernization of Spain, 1830–1930*, pp. 75–89. New York: Columbia University Press, 1987.

Casini, P. *Newton e la coscienza europea*. Bologna: Il Mulino, 1984.

Castronovo, V., F. Amatori, F. Silva, R. Artoni & F. Russolillo. *Storia dell'IRI*. 6 volumes. Rome: GLF Editori Laterza, 2012–15.

Cesarano, F. *Gli accordi di Bretton Woods. La costruzione di un ordine mondiale internazionale*. Bari: Laterza, 2000.

Chandler, A. *Inventing the Electronic Century*. New York: Free Press, 2001.

Chandler, A. *Scale and Scope: The Dynamics of Industrial Capitalism*. Cambridge, MA: Harvard University Press, 1990.

Chandler, A. *Strategy and Structure*. Eastford, CT: Martino, 2013 [first published 1962].

Chandler, A. *The Visible Hand*. Cambridge, MA: Harvard University Press, 1993 [first published 1977].

Chandler, A., F. Amatori & T. Hikino. *Big Business and the Wealth of Nations*. Cambridge: Cambridge University Press, 1997.

Chow, G. *Interpreting China's Economy*. Singapore: World Scientific, 2010.

Ciocca, P. *Ricchi per sempre? Una storia economica d'Italia (1796–2005)*. Turin: Bollati-Boringhieri, 2007.

Clark, G., K. O'Rourke, & A. M. Taylor. *Made in America? The New World, the Old and the Industrial Revolution*. NBER Working Paper 14077. Cambridge, MA: National Bureau of Economic Research, 2008.

Clark, G. *The Balance Sheets of Imperialism*. New York: Columbia University Press, 1936.

Clavin, P. *The Failure of Economic Diplomacy: Britain, Germany, France and the US, 1931–1936*. Basingstoke: Palgrave Macmillan, 1996.

Clayton, A. *The British Empire as a Superpower 1919–39*. Athens, GA: University of Georgia Press, 1986.

Coase, R. H. "The Nature of the Firm". *Economica* (1937) 4:16, pp. 386–405.

Cohen, J., "The 1927 Revaluation of the Lira. A Study in Political Economy", *Economic History Review*, 1972 (25), pp. 642–54.

Colli, A. *Dynamics of International Business*. London: Routledge, 2016.

Colli, A. *The History of Family Business, 1850–2000*. Cambridge: Cambridge University Press, 2003.

Collier, P. *Exodus: How Migration is Changing our World*. Oxford: Oxford University Press, 2013.

Comfort, N. *The Slow Death of British Industry: A Sixty-Year Suicide 1952–2012*. London: Biteback, 2012.

Costigliola, F. "The United States and the Reconstruction of Germany in the 1920s". *Business History Review* (1976) 50:4, pp. 477–502.

Cottarelli, C.& M. Guerguil (eds). *Designing a European Fiscal Union*. London: Routledge, 2014.

Crafts, N. "Patterns of Development in Nineteenth Century Europe". *Oxford Economic Papers* (1984) 36, pp. 438–58.

Crafts, N. F. R. "Industrial Revolution in England and France: Some Thoughts on the Question 'Why was England First'". *Economic History Review* (1977) 30:3, pp. 429–41.

Crafts, N. & G. Toniolo (eds). *Economic Growth in Europe Since 1945*. Cambridge: Cambridge University Press, 1996.

Crafts, N. & N. W. C. Woodward (eds). *The British Economy Since 1945*. Oxford: Oxford University Press, 1991.

Crepaz, M. M. L. *Trust Beyond Borders: Immigration, the Welfare State and Identity in Modern Societies*. Ann Arbor, MI: University of Michigan Press, 2008.

Crouch, C. *The Strange Non-Death of Neoliberalism*. Cambridge: Polity, 2011.

Cunha, A. *et al.* (eds). *An Inside View of the CAP Reform Process*. Oxford: Oxford University Press, 2011.

Darwin, J. *Britain and Decolonization: The Retreat from Empire in the Post-War World*. Basingstoke: Macmillan, 1988.

David, P. A. "Clio and the Economics of QWERTY". *American Economic Review* (1985) 75:2, pp. 332–7.

David, P. A. "Path Dependence: A Foundational Concept for Historical Social Science". *Cliometrica* (2007) 1:2.

Davies, R. W., M. Harrison & S. G. Wheatcroft (eds). *The Economic Transformation of the Soviet Union, 1913–1945*. Cambridge: Cambridge University Press, 1994.

Davis, L. E. & R. A. Huttenback. *Mammon and the Pursuit of Empire: The Economics of British Imperialism*. Cambridge: Cambridge University Press, 1988.

De Grauwe, P. *The Economics of the Monetary Union*. Oxford: Oxford University Press, 2014.

De Haan, J., S. Oosterloo & D. Schoenmaker (eds). *Financial Markets and Institutions: A European Perspective*. Cambridge: Cambridge University Press, 2015.

De Vries, J. *The Industrious Revolution: Consumer Behaviour and the Household Economy, 1650 to the Present*. Cambridge: Cambridge University Press, 2008.

Deane, P. & W. A. Cole. *British Economic Growth 1688–1959*. Cambridge: Cambridge University Press, 1962.

Deaton, A. *The Great Escape: Health, Wealth and the Origins of Inequality*. Princeton, NJ: Princeton University Press, 2015.

Dell, E. *The Schuman Plan and the British Abdication of Leadership in Europe*. Oxford: Oxford University Press, 1995.

Deng, K. G. "Development and its Deadlock in Imperial China, 221 BC–1840 AD". *Economic Development and Cultural Change* (2003) 51:2, pp. 479–522.

Di Nolfo, E. & B. Vigezzi (eds). *Power in Europe II: 1945–50*. Berlin: De Gruyter, 1992.

Dimsdale, N. & N. Horsewood. "A Model of the UK Economy in the Interwar Period". *European Economic Review* (1992) 36:2–3, pp. 702–09.

Dore, R. *Stock Market Capitalism: Welfare Capitalism: Japan and Germany versus the Anglo-Saxons*. Oxford: Oxford University Press, 2000.

Dore, R. *Taking Japan Seriously*. Stanford, CA: Stanford University Press, 1987.

Dormois, J. P. *The French Economy in the Twentieth Century*. Cambridge: Cambridge University Press, 2004.

Dormois, J. P. & M. Dintenfass (eds). *The British Industrial Decline*. London: Routledge, 1999.

Dornbusch, R., W. Nölling & R. Layard. *Postwar Economic Reconstruction and Lessons for the East Today*. Cambridge, MA: MIT Press, 1993.

Dowd, D. *The Twisted Dream: Capitalist Development in the US Since 1776*. Cambridge, MA: Winthrop, 1976.

Droz, B. *Histoire de la décolonisation au XX siécle*. Paris: Seuil, 2006.

Drummond, I. M. *Imperial Economic Policy 1917–39*. London: Allen & Unwin, 1974.

Duby, G. *Atlante storico*. Turin: Sei, 1995.

Edgerton, D. *Science, Technology and British Industrial "Decline". 1870–1970*. Cambridge: Cambridge University Press, 1996.

Edwards, J. & S. Ogilvie. "Universal Banks and German Industrialization: A Reappraisal". *Economic History Review* (1996) 49:3, pp. 427–46.

Eichengreen, B. *Essays in the History of International Finance 1919–39*. Cambridge: Cambridge University Press, 1990.

Eichengreen, B. *The European Economy Since 1945: Coordinated Capitalism and Beyond*. Princeton, NJ: Princeton University Press, 2006.

Eichengreen, B. *Globalizing Capital: A History of the International Monetary System*. Princeton, NJ: Princeton University Press, 2008.

Eichengreen, B. *Golden Fetters: The Gold Standard and the Great Depression 1919–1939*. Oxford: Oxford University Press, 1992.

Eichengreen, B. (ed.). *The Gold Standard in Theory and History*. London: Routledge, 1997.

Eichengreen, B. *Hall of Mirrors: The Great Depression, the Great Recession and the Uses and Misuses of History*. Oxford: Oxford University Press, 2015.

Eichengreen, "Institutions and Economic Growth", in N. Crafts & G. Toniolo (eds), *Economic Growth in Europe since 1945*, pp. 38–72. Cambridge: Cambridge University Press, 1996.

Eichengreen, B. "The Origins and Nature of the Great Slump Revisited". *Economic History Review* (1992) 45:2, pp. 213–39.

Eichengreen, B. *Reconstructing Europe's Trade and Payments: The European Payments Union*. Manchester: Manchester University Press, 1993.

Eichengreen, B., W. Lim, Y. C. Park & D. H. Perkins. *The Korean Economy: From a Miraculous Past to a Sustainable Future*. Cambridge, MA: Harvard University Press, 2015.

Ellwood, D. W. *Rebuilding Europe: Western Europe, America and Postwar Reconstruction*. London: Routledge, 1992.

Engerman, S. & R. E. Gallman (eds). *The Cambridge Economic History of the United States, Volumes 1–3*. Cambridge: Cambridge University Press, 1996–2000.

Engwall, L. & V. Zamagni (eds). *Management Education in Historical Perspective*. Manchester: Manchester University Press, 1998.

Erikson, E. *Between Monopoly and Free Trade: The English East India Company 1600–1757*. Princeton, NJ: Princeton University Press, 2014.

Esping-Andersen, G. *Politics Against Market*. Princeton, NJ: Princeton University Press, 1985.

Estrin S. & P. Holmes. *French Planning in Theory and Practice*. London: Allen & Unwin, 1983.

Fauri, F. *L'integrazione economica europea 1947–2006*. Bologna: Il Mulino, 2006.

Federico, G. & A. Teña. "Was Italy a Protectionist Country?", *European Review of Economic History* 1998 (1), pp. 73–97.

Federico, G. *An Economic History of the Silk Industry 1830–1930*. Cambridge: Cambridge University Press, 2009.

Feinstein, C. H. (ed.). *Banking, Currency and Finance in Europe between the Wars*. Oxford: Oxford University Press, 1995.

Feinstein, C. H., P. Temin & G. Toniolo. *The European Economies Between the Wars*. Oxford: Oxford University Press, 1997.

Feldman, G. D. *The Great Disorder: Politics, Economics and Society in the German Inflation 1914–1924*. Oxford: Oxford University Press, 1997.

Felice, D. *Oppressione e libertà. Filosofia e anatomia del dispotismo nel pensiero di Montesquieu*. Pisa: ETS, 2000.

Felice, E. *Ascesa e declino. Storia economica d'Italia*. Bologna: Il Mulino, 2015.

Felice, E. *Perché il Sud è rimasto indietro*. Bologna: Il Mulino, 2013.

Felloni, G. *Profilo di storia economica dell'Europa dal medioevo all'età contemporanea*. Turin: Giappichelli, 1997.

Fenoaltea, S. "Le ferrovie e lo sviluppo industriale italiano 1861–1913". In G. Toniolo (ed.), *L'economia italiana 1861–1940*, pp. 69–104. Bari: Laterza, 1978.

Fenoaltea, S. *The Reinterpretation of Italian Economic History: From Unification to the Great War*. Cambridge: Cambridge University Press, 2011.

Ferguson, N. *Empire: The Rise and Demise of the British World Order and the Lessons for Global Power*. New York: Basic Books, 2002.

Ferguson, N. *The Great Degeneration: How Institutions Decay and Economies Die*. London: Penguin, 2013.

Ferguson, N. "The Second World War as an Economic Disaster". In M. J. Oliver & D. Aldcroft (eds), *Economic Disasters of the Twentieth Century*, pp. 83–132. Cheltenham: Elgar, 2007.

Fieldhouse, D. K. *Colonialism 1870–1945*. New York: St Martin's Press, 1981.

Findlay, R. & K. O'Rourke. *Power and Plenty: Trade, War and the World Economy in the Second Millennium*. Princeton, NJ: Princeton University Press, 2007.

Fisher, M. H. *Migration: A World History*. Oxford: Oxford University Press, 2014.

Flandreau, M. & F. Zumer. *The Making of Global Finance*. Paris: OECD, 2004.

Flath, D. *The Japanese Economy*. Oxford: Oxford University Press, 2014.

Fogel, W. & S. L. Engerman. *Time on the Cross: The Economics of the American Negro Slavery*. Boston, MA: Norton, 1974.

Fohlin, C. "Capital Mobilisation and Utilisation in Latecomer Economies: Germany and Italy Compared". *European Review of Economic History* (1999) 3:2, pp. 139–74.

Foreman Peck, J. "A Model of Later Nineteenth Century European Economic Development". *Revista de Historia Economica* (1995) (13)3: pp. 441–71.

Foreman Peck, J. *History of the World Economy*. New York: Prentice Hall, 1995.

Freeman, C. & F. Louçã. *As Time Goes By: From the Industrial Revolutions to the Information Revolution*. Oxford: Oxford University Press, 2002.

Furubotn, E. & R. Richter. *Institutions and Economic Theory: The Contribution of the New Institutional Economics*. Ann Arbor, MI: University of Michigan Press, 2005.

Galbraith, J. K. *The Great Crash*. New York: Harcourt, 1955.

Galgano, F. *Lex Mercatoria*. Bologna: Il Mulino, 1993.

Gall, L. *The Deutsche Bank 1870–1995*. London: Weidenfeld & Nicolson, 1995.

Gallarotti, G. *The Anatomy of an International Monetary Regime: The Classical Gold Standard 1880–1914*. Oxford: Oxford University Press, 1995.

Garin, E. (ed.). *L'uomo del Rinascimento* (9th edn). Rome: Laterza, 2005.

Garside, W. R. (ed.). *Capitalism in Crisis: International Responses to the Great Depression*. Basingstoke: Macmillan, 1993.

Garvy, G. "Keynes and the Economic Activists of pre-Hitler Germany". *Journal of Political Economy* (1975) 83:2, pp. 391–405.

Gatrell, P. *Government, Industry and Rearmament in Russia, 1900–1914*. Cambridge: Cambridge University Press, 1994.

Gatrell, P. *The Tsarist Economy 1850–1917*. London: Macmillan, 1986.

Genovesi, A. *Lezioni di Commercio o sia d'Economia Civile* [1765] Milan: Vita e Pensiero, 2013.

Gerschenkron, A. *An Economic Spurt that Failed*. Princeton, NJ: Princeton University Press, 1977.

Gerschenkron, A. *Economic Backwardness in Historical Perspective*. Cambridge, MA: Harvard University Press, 1962.

Gifford, P. & W. R. Louis. *Decolonization and African Independence: The Transfers of Power, 1960–1980*. New Haven, CT: Yale University Press, 1988.

Gillingham, J. *Coal, Steel and the Rebirth of Europe 1945–1955: The Germans and the French from Ruhr Conflict to Economic Community*. Cambridge: Cambridge University Press, 1991.

Gimbel, J. *The Origins of the Marshall Plan*. Stanford, CA: Stanford University Press, 1976.

Goldstein, A. *Il miracolo coreano*. Bologna: Il Mulino, 2013.

Goldstone, J. A. *Why Europe? The Rise of the West in World Economy 1500–1850*. New York: McGraw Hill, 2008.

Goldthwaite, R. A. *The Building of Renaissance Florence: An Economic and Social History*. Baltimore, MD: Johns Hopkins University Press, 1982.

Good, D. F. *The Economic Rise of the Habsburg Empire 1750–1914*. Berkeley, CA: University of California Press, 1984.

Good, D. F. & T. Ma. "The Economic Growth of Central and Eastern Europe in Comparative Perspective, 1870–1989". *European Review of Economic History* (1999) 3:2, pp. 103–37.

Goody, J. *The Eurasian Miracle*. Cambridge: Polity, 2009.

Gourvish, T. R. & N. Tiratsoo (eds). *Missionaries and Managers: America Influences on European Management Education 1945–60*. Manchester: Manchester University Press, 1998.

Graham, A. (ed). *Government and Economies in the Postwar World: Economic Policies and Comparative Performance 1945–85*. London: Routledge, 1990.

Granovetter, M. "Coase Revisited: Business Groups in the Modern Economy". *Industrial and Corporate Change* (1995) 4:1, pp. 93–130.

Grantham, G. "The French Cliometric Revolution: A Survey of Cliometric Contributions to French Economic History". *European Review of Economic History* (1997) 1: 1:3, pp. 353–405.

Graziosi, A. "Building the First System of State Industry in History: Piatakov's VSNKh and the Crisis of NEP". *Cahiers du monde russe et sovietique* (1991) 32:4, pp. 539–80.

Graziosi, A. *L'Unione Sovietica, 1914–1991*. Bologna: Il Mulino, 2011.

Gregory, P. *Before Command: An Economic History of Russia from Emancipation to the First Five-year Plan*. Princeton, NJ: Princeton University Press, 1994.

Gregory, P. & R. C. Stuart. *Soviet Economic Structure and Performance*. New York: Addison Wesley, 1986.

Grief, A. "The Birth of Impersonal Exchange: The Community Responsibility System and Impartial Justice". *Journal of Economic Perspective* (2006) 20:2, pp. 221–36.

Greif, A. *Institutions and the Path to the Modern Economy: Lessons from Medieval Trade*. Cambridge: Cambridge University Press, 2006.

Grief, A. & M. Iylgun. "Social Organization, Violence and Modern Growth". *American Economic Review Papers and Proceedings* (2013) 103:3, pp. 534–8.

Griffith, R. T. (ed.). *Explorations in OEEC History*. Paris: OECD, 1997.

Hall, J. A. *Powers and Liberties*. Oxford: Oxford University Press, 1985.

Hanson, D. *Limits to Free Trade: Non-Tariff Barriers in the EU, Japan and US*. Cheltenham: Elgar, 2010.

Hanson, P. *The Economic Development of Russia: Between State Control and Liberalization*. Working Paper 32. Rome: ISPI, 2008.

Hargreaves, J. D. *Decolonization in Africa*. Harlow: Longman, 1997.

Harrison, M. *Accounting for War: Soviet Production, Employment and the Defence Burden, 1940–45*. Cambridge: Cambridge University Press, 1996.

Harrison, M. (ed.). *The Economics of World War II: Six Great Powers in International Comparison*. Cambridge: Cambridge University Press, 1998.

Harrison, M. "Resource Mobilization for World War II: The USA, UK, USSR and Germany, 1938–1945". *Economic History Review* (1988) 41:2, pp. 171–92.

Harrison, P. *The Rise and Fall of the Soviet Economy: An Economic History of the USSR from 1945*. Harlow: Longman, 2003.

Hartmann, H. & C. R. Unger (eds). *A World of Populations*. New York: Berghahn, 2014.

Hartwell, M. *The Industrial Revolution and Economic Growth*. London: Methuen, 1971.

Hatton, T. "Unemployment Benefits and the Macroeconomics of the Interwar Labour Market: A Further Analysis". *Oxford Economic Papers* (1983) 35:3, pp. 486–505.

Hatton, T. & J. G. Williamson. *Migration and International Labor Market, 1850–1939*, London: Routledge, 1994.

Hatton, T. J. & J. G.Williamson. "What Drove the Mass Migrations from Europe in the Late Nineteenth century?". *Population and Development Review* (1994) 20:3, pp. 533–59.

Hayes, P. *Industry and Ideology: I.G. Farben in the Nazi Era*. Cambridge: Cambridge University Press, 1987.

Headrick, D. R. *Power over Peoples: Technology, Environments and Western Imperialism 1400 to the Present*. Princeton, NJ: Princeton University Press, 2010.

Hentschel, V. "Indicators of Real Effective Exchange Rates of Major Trading Nations from 1922 to 1937". *German Yearbook on Business History 1988*. Berlin: Springer, 1990.

293

Herrigel, G. *Industrial Constructions: The Sources of German Industrial Power.* Cambridge: Cambridge University Press, 1996.

Hicks, J. "Education in Economics". An Address to the Manchester Statistical Society: Manchester: Norbury, Lockwood, 1941.

Hicks, J. *A Theory of Economic History.* Oxford: Oxford University Press, 1969.

Hilferding, R. *Das Finanzkapital.* Vienna: Wiener Volksbuchhandlung, 1910.

Hogan, M. J. *The Marshall Plan: America, Britain and the Reconstruction of Western Europe.* Cambridge: Cambridge University Press, 1987.

Holtfrerich, C. L. *German Inflation 1914–1923.* Berlin: De Gruyter, 1986.

Horie, S. *The International Monetary Fund: Retrospect and Prospect.* London: Macmillan, 1964.

Horn, J., L. N. Roseband & M. Roe Smith, *Reconceptualizing the Industrial Revolution.* Cambridge MA: MIT Press, 2010.

Houwink ten Cate, J. "Reichsbank President Hjalmar Schacht and the Reparation Payments (1924–1930)". *German Yearbook on Business History 1988.* Berlin: Springer, 1990.

Huang, Y. *Capitalism with Chinese Characteristics.* Cambridge: Cambridge University Press, 2008.

Hubbard, G. & T. Kane. *Balance: The Economics of Great Powers from Ancient Rome to Modern America.* New York: Simon & Schuster, 2013.

Huberman, M. "Labor Movements". In L. Neal & J. G. Williamson (eds) *Cambridge History of Capitalism,* Vol. II, pp. 348–83. Cambridge: Cambridge University Press, 2014.

Hudson, P. *The Industrial Revolution 1760–1830.* Oxford: Oxford University Press, 1992.

Hudson, P. (ed.). *Regions and Industries: A Perspective on the Industrial Revolution in Britain.* Cambridge: Cambridge University Press, 1989.

Hughes, J.& L. Cain. *American Economic History* (8th edn). Harlow: Pearson, 2010.

Hutton, G. *We Too Can Prosper: The Promise of Productivity.* London: Allen & Unwin, 1953.

Imai, M. *Kaizen: The Key to Japan's Competitive Success.* New York: McGraw Hill, 1986.

Jalan, B. *The Future of India: Politics, Economics and Governance.* New Delhi: Viking, 2005.

James, H. *The German Slump: Politics and Economics 1924–1936.* Oxford: Clarendon Press, 1986.

Jensen J. & F. Miszlivetz (eds). *Reframing Europe's Future: Challenges and Failures of the European Construction.* London: Routledge, 2014.

Johnson, S. & P. Temin. "The Macroeconomics of NEP". *Economic History Review* (1993) 46:4, pp. 750–67.

Jones, E. L. *Growth Recurring: Economic Change in World History.* Oxford: Oxford University Press, 1988.

Jones, G. *The Evolution of International Business.* Andover: Cengage Learning, 1996.

Jones, G. & J. Zeitlin (eds). *The Oxford Handbook of Business History.* Oxford: Oxford University Press, 2008.

Jones, K. *Reconstructing the World Trade Organization for the Twenty-First Century: An Institutional Approach.* Oxford: Oxford University Press, 2015.

Kaiser, D. *Economic Diplomacy and the Origin of the Second World War.* Princeton, NJ: Princeton University Press, 1980.

Kaiser, M. & E. A. Radice. *The Economic History of Eastern Europe 1919–1975.* Oxford: Oxford University Press, 1985.

Kaplan, J. J. & G. Schleiminger. *The European Payments Union: Financial Diplomacy in the 1950s*. Oxford: Oxford University Press, 1989.

Kelly, M., J. Mokyr & C. O'Grada. "Precocious Albion: A New Interpretation of the British Industrial Revolution". *Annual Review of Economics* (2014) 6, pp. 363–89.

Kemp, T. *The French Economy 1913–1939: The History of a Decline*. London: Prentice Hall, 1972.

Kennedy, P. *The Rise and Fall of the Great Powers*. London: Vintage, 1988.

Kennedy, W. *Industrial Structure, Capital Markets and the Origin of British Economic Decline*. Cambridge: Cambridge University Press, 1987.

Kershaw, I. (ed.). *Weimar: Why Did German Democracy Fail?* London: Weidenfeld & Nicolson, 1990.

Keynes, J. M. *Essays in Persuasion,* New York: Norton, 1963.

Keynes, J. M. *The Economic Consequences of the Peace*. London: Macmillan, 1919.

Keynes, J. M. *The General Theory of Employment, Interest and Money*. London: Macmillan, 1936.

Kindleberger, C. P. *Economic Growth in France and Britain, 1851–1950*. Cambridge, MA: Harvard University Press, 1964.

Kindleberger, C. P. *Europe's Postwar Growth*. Cambridge, MA: Harvard University Press, 1967.

Kindleberger, C. P. *A Financial History of Western Europe*. London: Routledge, 2006.

Kindleberger, C. P. *Manias, Panics and Crashes: A History of Financial Crises* (6th edn). London: Palgrave Macmillan, 2011.

Kindleberger, C. P. *The World in Depression 1929–1939*. Berkeley, CA: University of California Press, 1973.

Kirby, M. W. "Institutional Rigidities and Economic Decline: Reflections on the British Experience". *Economic History Review* (1992) 45:4, pp. 637–60.

Klein, B. H. *Germany's Economic Preparation for War*. Cambridge, MA: Harvard University Press, 1959.

Krober, A. R. *China's Economy: What Everyone Needs to Know*. New York: Oxford University Press, 2016.

Krugman, P. *The Return of Depression Economics and the Crisis of 2008*. New York: Norton, 2009.

Kuisel, R. F. *Capitalism and the State in Modern France*. Cambridge: Cambridge University Press, 1991.

Kuran, T. *The Long Divergence: How Islamic Law Held Back the Middle East*. Princeton, NJ: Princeton University Press, 2011.

Landes, D. *The Unbound Prometheus*. Cambridge: Cambridge University Press, 1969.

Landes, D. "Does it Pay to Be Late?". In J. Batou (ed.), *Between Development and Underdevelopment. The Precocious Attempts at Industrialization of the Periphery 1800–1870*, pp. 43–66. Geneva: Droz, 1991.

Lazonick, W. H. *Business Organization and the Myth of the Market Economy*. Cambridge: Cambridge University Press, 1993.

Leonardi, R. *Cohesion Policy in the EU: The Building of Europe*. London: Palgrave Macmillan, 2005.

Leonardi, R. *Convergence, Cohesion and Integration in the EU*. London: Palgrave Macmillan, 1995.

Lepenies, P. *The Power of a Single Number: A Political History of GDP*. New York: Columbia University Press, 2016.

Levy-Leboyer, M. & F. Bourguignon. *L'économie française au XIX siècle*. Paris: Economica, 1985.

Lewis, W. A. "Economic Development with Unlimited Supplies of Labour". *The Manchester School* (1954) 22(2) pp. 139–91.

Lincoln, J. R. & M. L. Gerlach. *Japan's Network Economy: Structure, Persistence and Change*. Cambridge: Cambridge University Press, 2008.

Locke, R. *The End of the Practical Man: Entrepreneurship and Higher Education in Germany, France and Great Britain, 1880–1940*. Greenwich: JAI Press, 1984.

Lombardo, G. *L'Istituto Mobiliare Italiano*. Bologna: Il Mulino, 1998.

Lopez-Claros A. & V. Perotti. *Does Culture Matter for Growth?* Policy Research Working Paper 7092. Washington, DC: World Bank, 2014.

Low, D. A. *Eclipse of Empire*. Cambridge: Cambridge University Press, 1991.

Lucassen, L. & J. Lucassen. "Quantifying and Qualifying Cross-Cultural Migrations in Europe Since 1500: A Plea for a Broader View". In F. Fauri (ed.), *The History of Migration in Europe: Perspectives from Economics, Politics and Sociology*, pp. 11–38. London: Routledge, 2015.

MacPherson, W. J. *The Economic Development of Japan 1868–1941*. Cambridge: Cambridge University Press, 1994.

Maddison, A. *Monitoring the World Economy, 1820-1992*. Paris: OECD, 1995.

Maddison, *The World Economy*, Vols 1 and 2. Paris: OECD, 2006.

Malanima, P. "When Did England Overtake Italy? Medieval and Early Modern Divergence in Prices and Wages". *European Review of Economic History* (2013) 17:1, pp. 45–70.

Malanima, P. *Economia preindustriale. Mille anni: dal IX al XVIII secolo*. Milan: Bruno Mondadori, 1995.

Malanima, P. *L'economia italiana. Dalla crescita medioevale alla crescita contemporanea*. Bologna: Il Mulino, 2002.

Malanima, P. & V. Zamagni (eds). Special issue on 150 years of the Italian economy. *Journal of Modern Italian Studies* (2010) 15(1).

Malode Molina, J. L. & P. Martina Aceña (eds). *The Spanish Financial System: Growth and Development since 1900*. London: Palgrave Macmillan, 2011.

Mandeville, *The Fable of the Bees*. [1714], Oxford: Clarendon Press, 1924.

Manning, P. *Migrations in History*. London: Routledge, 2012.

Martin Aceña, P. "Spain During the Classical Gold Standard Years, 1880–1914". In M. Bordo & F. Capie (eds), *Monetary Regimes in Transition*, pp. 135–72. Cambridge: Cambridge University Press, 1994.

Marx, K. *Capital* vol. 1. [1867 edition]

McCloskey, D. *Bourgeois Dignity: Why Economics Can't Explain the Modern World*. Chicago, IL: Chicago University Press, 2010.

McNeill, W. H. *Greece: American Aid in Action 1947–1956*. New York: Twentieth Century Fund, 1957.

Meier, C. (ed.). *The Marshall Plan and Germany: West German Economic Development Within the Framework of ERP*. Oxford: Berg, 1991.

Meier, C. "The Politics of Productivity: Foundation of American Foreign Policy after World War II". *International Organization* (1977) 31:4, pp. 607–33.

Meier, C. *Recasting Bourgeois Europe: Stabilization in France, Germany and Italy in the Decade after World War I*. Princeton, NJ: Princeton University Press, 2015.

Meier, C. "The Two Postwar Eras and the Conditions for Stability in Twentieth-century Europe". *American Historical Review* (1981) 86:2, pp. 327–52.

Metcalf, B. D. & T. R. Metcalf. *A Concise History of Modern India* (3rd edn). Cambridge. Cambridge University Press, 2012.

Middleton, R. *Towards the Managed Economy: Keynes, the Treasury and the Fiscal Policy Debate of the 1930s*. London: Methuen, 1985.

Mielants, E. H. *The Origins of Capitalism and the Rise of the West*. Philadelphia, PA: Temple University Press, 2007.

Milward, A. *The European Rescue of the Nation State*. London: Routledge, 1992.

Milward, A. *The New Order and the French Economy*. Oxford: Oxford University Press, 1970.

Milward, A. *The Reconstruction of Western Europe 1945–51*. Berkeley, CA: California University Press, 1984.

Milward, A. *War, Economy and Society, 1939–45*. Berkeley, CA: California University Press, 1979.

Minami, R. *The Economic Development of Japan*. Basingstoke: Macmillan, 1994.

Minot, B. "La chûte du premier gouvernement Blum et l'action des commissions des finances 1936–37". *Revue d'economie politique* (1982) 92:1, pp. 35–51.

Minsky, H. *Can "It" Happen Again? Essays on Instability and Finance*. London: Routledge, 2016.

Minsky, H. *The Financial Instability Hypothesis*. Working Paper 74. New York: Levy Economics Institute of Bard College, 1992.

Minsky, H. *J. M. Keynes*. New York: Columbia University Press, 1975.

Mitchell, B. R. *European Historical Statistics*. London: Macmillan, 1992.

Mitchell, B. R. *International Historical Statistics: Europe 1750–1988*. New York: Stockton Press, 1992.

Mitchell, B. R. *International Historical Statistics: Africa and Asia*. London: Macmillan, 1982.

Mitchell, B. R. *International Historical Statistics: The Americas and Australasia*. London: Macmillan, 1983.

Mitterauer, M. *Why Europe? The Medieval Origins of its Special Path*. Chicago, IL: University of Chicago Press, 2010.

Moggridge, D. E. *British Monetary Policy 1924–31: The Norman Conquest of $4.86*. Cambridge: Cambridge University Press, 1972.

Moggridge, D. E. *Maynard Keynes. An Economist's Biography*. London: Routledge, 1995.

Mokyr, J. *The Enlightened Economy: An Economic History of Britain 1700–1850*. New Haven, CT: Yale University Press, 2012.

Mokyr, J. *The Lever of Riches*. Oxford: Oxford University Press, 1992.

Molteni, C. & M. G. Pecorari. "I Kinyuu Keiretsu in Giappone: evoluzione storica, struttura attuale e implicazioni economiche". *Annali di storia d'impresa* (1993) v. 9, pp. 155–77.

Morikawa, H. *A History of Top Management in Japan: Managerial Enterprises and Family Enterprises*. Oxford: Oxford University Press, 2001.

Morishima, M. *Why Has Japan Succeeded? Western Technology and the Japanese Ethos*. Cambridge: Cambridge University Press, 1984.

Morris, C. T. "How Fast and Why Did Early Capitalism Benefit the Majority?" *Journal of Economic History* (1995) 55:2, pp. 211–26.

Mosconi, F. *The New European Industrial Policy*. London: Routledge, 2015.

Muzzarelli, M. G. *Il denaro e la salvezza. L'invenzione del Monte di Pietà*. Bologna: Il Mulino, 2001.

Neal, L. *A Concise History of International Finance: From Babylon to Bernanke*. Cambridge: Cambridge University Press, 2015.

Neal, L. & J. G. Williamson (eds). *The Cambridge History of Capitalism, 2 vols*. Cambridge: Cambridge University Press, 2014.

Nelson, R. "The Complex Economic Organization of Capitalist Economies". *Capitalism and Society* (2011) 6:1, Article 2.

North, D., *Understanding the Process of Economic Change*. Princeton, NJ: Princeton University Press, 2005.

Nuñez, C. E. *La fuente de la riqueza: Educacion y desarrollo economico en la España contemporanea*. Madrid: Alianza, 1992.

O'Brien, P. "The Costs and Benefits of British Imperialism 1846–1914". *Past & Present* (1988) 125, pp. 186–92.

O'Brien, P. "Deconstructing the British Industrial Revolution as a Conjuncture and Paradigm for Global Economic History". In J. Horn, L. N. Roseband & M. Roe Smith (eds), *Reconceptualizing the Industrial Revolution*, pp.21–46. Cambridge, MA: MIT Press, 2010.

O'Brien, P. "Do We Have a Typology for the Study of European Industrialization in the Nineteenth Century?". *Journal of European Economic History* (1986) 15:2, pp. 291–333.

O'Brien, P. & C. Keyder. *Economic Growth in Britain and France 1780–1914: Two Paths in the Twentieth Century*. London: Allen & Unwin, 1978.

O'Rourke, J. & G. Williamson. "Around the European Periphery 1870–1913: Globalization, Schooling and Growth". *European Review of Economic History* (1997) 1:2, pp. 153–90.

Obstfeld, M. & A. M. Taylor. *Global Capital Markets: Integration, Crisis and Growth*. Cambridge: Cambridge University Press, 2004.

Offe, C. *Il tunnel: L'Europa dell'est dopo il comunismo*. Rome: Donzelli, 1993.

Offer, A. "The British Empire: A Waste of Money?". *Economic History Review* (1993) 46:2, pp. 215–38.

Oliver, M. J. & D. H. Aldcroft (eds). *Economic Disasters of the Twentieth Century*. Cheltenham: Elgar, 2008.

Olivi, B. *L'Europa difficile*. Bologna: Il Mulino, 1998.

Overy, R. J. *The Interwar Crisis 1919–39* (2nd edn) Harlow: Pearson, 2007.

Overy, *The Nazi Economic Recovery 1932–1938*. Cambridge: Cambridge University Press, 1996.

Overy, R. J. *The Origins of the Second World War*. Harlow: Longman, 1987.

Overy, R. J. *War and Economy in the Third Reich*. Oxford: Oxford University Press, 1994.

Parker, R. A. "Economics, Rearmament and Foreign Policy: The UK Before 1939". *Journal of Contemporary History* (1975) 10:4, pp. 637–47.

Parker, R. E. *Reflections on the Great Depression*. Cheltenham, Elgar, 2002.

Parsons, C. A. & T. M. Smeeding (eds). *Immigration and the Transformation of Europe*. Cambridge: Cambridge University Press, 2006.

Parthasarathi, P. *Why Europe Grew Rich and Asia Did Not: Global Economic Divergence*. Cambridge: Cambridge University Press, 2011.

Patel, K. K. (ed.). *Fertile Ground for Europe? The History of European Integration and the Common Agricultural Policy Since 1945*. Baden Baden: Nomos Verlagsgesellschaft, 2009.

Peden, G. C. "Keynes, the Treasury and Unemployment in the Late 1930s". *Oxford Economic Papers* (1980) 32:1, pp. 1–18.

Perez, C. *Technological Revolutions and Financial Capital: The Dynamics of Bubbles and Golden Ages*. Cheltenham: Elgar, 2003.

Pervillé, G. *De l'Empire à la décolonisation*. Paris: Hachette, 1995.

Petri, R. "Innovazioni tecnologiche tra uso bellico e mercato civile". In V. Zamagni (ed.), *Come perdere la guerra e vincere la pace*. Bologna: Il Mulino, 1997.

Petri, R. *Storia economica d'Italia: Dalla grande guerra al miracolo economico (1918–1963)*. Bologna: Il Mulino, 2002.

Pierenkemper, T. & R. Tilly. *The German Economy During the Nineteenth Century*. Oxford: Berghahn, 2005.

Piffaretti, N. *Reshaping the International Monetary Architecture: Lessons from Keynes' Plan*. Policy Paper 5034. Washington, DC: World Bank, 2009.

Piketty, T. *Capital in the Twenty-First Century*. Cambridge, MA: Harvard University Press, 2014.

Piketty, T. & E. Saez. "Income Inequality in the USA, 1913–1998". *Quarterly Journal of Economics* (2003) 118, pp. 1–39.

Pollard, S. *British Prime and British Decline*. London: Arnold, 1990.

Pollard, S. "Capital Exports, 1870–1914: Harmful or Beneficial?". *Economic History Review* (1985) 38:4, pp. 489–514.

Pollard, S. (ed.). *The Gold Standard and Employment Policies Between the Wars*. London: Methuen, 1970.

Pollard, S. *Peaceful Conquest*. Oxford: Oxford University Press, 1981.

Pollard, S. *The Wasting of the British Economy: British Economic Policy 1945 to the Present*. London: Routledge, 1982.

Pomeranz, K. *The Great Divergence: Europe, China and the Making of the Modern World Economy*. Princeton, NJ: Princeton University Press, 2000.

Poni, C. "Espansione e declino di una grande industria: le filature di seta a Bologna tra XVII e XVIII secolo", in *Problemi d'acque a Bologna in età moderna*. Bologna: Istituto per la Storia di Bologna, 1983.

Prados de la Escosura, L. "Long Run Economic Growth in Spain Since 1800: An International Perspective". In A. Szirmai, B. van Ark & D. Pilat (eds), *Explaining Economic Growth: Essays in Honor of Angus Maddison*. Amsterdam: North-Holland, 1993.

Prados de la Escosura, L. "Capitalism and Human Welfare". In L. Neal & J. G. Williamson (eds). *The Cambridge History of Capitalism, Vol 2*, pp. 501–29. Cambridge: Cambridge University Press, 2014.

Prados de la Escosura, L. *De imperio a nacion: Crecimiento y atraso economico en España (1780–1930)*. Madrid: Alianza, 1988.

Prados de la Escosura, L. *El progréso economico de la España*. Madrid: Fundacion BBVA, 2003.

Prados de la Escosura, L. "Gerschenkron Revisited: European Patterns of Development in Historical Perspective". Working Paper 05–79 (10). Madrid: Economic History Department, University Carlos III, 2005.

Preda, D. "The Schuman Plan: The First Step to European Unity and the First Antitrust Law". *European Union Review* (2002) 7:2, pp. 61–78.

Price, R. *An Economic History of Modern France, 1730–1914*. London: Macmillan, 1981.

Ranieri, R. "Il Piano Marshall e la ricostruzione della siderurgia a ciclo integrale". *Studi Storici* (1996) 37:1, pp. 415–90.

Redmond, J. "An Indicator of the Effective Exchange Rate of the Pound in the 1930s". *Economic History Review* (1980) 33:1, pp. 83–91.

Redmond, J. "The Gold Standard between the Wars". In S. N. Broadberry & N. F. R. Crafts (eds), *Britain in the International Economy*, pp. 346–68. Cambridge: Cambridge University Press, 1992.

Reinhard, W. *A Short History of Colonialism.* Manchester: Manchester University Press, 2011.

Reszat, B. *European Financial Systems in the Global Economy.* Chichester: Wiley, 2005.

Rieber, A. R. *Merchants and Entrepreneurs in Imperial Russia.* Chapel Hill, NC: University of North Carolina Press, 1982.

Riesser, J. *The German Banks and their Concentration.* Washington, DC: Government Printing Office, 1911.

Ristuccia, C. "1935 Sanctions Against Italy: Would Coal and Oil Have Made the Difference?". *European Review of Economic History* (2000) 4:1, pp. 85–110.

Ritschl, A. "Reparation Transfers, the Borchardt Hypothesis and the Great Depression in Germany, 1929–32: A Guided Tour for Hard-Headed Keynesians". *European Review of Economic History* (1998) 2:1, pp. 49–72.

Ritter, G. A. *Storia dello stato sociale.* Bari: Laterza, 1996.

Rodrik, D. & A. Subramanian. *From "Hindu Growth" to Productivity Surge: The Mystery of the Indian Growth Transition.* Working Paper 0477. Washington, DC: International Monetary Fund, 2004.

Roe, M. J. *Strong Managers Weak Owners: The Political Root of American Corporate Finance.* Princeton, NJ: Princeton: University Press, 1994.

Romano, L. & F. Traù. "Il ruolo delle istituzioni nello sviluppo manifatturiero del mondo emergente. Tre 'modelli' di intervento pubblico negli anni successivi al secondo dopoguerra". *Rivista di Storia Economica* (2014) 30: pp. 121–60.

Roselli, A. *Money and Trade Wars in Interwar Europe.* London: Palgrave Macmillan, 2014.

Rosenberg, N. & L. B. Birdzell. *How the West Grew Rich.* New York: Basic Books, 1987.

Rosenthal, J. L. & R. B. Wong. *Before and Beyond Divergence: The Politics of Economic Change in China and Europe.* Cambridge, MA: Harvard University Press, 2011.

Rostow, W. W. *The Stages of Economic Growth.* Cambridge: Cambridge University Press, 1960.

Rowland, B. M. (ed.). *Balance of Power or Hegemony? The Interwar Monetary System.* New York: New York University Press, 1976.

Rowland, B. M. *Commercial Conflict and Foreign Policy: A Study in Anglo-American Relations 1932–38.* New York: Garland, 1987.

Rubinstein, W. D. *Capitalism, Culture and Economic Decline in Britain, 1750–1990.* London: Routledge, 1993.

Rudolph, R. L. *Banking and Industrialization in Austria–Hungary.* Cambridge: Cambridge University Press, 1976.

Sabel, C. F. & J. Zeitlin. *World of Possibilities: Flexibility and Mass Production in Western Industries.* Cambridge: Cambridge University Press, 1997.

Sanborn, J. A. *Imperial Apocalypse: The Great War and the Destruction of the Russian Empire.* Oxford: Oxford University Press, 2014.

Sanderson, M. *The Universities and British Industry 1850–1970.* London: Routledge, 1972.

Sauvy, A. *Histoire économique de la France entre les deux guerres*. Paris: Economica, 1965.

Schubert, A. *The Credit-Anstalt Crisis of 1931*. Cambridge: Cambridge University Press, 1991.

Schuker, S. *American "Reparations" to Germany*. Princeton, NJ: Princeton University Press, 1988.

Schulze, M. S. "Origins of Catch up Failure: Comparative Productivity Growth in the Hapsburg Empire, 1870–1910". *European Review of Economic History* (2007) 11:2, pp. 189–218.

Schulze, M. S. "Patterns of Growth and Stagnation in late Nineteenth-Century Habsburg Economy". *European Review of Economic History* (2000) 4:1, pp. 311–40.

Schulze, M. S. *Western Europe: Economic and Social Change Since 1945*. Harlow: Longman, 1999.

Schumpeter, J. A. *The Theory of Economic Development*. Piscataway, NJ: Transaction, 2008 [first published in German 1911; first English edn 1934].

Schweitzer, A. "Plans and Markets: Nazi Style". *Kyklos* (1977) 30:1, pp. 88–115.

Scranton, P. *Endless Novelty: Production and American Industrialization 1865–1925*. Princeton, NJ: Princeton University Press, 1997.

Scranton, P. & P. Fridenson. *Reimagining Business History*. Baltimore, MD: Johns Hopkins University Press, 2013.

Sen, A. *The Argumentative Indian: Writings on Indian History, Culture and Identity*. London: Penguin, 2005.

Sheldrake, J. & P. D. Webb. *State and Market: Aspects of Modern European Development*. Aldershot: Dartmouth, 1993.

Sherer, D. R. *Industry, State and Society in Stalin's Russia 1926–34*. Ithaca, NY: Cornell University Press, 1996.

Sherman, M. *Short History of Financial Deregulation in the United States*. London: Centre for Economic Policy Research, 2009.

Shucksmith, M., K. J. Thomson & D. Roberts (eds). *The CAP and the Regions: The Territorial Impact of the Common Agricultural Policy*. Wallingford: Centre for Agriculture and Biosciences International, 2005.

Silei, G. "Dalle assicurazioni sociali alla *Social Security*: Politiche sociali in Europa e negli Stati Uniti fra le due guerre (1919–1939)". In V. Zamagni (ed.), *Povertà e innovazioni istituzionali in Italia dal Medioevo ad oggi*, pp. 751–74. Bologna: Il Mulino, 2000.

Sinn, H. W. *The Euro Trap: On Bursting Bubbles, Budgets and Beliefs*. Oxford: Oxford University Press, 2014.

Skidelsky, R. *John Maynard Keynes 1883–1946: Economist, Philosopher, Statesman*. London: Macmillan, 2003.

Sklar, M. J. *The Corporate Reconstruction of American Capitalism, 1890–1916*. Cambridge: Cambridge University Press, 1988.

Stein, R. S. & J. Powers. *The Energy Problem*. Singapore: World Scientific, 2011.

Stiefel, D. "The Reconstruction of the Credit-Anstalt". In A. Teichova & P. Cottrell (eds), *International Business in Central Europe, 1918–1939*, pp. 415–30. Leicester: Leicester University Press, 1983.

Stiglitz, J. E. *The Economic Role of the State*. Oxford: Blackwell, 1989.

Stögbauer, C. "The Radicalisation of the German Electorate: Swinging to the Right and the Left in the Twilight of the Weimar Republic". *European Review of Economic History* (2001) 5:2, pp. 251–80.

Stögbauer, C. & K. J. Komlos, "Averting the Nazi Seizure of Power: A Counterfactual Thought Experiment". *European Review of Economic History* (2004) 8:2, pp. 173–99.

Sutton, A. C. *Western Technology and Soviet Economic Development 1917 to 1930*. Stanford, CA: Hoover Institution, 1968.

Sutton, A. C. *Western Technology and Soviet Economic Development 1930 to 1945*. Stanford, CA: Hoover Institution, 1971.

Sutton, A. C. *Western Technology and Soviet Economic Development 1945 to 1965*. Stanford, CA: Hoover Institution, 1973.

Swinnen, J. F. M. (ed.) *The Political Economy of the 2014–2020 CAP*. Brussels: Centre for European Policy Studies, 2015.

Sylla, R. & G. Toniolo (eds). *Patterns of Industrialization in Nineteenth-Century Europe*. London: Routledge, 1991.

Taylor, A. M. & J. G. Williamson. "Convergence in the Age of Mass Migration". *European Review of Economic History* (1997) 1:1, pp. 27–63.

Taylor, F. *The Downfall of Money: Germany's Hyperinflation and the Destruction of the Middle Class*. London: Bloomsbury, 2014.

Teichova, A. (ed.) *Central Europe in the Twentieth Century*. London: Scolar, 1997.

Temin, P. "The Beginning of the Depression in Germany". *Economic History Review* (1971) 24:2, pp. 240–8.

Temin, P. "The German Crisis of 1931: Evidence and Tradition". *Cliometrica* (2008) 2:1, pp. 5–17.

Temin, P. *Lessons from the Great Depression*. Cambridge, MA: MIT Press, 1991.

Temin, P. "Soviet and Nazi Economic Planning in the 1930s". *Economic History Review* (1991) 44:4, pp. 573–93.

Temin, P. & D. Vines. *The Leaderless Economy: Why the World System Fell Apart and How to Fix it*. Princeton, NJ: Princeton University Press, 2013.

Teña, A. "Proteccion y competitividad en España e Italia, 1890–1960". In L. Prados de la Escosura & V. Zamagni (eds), *El desarrollo economico en la Europa del sur: España e Italia en perspectiva historica*, pp. 321–58. Madrid: Alianza, 1992.

Teulings, C. & R. Baldwin (eds). *Secular Stagnation: Facts, Causes and Cures*. London: Centre for Economic Policy Research, 2014.

Tew, B. *Evolution of the International Monetary System*. London: Routledge, 1988.

Thygesen, N., K. Velupillai & S. Zambelli (eds). *Business Cycles: Theories, Evidence and Analysis*. London: Macmillan, 1991.

Tilly, R. "German Economic History and Cliometrics: A Selective Survey of Recent Tendencies". *European Review of Economic History* (2001) 5:2, pp. 151–87.

Todeschini, G. *Franciscan Wealth*. St. Bonaventure, NY: Franciscan Institute, 2009.

Tomlinson, J. *Democratic Socialism and Economic Policy: The Attlee Years*. Cambridge: Cambridge University Press, 1997.

Tone, A. *The Business of Benevolence: Industrial Paternalism in Progressive America*. Ithaca, NY: Cornell University Press, 1997.

Toninelli, P. A. (eds). *Lo sviluppo economico moderno dalla rivoluzione industriale alla crisi energetica (1750–1973)*. Venice: Marsilio, 1997.

Toninelli, P. A. (ed.). *The Rise and Fall of State-Owned Enterprises in the Western World*. Cambridge: Cambridge University Press, 2000.

Toniolo, G. *An Economic History of Liberal Italy, 1850–1918*. London: Routledge, 2014.

Toniolo, G. *L'economia dell'Italia fascista*. Bari: Laterza, 1980.

Toniolo, G. (ed.). *Oxford Handbook of the Italian Economy Since Unification*. Oxford: Oxford University Press, 2013.

Tortella, G. "Patterns of Economic Retardation and Recovery in South-Western Europe in the Nineteenth and Twentieth Centuries". *Economic History Review* (1994) 47(1), pp. 1–21.

Tortella, G. *The Development of Modern Spain*. Cambridge, MA: Harvard University Press, 2000.

Turner, H. A. *German Big Business and the Rise of Hitler*. Oxford: Oxford University Press, 1985.

Turner, J. D. *Reconstruction in Post-war Germany: British Occupation Policy and the Western Zones, 1945–55*. Oxford: Oxford University Press, 1989.

Urwin, D. W. *The Community of Europe: A History of European Integration since 1945*. Harlow: Longman, 1991.

Vague, R. *The Next Economic Disaster: Why it's Coming and How to Avoid it*. Philadephia, PA: University of Pennsylvania Press, 2014.

Van Ark, B., M. O'Mahoney & M. P. Timmer. "The Productivity Gap Between Europe and the United States: Trends and Causes". *Journal of Economic Perspectives* (2008) 22:1, pp. 25–44.

Van der Wee, H. & J. Blomme. *An Economic Development of Belgium since 1870*. Cheltenham: Elgar, 1997.

Van Dormael, A. *Bretton Woods: Birth of a Monetary System*. New York: Holmes & Meier, 1978.

Van Duijn, J. *The Long Wave in Economic Life*. London: Routledge, 1983.

Van Riel, A. & A. Schram. "Weimar Economic Decline, Nazi Economic Recovery and the Stabilization of Political Dictatorship". *Journal of Economic History* (1993) 53:1, pp. 71–105.

Voigtländer, N. & H.-J. Voth, "How the West Invented Fertility Restriction", *American Economic Review*, 2013, 103, (6), pp. 2227–64.

Von Helten, J. J. & Y. Cassis (eds). *Capitalism in a Mature Economy: Financial Institutions, Capital Exports and British Industry, 1870–1939*. Aldershot: Ashgate, 1990.

Von Krüdener, J. (ed.). *Economic Crisis and Political Collapse: The Weimar Republic*. Oxford: Oxford University Press, 1990.

Wakatobe, M. *Japan's Great Stagnation and Abenomics*. London: Palgrave Macmillan, 2015.

Wallerstein, I. *The Modern World System, Volume III*. Berkeley, CA: University of California Press, 2011.

Weder, M. *Some Observations on the Great Depression in Germany*. Discussion Paper 3716. Washington, DC: Center for Economic and Policy Research, 2003.

Werth, N. *Storia dell'Unione Sovietica. dall'impero russo alla Comunità degli Stati Indipendenti, 1900–1991*. Bologna: Il Mulino, 1993 [originally published in French].

Wexler, I. *The Marshall Plan Revisited: The European Recovery Program in Economic Perspective*. Westport, CT: Greenwood, 1983.

White, E. N. *Crashes and Panics: The Lessons from History*. Homewood, IL: Irwin, 1990.

Wicker, E. *The Banking Panics of the Great Depression*. Cambridge: Cambridge University Press, 1996.

Wiener, M. J. *English Culture and the Decline of the Industrial Spirit*. Cambridge: Cambridge University Press, 2004.

Williams, D. "London and the 1931 Financial Crisis". *Economic History Review* (1963) 15:3, pp. 513–28.

Williamson, O. *The Economic Institutions of Capitalism: Firms, Markets, Relational Contracting*. New York: Free Press, 1985.

Wixforth, H. & D. Ziegler. "*Bankenmacht*: Universal Banking and German Industry in Historical Perspective". In Y. Cassis, G. D. Feldman & O. Olsson (eds), *The Evolution of Financial Institutions and Markets in Twentieth-Century Europe*, pp. 249–72. Aldershot: Scolar, 1995.

Wozniak Boyle, J. *Conditional Leadership: the EU Commission and European Regional Policy*. Lanham, MD: Lexington, 2006.

Wrigley, E. A. *Energy and the English Industrial Revolution*. Cambridge: Cambridge University Press, 2010.

Wyplosz, C. "EMU: Why and How It Might Happen". *Journal of Economic Perspectives* (1997) 11(4), pp. 3–21.

Yueh, L. *China's Growth: The Making of an Economic Superpower*. Oxford: Oxford University Press, 2013.

Zaleski, E. *Stalinist Planning for Economic Growth, 1933–1952*. Chapel Hill, NC: University of North Carolina Press, 1980.

Zamagni, S. "The Lesson and Warning of a Crisis Foretold: A Political Economy Approach". *International Review of Economics* (2009) 56:3, pp. 315–34.

Zamagni, S. *Mercato*. Turin: Rosenberg & Sellier, 2014.

Zamagni, S. & V. Zamagni. *Cooperative Enterprise: Facing the Challenge of Globalization*. Cheltenham: Elgar, 2010.

Zamagni, V. (ed.). *Come perdere la guerra e vincere la pace*. Bologna: Il Mulino, 1997.

Zamagni, V. (ed.). *Finance and the Enterprise*. London: Academic Press, 1992.

Zamagni, V. "Ferrovie e integrazione del mercato nazionale nell'Italia post-unitaria". In *Studi in onore di Gino Barbieri*, pp. 1635–1649. Salerno: IPEM, 1983.

Zamagni, V. "Funzioni e strumenti del welfare state in prospettiva storica". In D. Da Empoli & G. Muraro (eds), *Verso un nuovo stato sociale*, pp. 3–15. Milan: Angeli, 1997.

Zamagni, V. "L'economia sociale di mercato nella storia". In V. Zamagni, A. Quadrio Cuzio & M Vitale (eds), *Economia sociale di mercato e umanesimo d'impresa*. Milan: Inaz, 2012.

Zamagni, V. "Un'analisi macroeconomica degli effetti della guerra". In V. Zamagni (ed.), *Come perdere la guerra e vincere la pace*, pp. 13–54. Bologna: Il Mulino, 1997.

Zamagni, V. *An Economic History of Italy 1860–1990*. Oxford: Clarendon Press, 1993.

Zamagni, V. *Finmeccanica. Competenze che vengono da lontano*. Bologna: Il Mulino, 2009.

Zamagni, V. "Institutional Innovations and Economic Growth in Europe in the Post-world War II Era". In A. Bonoldi & A. Leonardi.(eds), *Recovery and Development in the European Periphery (1945–1960)*, pp. 17–27. Bologna: Il Mulino, 2009.

Zamagni, V. & P. Porta (eds). *Economia*, Appendix VIII of the Italian Encyclopedia Treccani devoted to Italian Economic Thinking. Roma: Istituto dell'Enciclopedia Italiana, 2012.

Zan L., F. Rossi & S. Zambon. *Il "discorso del maneggio": Pratiche gestionali e contabili all'Arsenale di Venezia, 1580–1643*. Bologna: Il Mulino, 2006.

Zarnowitz, V. *Business Cycles: Theory, History, Indicators and Forecasting*. Chicago, IL: Chicago University Press, 1992.

Zeitlin, J. & G. Herrigel (eds). *Americanization and its Limits: Reworking US Technology and Management in Postwar Europe and Japan*. Oxford: Oxford University Press, 1999.

Index